Laws Relating to Cooperative Societies

A Commentary

Laws Relating to Cooperative Societies
A Commentary

Indian Contract Act • Negotiable Instruments Act • The Transfer of Property Act • Banking Regulation Act • Consumer Protection Act • Indian Evidence Act • Banker's Book Evidence Act • Income Tax Act • Limitation Act • The Indian Penal Code • Civil Procedure Code • The Industrial Dispute Act • The Payment of Wages Act • Workmen's Compensation Act • Factories Act • Sale of Goods Act

RISH PAL NAINTA
B.A. (Hon's) LLM.,
P.G.D.P.M. & L.W., P.G.D.J.M.C.,
Ph.D. (Law)
Lecturer (Law), Agriculture Cooperative Staff Training Institute,
Sangti, Summer Hill, Shimla
Formerly, Lecturer (Law)
Institute of Cooperative Management
(Government of India)

Foreword by

PROFESSOR B. R. SHARMA
Chairman,
Department of Laws,
Himachal Pradesh University, Shimla

DEEP & DEEP PUBLICATIONS PVT. LTD.
F-159, Rajouri Garden, New Delhi - 110 027

LAWS RELATING TO COOPERATIVE SOCIETIES

ISBN 81-7629-511-6

Typeset by THE COMPOSERS, 20/5, West Patel Nagar, Delhi - 110 064

Printed in India at MAYUR ENTERPRISES,
WZ Plot No. 3, Gujjar Market, Tihar Village, New Delhi - 110 018.

Published by DEEP & DEEP PUBLICATIONS PVT. LTD.,
F-159, Rajouri Garden, New Delhi - 110 027
Phones : 25435369, 25440916
E-mails : ddpbooks@yahoo.co.in • deep98@del3.vsnl.net.in
Showroom :
2/13, Ansari Road, Daryaganj, New Delhi -110 002 • Telefax : 23245122

*"Dedicated with all my love
and regards to my beloved Father—*

SHRI JAIKARAN DAS
*(who is, alas, no more)
who is the real brain behind our family.
What I am and ever hope to be,
I owe it to him".*

Contents

Foreword

Cooperative legislation has been receiving attention of the government at various points of time with the basic objective of involving people at the grass-root level so as to help them in availing the facilities provided by the cooperatives. The societies formed under the cooperative legislation acquire legal status and are permitted to raise funds and carry on business in a corporate character. For a better and smooth functioning of the cooperative societies it is essential that its members, office bearers, officers, agents and other servants have adequate knowledge not only of the Cooperative Societies Act but also of other related laws. The functional mechanism of cooperative societies is also dependent upon the provisions of several other laws. For example, while deciding disputes the provisions of other laws like Indian Evidence Act, Indian Arbitration Act and the Indian Limitation Act provide enough guidance. The Law of Contact, the Law of Negotiable Instrument, the laws relating to transfer of property, the laws relating to banking, consumer protection, the Banker's Book Evidence Act, the Income Tax Act and also the law of crimes including the provisions of Civil Procedure Code, the Industrial Disputes Act, the Payment of Wages Act, Workmen's Compensation Act, the Factories Act and Sale of Goods Act are widely attracted in the day to day functioning of the cooperative societies vis-á-vis its dealing with the public at large. The enactment of the Multi-State Cooperative Societies Act, 2002 is definitely going to add new dimensions to the cooperative movement in the present day liberalized economy.

The present book which is a commentary on the allied laws relating to cooperative societies written by Dr. R.P. Nainta makes a commendable effort in this direction. Dr. Nainta has not only stated the relevant provisions of different laws but has also critically analysed these provisions and its relevance to the cooperative societies. All these provisions of different laws play a vital role in improving the functional mechanism of the cooperative societies and help in making this institution accountable to the public at large. I have no doubt in my mind that Dr. Nainta has made a good attempt to bring all these provisions together in this book, which in the ultimate analysis will be useful not only to the cooperative institutions but to all those who may be interested in knowing more about the legal mechanism governing the functional/operational set up of the cooperative societies in India. I am also confident that the present book would prove useful to the students of law, government departments, cooperative societies, lawyers and judges. Therefore, Dr. Nainta deserves all praise for putting all efforts in bringing out the present book.

PROF. B. R. SHARMA
Chairman,
Department of Laws,
Himachal Pradesh University, Shimla

Introduction

The Nation has completed over five decades of independence. During this period, there has been a tremendous growth of the state activities in the social, economic and political fields. When the nation attained the independence, on August 15, 1947, Pandit Nehru, the first Prime Minister of India promised to "wipe every tear from every eye." The basic thrust of Nehru's approach aimed at ending the exploitation of common masses; to promote the welfare of the people; and establish a social order in which justice, social, economic and political could transform the national life. Cooperative movement was envisioned as an instrument of socio-economic policy. Nehru felt that in the changed context of self-rule in the country cooperative law needed changes of fundamental nature so as to strengthen the cooperatives by providing a greater role for the non-official. In nutshell, Nehru advocated simplification of cooperative legislation so as to involve people at the grass-root level enabling them to avail the facility provided by cooperatives.

This was not the first time that cooperative legislation was conceived to regulate the working of the cooperatives. In fact, the era of cooperative legislation in India commenced with the enactment of *Cooperative Societies Act,* 1904. This legislation was the result of the studies made by Sir Fredrick Nicholson into the possibilities of starting a system of agricultural banking. Besides, the legislation was also needed to take cooperative societies out of the purview of the general law on the subject. In addition, it was also considered desirable to confer on these societies more privileges which could help them in their operation as well as discourage capitalistic formations. The societies formed under this maiden legislation were given legal recognition and authorized to raise funds and carry on business in a corporate character. The legislation provided for appointment of Registrar by provincial government. With the passage of time, many shortcomings of the present legislation came into being including its non-application to non-credit societies. Also the legislation did not provide for a Central or Federal Cooperative Structure, which was the need of the hour. Thus, the New Act of 1912 amended the law. When diarchy was established under the Constitutional Reforms of 1919, Cooperative was made a transferred subject. Thereafter, States like Bombay and Madras enacted their own legislation on Cooperation. In 1942, the Central Government enacted The Multi State

Cooperative Societies Act. The Act provided for the incorporation, regulation and winding up of cooperative societies.

Cooperation became a subject concerning Ministry of Food and Agriculture in the Government of India after independence with the creation of a small cell for cooperation. The creation of a separate Department in the Central Government in December 1958 provided a new impetus to the direction and growth of cooperative movement. The Committee on Cooperation constituted by the Government in 1965 also made important recommendations for incorporation of cooperative principles in Cooperative law, devaluation of powers of Registrar, promotion of Cooperative leadership and development of genuine types of cooperative societies. However, the subsequent developments showed that the government has been tightening its hold on cooperative institutions through incorporation of provisions in cooperative laws.

The five-year plans formulated by the Government of India including the existing Ninth Plan have always continued to lay special emphasis on cooperatives. In view of all these efforts, the cooperative societies established under respective legislations in different parts of the country have recorded considerable progress in recent years in the supply of agricultural inputs, distribution of consumers' articles, housing, credit, banking and storage.

The latest development in the area of cooperative movement in the country has been the setting up of a high level committee by the Planning Commission of India for making a reappraisal of the existing cooperative set-up. One of the significant recommendations of the committee relates to the formulation of a *Model Cooperative Societies Act*. The recommendation has also received approval of the Central Government and has been circulated to all the State Governments. The new Model Act envisages autonomy to the cooperative societies and frees them from State control. The basic aim of this formulation is to improve the working of the societies eliminate delay in decision-making. It is significant to point out here that the recommendation of the High Level Committee regarding formulation of Model Act have been emulated by the Andhra Pradesh Government which has enacted the new *Andhra Pradesh Mutually Aided Cooperative Societies Act, 1995*. The present Central Government have enacted the new Model Act which is known as Multi State Co-operative Societies Act, 2002 (39 of 2002) into law so that cooperative institutions get chance to grow independently which is not only essential but desirable in the liberalized economy.

The rising numerical strength of cooperative institutions, the larger number of sectors in which they are functioning, their extended territorial and membership coverage, their higher command over financial resources and expanded volume and variety of their operations call for a careful and better understanding of the Cooperative Societies Act and also of "Related Laws" applicable in their working and dealings. The awareness of the members, office-bearers, officers, agents and servants of cooperative societies with regard to the legal right and obligation, necessitates a closer examination with reference to the provisions of not only the Cooperative Societies Act, but also of "Related Laws". The working of a cooperative society and the application of the special law enacted for the purpose, are to a considerable extent, dependent upon the provision of several other laws. For example, a cooperative society while lending money or supplying goods or arranging sale of goods produced by its members establishes contractual relationship not only with members, but also with outsiders and the respective rights and obligations of the parties are governed by the provisions of the Contract Act, Sale of Goods Act and Transfer of Properties Act. Similarly, the Registrar or a person delegated with his powers is considered to be a civil court for summoning and enforcing the attendance of witnesses, for discovery, for proof of facts by Affidavits and for issue of commission, etc. While deciding disputes, though the Indian Evidence Act, Indian Arbitration Act and the Indian Limitation Act are not required to follow, but basic principles of the said enactments are required to be followed.

In the course of business, money and properties of the cooperatives are being embezzled and records are tampered with to conceal such crimes. The provisions of Indian Penal Code relating to such crimes are directly attracted and the study of such provisions becomes necessary in order to deal with such offences expeditiously and effectively. There are also other enactments like Income Tax Act, which provides certain exemptions, but they are nowhere indicated in the Co-operative Societies Act. Ignorance of such provisions by those who are associated with the working of cooperative institutions might deprive such institutions of getting these exemptions and privileges.

The employment of workers and labourers in certain types of industrial and labour contract cooperative societies attracts the application of the provisions of various industrial and labour laws. The relief of benefit the workers are entitled to get under the terms of contract of employment and as a measure of social justice are nowhere provided in the Cooperative Societies Acts. On the other hand, adjudication of disputes between a cooperative society and its workers is excluded from the jurisdiction of the Registrar.

Cooperators working in Cooperative Banking Institutions must study the enactments, namely, Banker's Book Evidence Act, Banking Regulation Act and Negotiable Instrument Act.

A cooperator working in cooperative institutions, therefore, should not only have knowledge of the Cooperative Societies Act, but also, the knowledge of Related laws which are applicable to cooperative institutions.

In the present study an attempt is being made to provide first-aid guidance to a cooperator to enable him to associate himself and run a cooperative institution without any legal flaw. The growing diversified activities and the growing consciousness of members of a cooperative with regard to their rights and liabilities in relation to their institutions have made it all the more necessary for co-operators to know related laws to co-operatives.

The present book has been divided into 16 chapters, which includes all laws, which are applicable *vis-a-vis* enforceable to different co-operative institutions of the country. An attempt has been made to examine all relevant provisions with illustrations and comments, appropriate case law has been incorporated.

Chapter One examines the Indian Contract Act. The law of contract affects every person. Every one of us enters into contracts day after day or in day-to-day activities such as in making purchases, in making loans of an article and many other transactions of daily life. Such type of relationship is called legal relationship between the parties to a contract. The knowledge of the various provisions relating to contracts has a vital importance to an institution engaged in economic or social activities. Though, the Co-operative Societies Act are in force in different states as special laws governing all problems relating to their disputes, but the Co-operative Societies Act do not cover all aspects of the transactions of co-operative institutions relating to contractual rights and obligations, as well as the provisions of Contract Act, hence these institutions are bound by the provisions of general principles of the Contract Act.

Second Chapter discusses the provisions of the Negotiable Instrument Act. Here, an attempt is made to examine those provisions, which are applicable to co-operative institutions. Since, the co-operatives are dealing with credit business, so the co-operative law cannot decide the disputes relating to credit business. In banking business the relationship of banker and customer is not ordinary one, but those are contractual relationship. In this relationship both have agreed to honour, accept each other statement, version, failing which other have a right to file the case for non-fulfilment of obligation. These disputes cannot be decided by co-operative law. Such disputes can be decided by different courts in different situations, hence the study has a vital importance for co-operators of the country.

Third Chapter is an attempt to examine the provisions of the Transfer of Property Act. The co-operative societies while arranging sale establish contractual relationship with its members and outsiders also. The provisions of Transfer of Property Act govern the rights and obligations of the parties. Different kinds of mortgages and leases have been discussed in the chapter.

The Fourth Chapter throws light on the Banking Regulation Act applicable to co-operatives. Here an attempt has been made to understand the relationship of the customer with a bank. The Relationship of Banker with his customer is contractual one, not ordinary one, in case of breach of obligation, either of, has a right to file the case against each other. In this chapter, the cash reserve, maintenance of a percentage of assets, submission of returns inspection, power to give directions and certain penalties, which can be imposed on co-operative institution, have been highlighted.

Chapter Five throws light on the Consumer Protection Act. The disputes relating to deficiency of service and other allied activities in the cooperatives can be filed in consumer courts. An attempt has been made to understand the basic provisions of the Act. In the Definition of Person, the Co-operative

Society has also been incorporated. The court has held that compensation is to be given for loss or injury suffered by a consumer, due to negligence of the opposite party.

Chapter Six examines the Indian Evidence Act. A fact may be proved either by oral evidence of fact or by documentary evidence which means, there are two methods of proving a fact. One is by producing witnesses of fact, which is called oral evidence, and other, by producing a document, which records the fact, in question and which is called documentary evidence. Here the author has attempted to examine the provisions, which are applicable to co-operatives.

The Seventh Chapter attempts to examine Banker's Book Evidence Act. The banking system as it exists today is the outcome of many centuries and is not a development of any particular period. During the last two centuries the banking system started taking concrete shape. In cooperatives, the co-operative institutions, dealing with credit business are also governed under Banker's Book Evidence Act. The Co-operators of the co-operative institutions should have first hand knowledge of the Act, so that unnecessary litigation could be avoided. The appropriate provisions have been incorporated along with relevant case laws.

Chapter Eight examines the Income Tax Act. The main purpose of introducing the Income Tax Act, one of Direct Taxes, was to curb the accumulation of money with the riches while nothing or very little benefits go to the common man. By mobilizing income through this means, the developmental and other expenses of the government is being met. In this chapter an attempt is being made to study the legislation in generally and to know the provisions relating to cooperative societies, in specific.

Ninth Chapter sums-up discussion on the Indian Limitation Act. The author has touched only those provisions, which have a direct relation with co-operative institutions, but in most of the State Co-operative Societies Act, the Limitation Act has not been incorporated and discussed. Keeping in view, this aspect of importance, the Limitation Act has been incorporated and discussed in this present book.

Tenth Chapter sums-up discussion on the Indian Penal Code. The author has touched only those provisions which has a direct relation with co-operative institutions. Keeping in view, the functioning of co-operative societies of the country, the main provisions of Indian Penal Code relating to misappropriation, unlawful retention of property, additions, alterations and tampering of records, wrongful furnishing of documents and criminal breach of trust have been discussed in detail.

The Eleventh Chapter attempts to examine the relevant provisions of Civil Procedure Code. Though the cooperatives have their own legal system for deciding disputes between the parties, but the basic principles of civil procedure have to be followed. What procedures have to be followed have been discussed along with relevant laws like issue of summons to framing issues, recording of evidences, arguments and judgments.

Twelfth Chapter is devoted to a discussion on the Industrial Dispute Act. The basic objective of the Act is to make provision for the investigation and settlement of industrial disputes, including their adjudication. The Act envisages collective bargaining, contracts between union representing the workmen and the management, a matter of which is outside the realm of Co-operative Societies Act, the common law or the Indian law of contracts. No court have jurisdiction to try and adjudicate upon an industrial dispute, if it is concerned with the enforcement of certain rights or liability created under the Industrial Dispute Act.

The Thirteenth Chapter throws light on the Payment of Wages Act. An attempt has been made to examine the provisions where the payment of wages to the employees on due dates and expeditious disposal of claims relating to wages or any portion thereof wrongly withheld have been discussed. These disputes cannot be decided under co-operative law but can only be decided under Payment of Wages Act.

Chapter Fourteen is an attempt to examine the provisions of Workmen's Compensation Act, which are also applicable to co-operative institutions of the country. Since, these disputes cannot be decided under co-operative law, so the Act has a significant role to play. In this chapter, cheaper and quicker disposal of disputes relating to compensation through special tribunals and payment by certain classes of employers to their workmen of compensation for injury by accident and how much compensation can be awarded have been discussed.

Chapter Fifteen looks at the provisions of the Factories Act. The Co-operative Societies are also engaged in various activities and number of employees' are engaged in those activities. There is no provision relating to employee's working conditions, i.e. health, safety, welfare, working hours and wages in the Co-operative Societies Act. So, the disputes relating to their working conditions can be decided under Factories Act and not under the Co-operative Societies Act. Hence, the provisions of Factories Act are very important for those co-operative institutions which are engaged in production activities.

Last Chapter throws light on Sale of Goods Act. The Co-operative Societies, while supplying goods or arranging sale of goods produced by its members establishes contractual relationship not only with members, but also with outsiders, the rights and obligations of the parties are governed by the provisions of the Sales of Goods Act. The Legislation has a vital importance for co-operators.

The author would like to express his immense sense of gratitude to his teacher Prof. B.R. Sharma, Chairman, Department of Laws, Himachal Pradesh University, Shimla without whose guidance, the work would not have been completed in the present form.

I also gratefully acknowledge the help of the various authors whose works have been acknowledged. In this regard, mention must be made of Sh. R.K. Bangia, M.P. Tondon, P.L. Malik, Kailash Rai, Avtar Singh, H.R. Suneja, S.N. Shukla, S.P. Padhi, Rattan Lal Dhiraj Lal and National Council for

Co-operative Training for making significant contribution in the field. I once again acknowledge the help, which has been derived from their learned works.

I am grateful to my mother Smt. Ujjala Devi, my wife Indira Nainta and my little sons master Aayush Nainta and Abhinav Rishpal Nainta who willingly gave up the time, which would have been theirs in order to see the completion of this book. The services rendered by my brother Sh. Rajendra Nainta and Sh. Umesh Narta during the preparatory stages of this work cannot be forgotten. In fact, both these persons have rendered their services in reading and correcting the manuscript and offered their comments. Thanks are also due to Miss Alka Dixit for her painstaking work in typing out the manuscript.

The author also expresses his sincere thanks to Sh. G.S. Bhatia of Deep and Deep Publications Pvt. Ltd., New Delhi for bringing out this work in the present shape.

Shimla RISH PAL NAINTA

1

Indian Contract Act, 1872

A. THE OBJECTIVE OF STUDYING THE LAW OF CONTRACTS

The law of contract affect every person. Every one of us enters into contracts day after day or in day-to-day activities such as in making purchases, in making loans of an article and many other transactions of daily life. Such type of relationship is called legal relationship among the parties of a contract. The knowledge of the various provisions relating to contracts has a vital importance to an institution engaged in economic or socially activities. The co-operative societies in the present days have embarked upon economic activities relating to trade and commerce with substantially depend upon the fulfilment of promises. Of course, the co-operative societies acts are in force in different states as special laws governing all problems relating to their disputes. However, the Co-operative Societies Act do not cover all aspects of the transactions of co-operative institutions relating to contractual rights and obligations, as well as the provisions of contract act, hence these institutions are bound by the provisions of general principles of the contract Act.[1]

B. SCHEME OF THE INDIAN CONTRACT ACT

Broadly speaking, the act can be divided into two main groups viz.: (i) General Principles of contract, and (ii) Special kinds of contract.

(a) General Principles of Contract

The general principles of contract are all laid down in sections 1 to 75 of the act. All these sections can be grouped under the following sub-heads:

(i) Preliminary (Secs. 1, 2, 7, 23-25, 27 & 58).
(ii) Of the communication, acceptance and revocation of proposals (Secs. 2-8).
(iii) Of the contracts and voidable contract (Secs. 10-19(a) & 22-23).
(iv) Of void agreements (Secs. 11, 20-30, 32, 36, 56, 57 & 64-67).

1. See, S.P. Padhi, *Allied Laws for Cooperatives* (1968) at 1.

(v) Of contingent contracts (Secs. 31 & 36).
(vi) Of the performance of contract (Secs. 37-67).
(vii) Of certain relations resembling those created by contracts (quasi-contracts) (Secs. 68-72).
(viii) Of consequences of the breach of contract (Secs. 73-75).

(b) Special Kinds of Contracts

Above all this, the remaining part of the contract act deals with three particular kinds of contracts, viz.

(i) Contract of indemnity and Guarantee (Secs. 124-147).
(ii) Of Bailment (Secs. 148-181).
(iii) Of Agency (Secs. 182-238).

C. DEFINITION OF CONTRACT

The term, 'contract' is defined in section 2(h) of the Indian Contract Act, 1872 as follows:

An agreement enforceable by law is a contract. Thus for formation of a contract there must be—

(1) an agreement, and
(2) the agreement should be enforceable by law.

(a) Agreement

"Agreement" is defined as "every promises and every set of promises forming the consideration for each other" Section 2(e). 'Promise' is defined as an accepted proposal. Section 2(b) says: "A proposal, when accepted, becomes a promise." There should be at least two parties having identity of mind in relation to matter at the same time and in the same sense. This can be found from the term of the proposal or offer and the acceptance of it by the other party. Thus, it is very much clear that there can be no agreement unless there is an offer and acceptance of the terms by the parties to the agreement. In other words, it is the offer and acceptance that constitute the agreement.

(b) When Agreement becomes Contract

An agreement is regarded as a contract when it is enforceable by law.[2] The conditions of enforceability are stated in section 10. According to this section an agreement is a contract when it is made for some consideration, between parties who are competent, with their free consent and for a lawful object, section 10 is as follows:

2. Section 2 (h).

"All agreements are contracts if they are made by the free consent of parties competent to contract, for a lawful consideration and with a lawful object, and are not hereby expressly declared to be void."

Thus, every contract is an agreement, but every agreement is not a contract. An agreement becomes a contract when the following conditions are satisfied:

1. The parties are competent to contract.
2. There must be free consent among the parties of a contract.
3. The considera tion and object of a contract must be lawful.
4. They must not expressly be declared void.

All agreements are not enforced by law. For example,

- an agreement to dine in a friend's house, or
- an agreement to go to cinema together, or
- an agreement to give rupees one hundred to a charity.

Hence, it is necessary to ascertain from the provisions of the law of contract the nature of agreements which the law is prepared to enforce.

(c) Contract as Civil Obligation

The law of contract confines itself to the enforcement of voluntarily created civil obligation. It does not cover the whole range of civil obligations. There are many obligations of civil nature, like those imposed by law or created by the acceptance of a trust, whose violation may be actionable under the law of torts or of trusts, but they are outside the field of contract. The law of contract is also not able to take care of the whole range of agreement.

(d) Proposal or Offers

Section 2(a) defines, 'Proposal' as follows: "When one person signifies to another his willingness to do or to abstain from doing any thing, with a view to obtaining the assent of that other to such act or abstinence, he is said to make a proposal." The person who makes the proposal is called the promisor or "offer", the person to whom it is made is called the "proposee" or "offeree" and when he accepts it, he is called a "Promise". An offer which is expressed by conduct is called an "implied offer" and the one which is expressed by words, written or spoken, is called "express offer". An acceptance may likewise be made expressly or impliedly. An agreement in order to result in a contract, it should fulfil the following requirements:

(e) Intention

An intention that the 'agreement' shall result in legal relations, that is to say that the parties to the agreement should intend that it should be attended by legal consequences. There is no provision in the Indian Contract Act, nor has there been any reported decision in India, requiring that an offer or its acceptance should be made with the intention of creating legal relation. In

England it is settled Principle that, "to create a contract there must be a common intention of the parties to enter into legal obligations.[3]

(f) Supreme Court's View of Requirement of Intention

The Supreme Court of India has expressed its reservation about the need of this separate requirement of 'intention to contract' under the Contract Act. Going by the criticism which is already there in the west, the court found that it was a necessity of those systems where consideration was not a requisite of enforceability. Thus, it is still an open question whether the requirement of "intention to contract" is applicable under the Indian Contract Act in the way in which it has been developed in England.[4]

For agreement, the law adopts two tests; the first is whether the agreement satisfies certain formal requirements, i.e., whether it is written, signed, sealed and delivered over by one party to the other, if it is so required by law. Then, the law presumes that the parties did intend to enter into a contract. But since every contract cannot satisfy these formal requirements, another test is adopted, namely, that it should be supported by consideration.[5]

(g) Consideration

Section 25 of the Indian Contract Act opens with the declaration that "an agreement made without consideration is void."[6] In the words of Pollock, "Consideration is the price for which the promise of the other is bought, and the promise thus given for value is enforceable."

In *Thomas* v. *Thomas*[7] Justice Patterson, "consideration means something which is of some value in the eye of law. . . . It may be some benefit to the Plaintiff or some detriment to the defendant. *Lush Jin Carrier Misa*[8]. A valuable consideration in the sense of the law, may consist either in some right, interest, profit or benefit accruing to the one party, or some forbearance, detriment, loss, or responsibility given, suffered or undertaken by the other.

In section 2(d) of the Indian Contract Act, consideration is defined as follows: When, at the desire of the promisor, the promisee or any other person has done or abstained from doing, or does or abstains from doing, or promises to do or to abstain from doing, something, such act or abstinence or promise is called a consideration for the promise.

The definition of consideration in section 2(d) requires, in the first place, that the act or abstinence, which is to be a consideration for the promise, should be done at the desire of the promisor; secondly, that it should be done by promisee or any other person and, lastly, that the act or abstinence

3. Quoted in Avtar Singh, *Law of Contract (1996)* at 7.
4. *Id*. at 12. CWT *v*. Abdul Hussain Mulla Md. Ali, (1988) 3 SCC 569.
5. *Supra* note 1 at 4.
6. Pipraich Sugar Mills *v*. P.S. Mills Mazdoor Union, 1956, SCR 872.
7. (1882) 2QB, 851, 859.
8. (1875) LR 10 Ex. 153, 162.

may have been already executed or is in the process of being done or may be still executory, that is to say, it is promised to be done.

A consideration need not be adequate i.e., a full return for the promise, but it must be something of value in the eyes of law.

ILLUSTRATION

'A' agreed to sell a horse worth rupees one thousand for rupees five hundred and his consent was freely given, the agreement is a valid contract, although consideration was inadequate. But the inadequacy of consideration may be a relevant consideration in order to determine whether consent was given freely or not. There are, however, some exceptions to the general rule that a contract without consideration is void (section 25) and they are as follows:

(i) If it is expressed in writing and registered, if so required by the law of registration, and is made of natural love and affection between parties standing in a near relation to each other, e.g. a gift by a husband to his wife, but transfer of property by husband to wife due to quarrels and disagreements was held to be an un-enforceable contract.

(ii) If it is made to compensate a person who has already done something voluntarily to the promisor, or done some thing if the promisor was compellable to do, e.g. "A" putting off fire of 'B's house voluntarily and "B" thereafter making a promise to pay a reward; 'A' supported B's minors on during his absence on pilgrimage, 'B' after return making promise to compensate.

(iii) If it is a promise in writing and signed by the person to be charged therewith, or by his agent, to pay a debt barred by the law of limitation.

D. PARTIES COMPETENT TO CONTRACT

As per the provisions of section 11 of the Indian Contract Act, 1872 there are three basic conditions for determining the parties competent to contract, namely:

1. Every person, who is of the age of majority according to the law to which he is subject, further,
   (a) As per the provisions of Indian Majority Act, the person who attains the age of 18 years, shall be deemed to be a major, and
   (b) As per the provisions of court of Wards Act, the person who attains the age of 21 years shall be deemed to be a major.
2. Section 12 of the Act provides that a person, who understands the basic effects of the contract at a time of contract is a sound mind and shall be competent to contract.
3. He should not be prohibited to enter into a contract by such laws to which he is subject.

(a) Free Consent

According to section 10 free consent is an essential requirement of a contract. Section 14 defines "free consent."

(b) Definition of Free Consent

Consent is said to be when it is not caused by[9]:

(I) coercion, as defined in section 15, or
(II) undue influence, as defined in section 15, or
(III) fraud, as defined in section 17, or
(IV) misrepresentation, as defined in section 18, or
(V) mistake, subject to the provisions of section 20, 21 and 22 consent is said to be so caused when it would not have been given but for the existence of such coercion, undue influence, fraud, misrepresentation or mistake.

Section 2(i) says that, "an agreement which is enforceable by law at the option of the other or others is voidable contract.[10]

An agreement, the consent to which is caused by coercion is voidable at the option of the party whose consent was so caused. "Coercion" is the committing or threatening to commit, an act forbidden by the Indian Penal Code, or the unlawful detaining, or threatening to detain, any property, to the prejudice of any person whatever, with the intention of causing any person to enter into an agreement.

ILLUSTRATIONS

A, on board on English ship on the high seas, causes B to enter into an agreement by an act amounting to criminal intimidation under the Indian Penal Code.

A afterwards sues B for breach of contract at Delhi, A has employed coercion, although his act is not an offence by the law of England, and although section 506 of the Indian Penal Code, was not in force at the time when or place where the act was done.

(c) Definition of Undue Influence

Section 16 of the Act defines undue influence.

16(1) A contract is said to be induced by "undue influence" where the relations subsisting between the parties are such that one of the parties is in a position to dominate the will of the other and uses that position to obtain an unfair advantage over the other.

9. Section 14.
10. Nokhia *v.* State of H.P., AIR 1985 H.P. 88. Kailash Chandra Kotia *v.* Rajasthan State Industrial Development and Invest. Corpn. (1991)1 Raj. L.R. 174 Jodhpur Bench.

(2) In particular and without prejudice to the foregoing principle, a person is said to be able to dominate the will of another—

(a) where he holds a real or apparent authority over the other, or where he stands in a fiduciary relation to the other; or
(b) where he makes a contract with a person whose mental capacity is temporarily or permanently affected by reason of age, illness, or mental or bodily distress.

(3) Where a person who is in a position to dominate the will of another enters into a contract with him, and the transaction appears, on the face of it or on evidence adduced, to be unconscionable, the burden of proving that such contract was not induced by undue influence shall lie upon the person in a position to dominate the will of the other.

Nothing in this sub-section shall affect the provisions of section III of the Indian Evidence Act. In other words, undue influence means where the relationship between the parties are such that one of the parties is in a position to dominate the will of the other and uses that position to obtain the consent for a contract.

ILLUSTRATIONS

(a) 'A' applies to a banker for a loan at a time when there is stringency in the money market. The banker declines to make the loan except at an unusually high rate of interest. A accepts the loan on these terms. This is a transaction in the ordinary course of business, and the contract is not induced by undue influence.

(b) A, being in debt to B, the money-lender of his village, contracts a fresh loan on terms which appears to be unconscionable. It lies on B to prove that the contract was not induced by undue influence.

(d) Definition of Misrepresentation

Misrepresentation is defined in section 18: 'Misrepresentation' means and includes—

(i) the positive assertion, in a manner not warranted by the information of the person making it, of that which is not true though he believes it to be true;
(ii) any breach of duty which, without any intent to deceive, gains an advantage to the person committing it, or any one claiming under him, by misleading another to his prejudice, or to the prejudice of any one claiming under him; and
(iii) Causing, however innocently, a party to an agreement, to make a mistake as to the substance of the thing which is the subject of the agreement.

(e) Definition of Fraud

Intentional misrepresentation of facts, speaking broadly is called 'fraud'.

'Fraud' means and includes any of the following acts done with "intent to deceive" or to induce a person to enter into a contract—

(1) the suggestion that a fact is true when it is not true and the person making the suggestion does not believe it to be true;
(2) active concealment of a fact by person who has knowledge or belief of the fact;
(3) Promise made without any intention of performing it;
(4) Any other act fitted to deceive; and
(5) Any such act or omission as the law specially declares to be fraudulent.

ILLUSTRATIONS

(a) A sells, by auction, to B, a horse which A knows to be unsound. A says nothing to B about the horse's unsoundness. This is not fraud in A.

(b) A and B being traders, enter upon a contract, A has private information of a change in prices which would affect B's willingness to proceed with the contract. A is not bound to inform B.

(f) Definition of Mistake

Where the mistake does not defeat consent, but only misleads the parties, section 20 shall apply. This section provides:

"Where both the parties to an agreement are under a mistake as to a matter of fact essential to the agreement, the agreement is void."

ILLUSTRATION

A being entitled to an estate for the life of B agrees to sell it to C. B was dead at the time of an agreement, but both parties were ignorant of the fact. The agreement is void.

(g) Lawful Consideration and Object

The consideration and object of a contract is lawful, unless:

(a) It is forbidden by law, or
(b) It is of such nature, if permitted, would defeat the provisions of any law, or
(c) It involves or implies injury to the person or property to another, or
(d) The court regards it as immoral or is against the public policy.

In the presence of any of the four things as mentioned above, the consideration and object of a contract is said to be unlawful and such contracts are to be void.

E. WRITTEN AND REGISTERED CONTRACTS

An agreement made without consideration is void unless—

(a) It is in Writing and Registered

It is expressed in writing, and registered under the law for the time being in force for the registration of documents, and is made on account of natural love and affection between parties standing in a near relation to each other; or unless.

(b) It is Promise to Compensate for some thing done

It is a promise to compensate, wholly or in, a person who has already voluntarily done something for the promisor, or something which the promisor was legally compellable to do; or unless.

(c) It is a Promise to pay a Debt Barred by Limitation Law

It is a promise, made in writing and signed by the person to be charged therewith, or by his agent generally or specially authorised in that behalf, to pay wholly or in part a debt of which the creditor might have enforced payment but for the law of the limitation of suits. In any of these cases, such an agreement is a contract.

ILLUSTRATION

(a) A, for natural love and affection, promises to give his son B, Rs. 1,000. A puts his promise to B into writing and registers it. This is a contract.
(b) A promises, for no consideration, to give to B Rs. 1,000. This is a void agreement.

F. CONTRACTS EXPRESSLY DECLARED VOID

(1) If parties to a contract are not competent to contract.
(2) Where both the parties to a contract are under a mistake.
(3) If the consideration and objects are unlawful.
(4) If the consideration and objects of contract are unlawful in part or even.
(5) Agreement without consideration.
(6) Agreement in restraint of marriage.
(7) Agreement in restraint of trade.
(8) Agreement in restraint of legal proceedings.
(9) Agreement void for uncertainty.
(10) Agreement by way of wager.
(11) Enforcement of contracts contingent on an event happening.

(12) Agreements contingent on impossible events.
(13) Agreement to do impossible act.
(14) Reciprocal promise to do things legal and also other things illegal.
(15) Consequences of rescission of voidable contract.
(16) Obligation of person who has received advantage under void agreement, or contract that becomes void.
(17) Mode of communicating or revoking rescission of voidable contract.
(18) Effect of neglect of promise to afford promisor reasonable facilities for performance.

(a) Void Contracts

An agreement not enforceable by law is said to be void. In other words, a void contract is one which has no legal éffect. It confers no right on either party.[11]

ILLUSTRATIONS

(a) A by fraud induces B to make a contract with A. The contract is binding on A, unless B chooses to set it aside. B can set aside it at his option, where A has no such option.

(b) A promises to superintend on behalf of B, a legal manufacture of indigo, and an illegal traffic. In other articles, B promises to pay to A a salary of Rs. 10,000 a year. The agreement is void, the object of A's promise, and the consideration for B's promise, being in pawn unlawful.

(b) Voidable Contract

A "Voidable Contract" is one, which one of the parties may affirm, or reject, at his option; or, defined by the clause (i) of section 2. An agreement which is enforceable by law at the option of one or more of the parties thereto, but not at the option of the other or others.

The expression "voidable contract" refers to cases, in which—

(a) the contract is defective in its origin, and voidable from the very beginning; as, for example, where it has been induced by coercion, or undue influence, or fraud, or misrepresentation; and
(b) the contract ceases to be enforceable by one party, owing to some subsequent circumstances.[12]

In other words, A contract, which is binding unless one of the parties can put on end to at his option. His option can be exercised without reference to the other party and the contract is a binding, if he elects to treat it as binding and void if he elects to treat it as void.

11. See *Supra* note 3 at 223-68.
12. Subrahmanyan and Singhal, *Indian Contract Act* (1989) at 259.

ILLUSTRATION

(a) A employed by B subject to a wed notice on either side. It is binding unless either or party does not put it an end to at his option. Any of the parties (A & B) can exercise has option without any reference to other.

G. CONTINGENT CONTRACTS

The expression, 'contingent contracts' is defined in section 31 of the contract Act:

A "contingent contracts" is a contract to do or not to do something. If some event, collateral to such contract, does not happen.

ILLUSTRATION

(a) A contracts to pay B Rs. 10,000 if B's house is burnt. This is a contingent contract.

A contract which is subject to a certain or an absolute type of condition cannot be regarded or an absolute type of condition cannot be regarded as a contingent contract. A contract, for example, to pay a sum of money on the expiry of a time or on the death of a person is not a contingent contract because these events are of a certain nature. The time or the person in question will definitely expire and the money will become payable when the condition is of uncertain nature, then only the contract can be regarded as truly contingent.

Example: A contract to pay a sum of money on the destruction of a premises by fire, is a contingent contract, for that contingent may or may not happen. From this point of view, all contracts of insurance, are contingent contracts.[13]

Ordinarily, therefore, a contingent contract will contemplate a future event. But a contract may also relate to an event which has already happened and the only thing uncertain being that the parties do not know which way it happened.

Such a contract is only binding on happening or not happening of an event. The following are the contingent contracts:

(i) Enforcement of contracts contingent on an event happening.
(ii) Enforcement of contract contingent on an event not happening.
(iii) When event on which contract is contingent to be deemed impossible if it is the future conduct of a living person.
(iv) When contracts become void which are contingent on happening of specified event within fixed time.
(v) When contracts may be enforced which are contingent on specified event not happening within fixed time.
(vi) Agreement contingent on impossible events void.

13. Valiammal Rangarao *v.* Muthu Arunaswamy (1982) 3 SCC 508.

H. IMPLIED OR QUASI CONTRACTS

There are many situations in which law as well as Justice require that a certain person be required to conform to an obligation, although he has neither broken any contract nor committed any tort.

Example: A person in whose home certain goods have been left by mistake is bound to restore them. Such obligations are generally described, for want of a better or more appropriate name, as quasi-contractual obligations.

Such contracts are described as "certain relations resembling those created by contracts." When one person has benefited at the expense of another under such circumstances as to call for the repayment or the restoration of the benefit, the law imposes an obligation on him to make the repayment. Such repayments are called quasi-contracts, because although there is no contract or agreement between the parties, they are put in the same position as if there were a contract between them.

Example:

(1) A person incapable of contracting is liable for necessaries supplied to him, or on his behalf.

(2) Suits for money had and received: A right to sue for recovery of the money may arise—

 (a) Where the plaintiff paid the money to the defendant.

  (i) By mistake of fact.

  (ii) In pursuance of a contract, the consideration for which has failed. Failure of consideration must be distinguished from absence of consideration.

Example. If "X" pays "Y" Rupees fifty in return for which "Y" promises to deliver certain goods to "X" there is consideration, but if "Y" fails to carry out his promise, there is a total failure of consideration and "X" can recover rupees fifty. If part of the goods have been delivered, "X" cannot recover part of his purchase price, because the consideration has not totally failed. His remedy is an action for damages.

  (iii) Under coercion, undue influence and fraud.

 (b) When the plaintiff has paid to the third party money which another is bound to pay.

 (c) When defendant obtained money from third party e.g., agent making secret profits.

(3) A finder of goods lost by another must try to find the owner and must not appropriate the goods to his own use. He can, however, recover from the owner expenses incurred in protecting and preserving the property.

(4) A person enjoying benefit of non-gratuitous act is under an obligation to compensate the other party.

(5) 'An account stated.' This is an admission of indebtedness from which the law may imply an undertaking to pay e.g. an I.O.U.[14]

14. See, *Supra* note 1 at 10-11.

I. CONTRACTS OF BAILMENT

Bailment implies a sort of relationship in which the personal property of one person temporarily goes into the possession of another. The ownership of the articles or goods is in one person and the possession in another. The circumstances in which this happens are numerous.

Example: Delivering a cycle, watch or any other article for repair, or learning a cycle or car etc. At a stand, depositing luggage or books in a clock room, delivering gold to a Goldsmith for making ornaments, delivering garments to a dry cleaner, delivering goods for carriage, ware housing or storage and so forth, are all familiar situations which create the relationship of bailment.[15]

(a) Definition of Bailment

"Bailment" is defined in section 148 of the Indian Contract Act in the following terms:

A 'Bailment' is the delivery of goods by one person to another for some purpose, upon contract that they shall, when the purpose is accomplished, be returned or otherwise disposed of according to the directions of the person delivering them.

The person who delivers the goods is called the 'bailor' and the person to whom they are delivered is called the 'bailee.'

(b) Essential Features of Bailment

(i) Delivery of Possession

Section 149 explains the meaning of delivery of possession. "The delivery to the bailee may be made by doing any thing which has the effect of putting the goods in the possession of the intended bailee or of any person authorized to hold them on his behalf."

Delivery of possession is thus of two kinds, namely:

(i) actual delivery, and
(ii) constructive delivery.

(ii) Delivery should be upon Contract

Delivery of goods should be made for some purpose and upon a contract that when the purpose is accomplished the goods shall be returned to the bailor. The contract may be express or implied. Thus, where with the consent of the station master goods were stored on a railway company's was held liable when they were damaged by fire caused by a spark emitted by a passing engine.

(iii) Delivery should be upon some Purpose

Bailment of goods is always made for some purpose and is subject to the condition that when the purpose is accomplished the goods will be returned

15. *Ibid.*

to the bailor or disposed of according to his mandate. If the person to whom the goods are delivered is not bound to restore them to the person delivering them or to deal with them according to his directions, their relationship will not be that of bailor and bailee.

(J) CONTRACTS OF PLEDGE

Section 172 defines pledge:

The bailment of goods as security for payment of a debt or performance of a promise is called "pledge". The bailor in this case is called the "Pawner." The bailee is called the "Pawnee."

Thus a pledge is only a special kind of bailment, and the chief basis of distinction is the object of a contract. Where the object or the delivery of goods is to provide a security for a loan or for the fulfilment of on obligation that kind of bailment is called pledge.

The owner can make a valid pledge, but in the following cases, a person other than the owner can make a valid pledge:

(i) An agent with the consent of the owner, in possession of goods or documents.

(ii) A person having possession of goods under a voidable contract so long as the contract is not rescinded provided, the pawnee acts without notice of Pawner's defect of little.

(iii) Where a person pledges goods in which he has only a limited interest, the pledge is valid to the extent of that interest.

(iv) If, one of the several co-owners is in sale possession of the goods with the consent of the owners, he can make a valid pledge.

(a) Essential Ingredients of a Pledge

(i) Delivery of Possession

Delivery of the chattel pawned is a necessary element in the making of a Pawn. The property pledges should be delivered to the Pawnee. Thus, where the producer of a film borrowed a sum of money from a financier-distributor, and agreed to deliver the final prints of the film when ready, the agreement was held not to amount to a pledge, there being no actual transfer of possession. Delivery of the key of the godown where the goods are stored is an illustration of constructive delivery. Delivery of documents of title which would enable the pledgee to obtain possession is equally effective to create a pledge.

(ii) In Pursuance of Contract

Pledge is a conveyance pursuant to a contract, and it is essential to a valid pledge that delivery of the chattel shall be made by the pledger to the pledgee in pursuance of the contract of pledge.

K. CONTRACTS OF INDEMNITY AND GUARANTEE

(a) Contracts of Indemnity

Section 124 of the Indian Contract Act define indemnity as under:

A contract by which one party promises to save the other from loss caused to him by the conduct of the promisor himself or by conduct of any other person, is called a "Contract of indemnity."

ILLUSTRATION

A contract to indemnify B against the consequences of any proceedings which C may take against B in respect of a certain sum of 200 rupees. This is a contract of indemnity. The person who gives the indemnity is called the "indemnifier" and the person for whose protection it is given is called the "indemnity-holder" or, "indemnified".

Thus, the scope of indemnity is by the very process of definition restricted to causes where there is a promise to indemnify against loss, caused.

(a) by the promisor himself, or
(b) by any other person.

The definition excludes from its purview causes of loss arising from accidents like fire or perils of the sea loss must be caused by human agency.

(b) Contracts of Guarantee

"Contract of guarantee" is defined in section 126 of the Act as follows:

A 'Contract of guarantee' is a contract to perform the promise, or discharge the liability, of a third person in case of his default. The person who gives the guarantee is called "Surety", the person in respect of whose default the guarantee is given is called the "Principal debtor", and the person to whom the guarantee is given is called the "creditor". A guarantee may be either oral or written.

(c) Essential Features of Guarantee

I. Principal debt,
II. Consideration,
III. Misrepresentation and concealment, and
IV. Writing not necessary.

L. CONTRACTS OF AGENCY

Agency has to be distinguished from the relationship of vend or and purchaser. In both, physical possession passes from one party to the another, but in the case of a sale, the ownership and with it, the risk also passes, so that, if the goods perish after the property in the goods has passed to the buyer, the liability should be of the buyer only.

In the agency ownership continue with the Principal and he alone is responsible for loss of goods in the hands of the agent provided there is no fault nor any negligence on the part of the agent.

(a) Agent

'Agent' is defined in section 182 of the act in the following words: An agent is a person employed to do any act for another or to represent an other in dealings with third persons. The person for whom such act is done, or who is so represented is called the "Principal."

(b) Method of Creating Agency

In the words of Desai, J. of the Supreme Court: "The relation of agency arises whenever one person called the agent has authority to act on behalf of another called the principal and consents so to act. The relationship has its genesis in a contract."

The relationship of Principal and agent may be created in any of the following ways:

1. by express appointment;
2. by the conduct or situation of the parties;
3. by necessity of the case; or
4. by subsequent ratification of an unauthorized act.

(c) Implied Agency

Implied agencies arises from the conduct, situation or relationship of parties. Whenever a person places another in a situation in which that other is understood to represent or to act for him, he becomes an implied agent. Thus, where a woman allowed her son to drive a car for her, she paying all the expenses of maintenance and operation, it was held that the son was an implied agent of the mother and when he made a collision injuring his wife, the wife could sue the mother for the fault of her agent. A permission granted to a person to ferry a car from one place to another makes him an agent for that limited purpose so as to create liability for consequences of negligent driving. The borrower of a car would not occupy that position. Unauthorized pretensions do not have the effect implied agency includes:

(i) Agency by estoppel;
(ii) Agency by holding out; and
(iii) Agency of necessity.

2

Negotiable Instruments Act, 1881

A. DEFINITION

A negotiable instrument is a piece of paper which entitles a person to a sum of money and which is transferable from person to person by mere delivery. The person to whom it is so transferred becomes entitled to the money and also to the right to further transfer it.

The law relating to negotiable instruments is contained in the negotiable instruments act, 1881 which deals with promissory notes, Bills of exchange and cheque, as also hundis. For a person who takes a negotiable instrument in good faith and for value becomes the true owner even if he takes it from a thief or finder.

The great element of negotiability is the acquisition of property by your own conduct, not by another's, that if you take it bonafide and for value no body can deprive you of it. *Raephal* v. *The Bank of England* is an authority for this proposition.

Facts of the Case

Some bank notes of the bank of England were stolen in a robbery. The bank immediately prepared and distributed a list of the stolen notes. The Plaintiff who was a money changer in Paris, also received one such list. Twelve months after the receipt of this notice a man come to the Plaintiff to exchange a bank of England note. The Plaintiff had no recollection of the notice and completely forgetting it cashed the note. The note turned out to be stolen one. It was held that the Plaintiff, having taken the note in good faith, was entitled to its payment. He was no doubt some-what negligent, but he had acted honestly.[1]

This Principle applies only when the instrument is negotiable, which means, that the instrument should be such or in such a state that it can be transferred like cash by simple delivery. If it requires something other than delivery e.g., endorsement, then it is not negotiable till it is properly indorsed.

1. Quoted in, Avtar Singh, 'Negotiable Instruments (1979) at 709-10.

ILLUSTRATION

One G, by means of a fraud, obtained a cheque from the defendant forester. The cheque was made payable to G or order. G gave the cheque to the Plaintiff in payment of his own debt, but forgot to indorse it. The Plaintiff had no notice of the fraud then, but, before he could obtain G's endorsement, he was given notice of fraud. Accordingly the Plaintiff could not get a good title.

Section (13) of Negotiable Instruments Act, 1881 provides that negotiable instruments includes Promissory note, bill of exchange and cheque, whether payable to be bearer or order. Thus, though the section speaks of only three kinds of instruments, it does not mean that there can not be any other negotiable instruments than these three. Indeed, every document which entitles a person to a sum of money and which is transferable by mere delivery, is entitle to be called "Negotiable Instruments."

B. DOCTRINE OF NEGOTIABILITY

There are three essential qualities attached to a negotiable instrument:

(i) Negotiable instrument must be transferable—which means the property in it—the legal ownership—must be transferable by mere delivery, accompanied, in the case of an instrument payable to order, by endorsement. No instrument of transfer is required and no notice of transfer need to given to the party/parties liable on the instrument.

(ii) It must be given in good faith and for value without notice of any defect in the title of the transferor, an indefeasible title against all comers. Also the title passes free from equities and counter-claims between previous parties of which the transferee has no notice.

(iii) It must contain a right of action in itself the possessor of it is deemed to be the true owner capable of enforcing any claims thereon he is under no duty to justify his title in the first instance.

C. MEANING OF DELIVERY

Delivery is defined as a transfer of possession from one person to another and is essential for the negotiation of a negotiable instrument. As per section 46 of the Negotiable Instruments, Delivery can be of two types.

(a) Actual Delivery; and
(b) Constructive Delivery.

(a) Actual Delivery

Actual delivery takes place by actual change of possession of the instrument from one person to another. The instrument must be handed over physically to whom it is actually intended to be delivered or to his authorized agent.

ILLUSTRATION

When A, the holder of a negotiable instrument payable to bearer, delivers it to B's agent to be kept for B, the instrument has been negotiated.

(b) Constructive Delivery

Constructive Delivery means that the instrument is not delivered or handed over to the person to whom it is so intended to be delivered but the possession of the instrument is in law deemed to have been transferred when delivery is completed by some act which changes the possession in the eyes of law from the transferor to the transferee. In such cases the question of intention comes in.

ILLUSTRATION

A, the holder of a negotiable instrument payable to bearer, which is in the hands of A's banker, directs the banker to transfer the instrument to B's account with him. The Banker, on accepting the instructions, now holds the instrument as agent of B. The instrument has been negotiated and B has become the holder of it. Whether the delivery is actual or constructive, assent of both the parties to the transaction is necessary for the delivery to be effective[2].

(c) Mode of Transfer

The mode of transfer provided by the Negotiable instruments act depends upon the character of the instrument. According to section 13, a negotiable instrument may be payable to:

(i) bearer, or
(ii) specified person or order,

while a bearer cheque passes by simple delivery, an order cheque passes by endorsement and delivery.

D. TYPES OF NEGOTIABLE INSTRUMENTS

Though the negotiable instruments possess the above mentioned features, they fall under two categories as follows:

(a) Negotiable Instruments by Statute, and
(b) Negotiable Instruments by custom or usage.

2. See. H.R. Suneja, 'Practice and Law of Banking, (1990) at 183-84.

(a) Negotiable Instruments by Statute

As already stated the negotiable instruments act states three instruments—promissory note, Bill of Exchange and cheque—as negotiable instruments. They are, therefore called negotiable instruments by statute.

(b) Negotiable Instruments by Custom or Usage

Some other instruments have acquired the character of negotiability by the custom or usage of trade. Section 137 of the Transfer of Property Act, 1882 also recognized that an instrument may be negotiable by law or custom. Thus in India Government Promissory notes, Shah Jog Hundis, delivery orders and railway receipts have been held to be negotiable by usage or custom of the trade.

E. KINDS OF NEGOTIABLE INSTRUMENTS

Section 13(1) of the Negotiable Instrument Act, 1881, provides that negotiable instruments include promissory note, bill of exchange and cheque, whether payable to bearer or order.

The section makes it clear that instruments payable to order are also negotiable. But it should be noted that an order instrument can only be negotiated by endorsements and the endorsement must be genuine.

Special feature of a "Negotiable Instrument"—(1) a negotiable instrument is transferable from hand to hand like money. The property in the instrument passes by endorsement and delivery, or by delivery only.

(2) In case of dishonour, the holder of the instrument is entitled to sue on the instrument in his own names.

(3) A *bonafide* holder of a negotiable instrument for value without notice gets it free from all the defects in the title of his transferor, subject to fraud and illegality in the transfer of the instrument.

(a) Promissory Note

Promissory note is defined by Section 4 of the Act.

A Promissory note is an instrument in writing containing an unconditional undertaking, signed by the maker, to pay a certain sum of money only to, or to the order of a certain person or to the bearer of the instrument.

ILLUSTRATION

A signs instrument in the following terms:

(a) I promise to pay B or order Rs. 500.
(b) I acknowledge myself to be indebted to B in Rs. 1,000, to be paid on demand, for value received.
(c) Mr. B, I.O.U. Rs. 1,000.

(d) I Promise to pay B Rs. 500, and all other sums which shall be due to him.

(e) I promise to pay B Rs. 500, first deducting there out any money which he may owe me.

(f) I promise to pay B Rs. 500. Seven days after my marriage with C.

(g) I Promise to pay B Rs. 500 on D's death, provided D leaves me enough to pay that sum.

(h) I promise to pay B Rs. 500 and to deliver to him my black horse on 1st January next.

The Instruments respectively marked (a) and (b) are promissory note. The instruments respectively marked (c), (d), (e), (f), (g) and (h) are not promissory note.

In *Balmukand* v. *Munna Lal Ranji Lal*[3] the court held that before a document is treated as promissory note it should be promissory note both in form and in intent. If indebtedness is acknowledged in a document in a defined sum of money payable 'on demand', that is enough to make the document a promissory note and the document need not necessarily say that the debtor promises to repay amount.

In *Bachan Singh* v. *Ram Avadh*[4] the court held that there must be an express undertaking upon the face of the instrument to pay the money before it can be held to be a promissory note. A mere implied undertaking will not do.

Thus a promissory note is a promise in writing by a person to pay a sum of money to a specified person or to his order. The usual form of a promissory note is like this.

Rs. 500	Shimla, November 7, 2000
Three months after date, I promise to pay Aayush Nainta or Bearer/Order, the sum of rupees five hundred for value received.	
	Nitin

Although this is the usual form, no particular form of words is requisite. It may take any other form. But in any case it must possess the following characteristics.

(1) Writing

The first essential is that all negotiable instruments must be in writing. An oral engagement to pay a sum of money is not an instrument, much less negotiable. The writing may be better in ink or in pencil even.

3. AIR 1970, P&H 516.
4. AIR 1949 All. 431.

(2) Promise to Pay

It must contain a promise to pay, A mere acknowledgment of debt is not a promissory note. Where a note was made in this form:

"I.O.U., E.A. Gay, the sum of Rupees two hundred for values received." Holding that it was not a Promissory note, the court said:

"In order to constitute a good Promissory note there should be an express Promise to pay the money . . . while such promise need not be expressed in any particular form of words, the language used must be such that the written undertaking to pay may be fairly deduced therefrom."

(3) Unconditional

The Promise to pay the money should be unconditional, or subject only to a condition which according to the ordinary experience of mankind is bound to happen.

(4) Money only

The instrument must be payable in money and money only. If the instrument contains a promise to pay something other than money or something, in addition to money, it will not be promissory note. The sum of money payable must also be certain.

The Act nowhere requires that the amount should be stated both in words and figures. But this has become usual. In recognition of this fact section 18 says that in case of discrepancy the amount stated in world will prevail[5].

(5) Certain Parties

The parties to the instrument must be designated with reasonable certainty. There are two parties to a promissory note, namely, the person who makes the note and is known as the maker and the payee to whom the promise is made. Both the maker and the payee must be indicated with certainty on the face of the instrument.

(6) Signed by the Maker

If the instrument has not been signed by the maker, then it is not a promissory note. So, it is essential that the instrument must be signed by the maker.

(a) Bill of Exchange

Section 5 defines bill of exchange. A 'bill of exchange' is an instrument in writing containing an unconditional order, signed by the maker, directing a certain person to pay a certain sum of money only to, or to the order of a certain person or to the bearer of the instrument. The usual form of a bill of exchange is given on next page:

5. See *Supra* Note 1 at 715.

Rs. 500.00 Shimla: November 7, 2000

Three months after date pay to Aayush or $\frac{\text{Bearer}}{\text{Order}}$ the sum of rupees five hundred, for value received.

To
Nitin Pal Singh
Shimla **Sahil**

Although this is the general form of a bill of exchange, no particular form is prescribed. Whatever form it may take, it must substantially comply with the requirements of section 5. In essence a bill of exchange is the order of a creditor upon his debtor requiring him to pay the money to the person specified.

The following are the essential ingredients[6] of the bill of exchange:

1. It must be in writing.
2. The bill of exchange must contain an order to pay. The order to pay may be in the form of a request, but it should be imperative.
3. The order to pay should be unconditional. The word "Unconditional" has already been explained in connection with "Promissory note" and the same consideration apply here.
4. The order must be to pay money and money only. The amount ordered to be paid must be certain.
5. A bill of exchange requires three parties. First, the person who makes the bill of exchange, called the drawer; second, the person to whom it is addressed, called the drawee and thirdly, the payee. All these parties must be indicated with reasonable certainty.
6. The bill must be signed by the drawer.

C. CHEQUE

Section 6 defines 'cheque'. It says:

A 'cheque' is a bill of exchange drawn on a specified banker and not expressed to be payable otherwise than on demand.

A cheque being a bill of exchange must possess all the essentials of a bill and should also meet the requirements of section 6.

(i) Essential Ingredients of a Cheque

1. Writing;
2. Unconditional order;
3. On a specified banker only;
4. Certain sum of money;
5. Payee to be certain;

6. *id.* at 717-18.

6. Signed by the drawer; and
7. Payable on demand.

In addition to satisfying the essentials of a bill of exchange a cheque must fulfil the requirements of section 6. In the first place, a cheque must be drawn upon a banker. Secondly, the cheque must be payable on demand.

A cheque has always to be made payable on demand, where as an ordinary bill of exchange can be made payable after a fixed period. A future dated cheque, being not payable on demand, may not be regarded as a cheque in the real sense of the word unless that date arrives and it becomes payable on demand.

F. PAYMENT OF CHEQUES AND PROTECTION TO THE PAYING BANKER

As we have understood that the banker-customer relationship is a contractual relationship with super-head obligation on the part of a banker to honour the customer's cheques as and when they are presented provided, of course, certain conditions are satisfied before payment is made by a banker.

The Negotiable Instruments Act, 1881 deals with payment of cheques and protection to the paying banker under various sections which include sections 10, 31, 85, 85A, 87, 89, 126-130.

G. DEFINITION OF HOLDER

Every instrument initially belongs to the payee and he is entitled to its possession. The payee can transfer it to any person in payment of his own debt. This transfer is known as negotiation. Negotiation takes place in two ways. A bearer instrument passes by simple delivery and the person to whom it is delivered becomes the holder. An order instrument, on the other hand, can be negotiated only by endorsement and delivery and the indorsee becomes the holder. Hence, holder means either the bearer or indorsee of an instrument.[7]

Section 8 of the Negotiable Instruments Act, 1882 deals with holder, which means:

The "holder" of a promissory note, bill of exchange or cheque means any person entitled in his own name to the possession thereof and to receive or recover the amount due thereon form the parties thereto.

Where the promissory note, bill of exchange or cheque is lost or destroyed, its holder is the person so entitled at the time of such loss or destruction. In other words, the person who was entitled to receive payment at the time the instrument was lost, will continue to be regarded as its holder; the finder does not become its holder.

---

7. *id.* at 724.

H. DEFINITION OF HOLDER IS DUE COURSE

The "despotic but necessary principle" relating to negotiable instruments is that "a person taking a negotiable instrument in good faith and for value obtains a valid title though he takes from one who had none", or who was merely thief. "The property in a negotiable instrument is acquired by any one who takes it *bonafide*, and for value, notwithstanding any defect of title in the person from whom he took it." Now such a person who takes an instrument "in good faith and for value" becomes the true owner of the instrument and is known as a "holder in due consideration". According to section 9, "Holder in due course means any person who for consideration became the possessor of a Promissory note, bill of exchange or cheque if payable to bearer, or the payee or indorsee thereof, if payable to order, before the amount mentioned in it became payable and without having sufficient cause to believe that any defect existed in the title of the person from whom he derived his title.

The phrase "in good faith and for value" has been split up by section 9 into four elements all of which must concur to make a holder in due course. They are:

1. The holder must have taken the instrument for value.
2. He must have obtained the instrument before its maturity.
3. The instrument must be complete and regular on its face.
4. He must have taken the instrument in good faith and without notice of any defect either in the instrument or in the title of the person negotiating it to him.

In *Sukhan Raj Khim Raja, a Firm of Merchants, Bombay* v. *N. Raja Gopalan*[8] the court held that the plaintiff was fully aware that the cheque had been dishonoured, and the endorsement in his favour was only after it was returned by the bank. Therefore, it had lost its negotiability. Hence, he cannot be a holder in due course. This essential characteristic having not been comprehended and more so, when the cheque had never been thereafter presented to the bank for encashment, the suit as laid, could not have been degreed at all.

In *Brajakirshore Dudt* v. *Purnachandra Panda*[9] the court held that three conditions are necessary to be holder in due course. Firstly, he must be a holder for consideration, secondly, the instrument must have been transferred to him before it becomes overdue, and thirdly, he must be a transferee in good faith and that he should not have any reason to believe that there was any defect in the title of the transferor.

I. MEANING OF NEGOTIATION

The transfer of an instrument by one party to another so as to constitute the transferee a holder is called "Negotiation." A bearer instrument is

8. (1989) ILW 401.
9. AIR 1957 at 153.

transferable by simple delivery (S.14). An instrument payable to order can be transferred by endorsement and delivery (S. 46).

J. ENDORSEMENT

(a) Definition of Endorsement

Section 15 defines endorsement follows: "When the maker or holder of a negotiable instrument signs the same, otherwise than as such maker, for the purpose of negotiation, on the back or face thereof or on a slip of paper annexure thereto, or so signs for the same purpose a stamped paper intended to be completed as a negotiable instrument, he is said to have endorsed the same and is called the endorser.

(b) Who may Indorses

Section 51 of the Negotiable Instrument Act, 1881 speaks that who may indorse. The payee of an instrument is the rightful person to make the first endorsement. Thereafter, the instrument may be indorsed by any party who has become the holder of the instrument. Ordinarily, the maker of a note and the drawer of a bill cannot indorse. But if any of them has become the holder in his own right, he may indorse the instrument.

(c) Kinds of Endorsement

According to the Negotiable Instrument Act, endorsements are of the following kinds:

(i) Endorsement in Blank

If the endorser signs his name only, the endorsement is said to be "in Blank" (section 16). The endorsement does not specify the name of endorsee with the effect that an instrument endorsed in blank becomes payable to the bearer (subject to the provisions as regards crossed cheques) even though originally payable to order (section 54) and no further endorsement is required for its negotiation.

ILLUSTRATION

If a cheque is payable to "X" or order and "X" merely signs on its back, such endorsement is called endorsement in blank such endorsement makes it a bearer cheque which may be further negotiated by mere delivery.

(ii) Endorsement in full

If in addition to his signature, the endorser adds a direction to pay the amount mentioned in the instrument to, or to the order of a specified person, the endorsement is said to be "endorsement in full." (Section 16)

ILLUSTRATION

If a cheque is payable to "X" or order and "X" adds the words pay to "Y" or pay to "Y" or "order". Such endorsement is called endorsement is full. The endorsement will then be payable to "Y" or his order and will necessitate endorsement by "Y" for its further negotiation.

According to section 55, "If a negotiable instruments, after having been endorsed in blank, is endorsed in full, the amount of it cannot be claimed from the endorser in full, except by the person to whom it has been endorsed in full or by one who derives title through such person.

ILLUSTRATION

A cheque is endorsed in blank by "X" and transferred to "Y" who endorses it in favour of "Z". The latter transfers it without any endorsement to 'Q'. If the cheque is dishonoured, 'Q' cannot sue 'Y' or 'Z'. He can sue 'X' only.

(iii) Conditional Endorsement

If the endorser of a negotiable instrument, by express words in the endorsement, makes his liability, or the rights of the endorsee to receive the amount due thereon, dependent on the happening of a specified event, although such event may never happen, such endorsement is called a conditional endorsement (Section 52).

Conditional endorsements do not make the instruments non-transferable. However, such endorsements are generally not used.

ILLUSTRATION

"Pay C if he returns from Bombay." Thus C gets the right to receive payment only on the happening of a particular event, i.e. if he returns from Bombay if the event does not take place, the endorsee cannot sue any of the parties.

(iv) Restrictive Endorsement

Generally, an endorsee of a negotiable instrument is fully competent to negotiate it further but section 50 permits restrictive endorsements which take away the negotiability of such instruments. "The endorsement may, by express words, restrict or exclude the right to negotiate or may merely constitute the endorsee an agent to endorse the instrument or to receive its contents for the endorser or for some other specified person." Such an endorsement prohibits further endorsement and is called "Restrictive endorsement."

ILLUSTRATION

If B endorses an instrument payable to bearer as follows, the right of C to further negotiate is excluded:

(a) Pay the contents to C only.
(b) Pay C for my use.
(c) Pay C or order for the account of B.
(d) The within must be created to C.

But the followings endorsements are not restrictive endorsements:

(a) Pay C.
(ii) Pay C value in account of X Bank.
because the endorser has not specifically restricted the negotiability of the instrument.

In *Kunjn Pillai* v. *Peria Swamil*[10] the court held that the endorsement of an instrument for collection passes the legal title to the transferee so as to enable him to demand, receive and sue for the money to be paid. It may be that the indorsee is bound to account to the endorser, but it does not justify the defendant to challenge the plaintiff's right to sue upon it. Similarly, actions can be maintained by agent, trustee or executor or an instrument, proved the full legal title vests in him by a proper endorsement. Notwithstanding that he may not have a beneficial interest in its proceeds. This is an exception to the ordinary law of urgency.

(v) Endorsement 'Sans Recourse'

An endorser of a negotiable instrument may by express words in the endorsement, exclude his own liability thereon (section 25). If the endorser does not want to incur any liability as endorser, he can insert a stipulation in his endorsement negating or limiting his liability.

ILLUSTRATION

(i) "Pay D or order without recourse to me".
(ii) "Pay D or order Sans Recourse".
(iii) "Pay D or order at his own risk".

These words will exclude the liability of the Endorser altogether.

(iv) Partial Endorsement

Section 56 deals with partial endorsement which says that an instrument cannot be indorsed for a part of its amount only.

10. (1969) 2 MLJ 148.

ILLUSTRATION

If the instrument is for Rs. 100 it cannot be indorsed for Rs. 50 only. But if the amount due has already been partly paid, a note to that effect may be indorsed on the instrument and it may then be negotiated for the balance.

K. CROSSING OF CHEQUES

When a cheque bears a cross its face two parallel transverse lines, the cheque is said to be crossed. The lines are usually drawn on the left hand top corner of the cheque. But they may be drawn anywhere.

Crossed cheques are dealt with in sections 123 to 131 of the Negotiable Instruments Act, 1881. It should be noted that crossings apply only to cheques. There is no facility for crossing a trade bill of exchange.

According to an instruction to a banker to pay the cheque to a banker, or to a specified person's bank account, and not in cash a cross the counter. The purpose of crossing is, of course, to minimise the risk of loss if the cheque is lost or stolen, especially when it is sent through post.

Crossing affects only the mode of payment of the cheque. Unless expressly stated so, crossing does not restrict the negotiability of a cheque.

(a) Kinds of Crossing

Crossing is basically of two kinds, namely—

(i) General Crossing.
(ii) Special Crossing.

(i) General Crossing

Section 123 which governs general crossing reads as:

"Where a cheque bears across its face an addition of the words 'and company' or any abbreviation thereof, between two parallel traverse lines, or of two parallel traverse lines simply, either with or without the words 'not negotiable', that addition shall be deemed a crossing, and the cheque shall be deemed to be crossed generally."

General crossings may appear as follows:

1. __________
   ____
   ____
2. and company
   ____
3. & Co
   ____
4. Not Negotiable.
   ____
   ____

5. A/C Payee.

(ii) Special Crossing

According to section 124, "where a cheque bears across its face an addition of the name of a banker, either with or without the words 'not negotiable' that addition shall be deemed a crossing and the cheque shall be deemed to be crossed specially and to be crossed to that banker."

The special crossing on the cheque is a direction to the paying banker to honour the cheque only when it is presented through the bank mentioned in the crossing and no other bank. Special crossing may appear as follows:

1. State bank of India
2. State bank of India
   A/C Payee
3. State Bank of India
   A/C Payee
   Not negotiable
4. State Bank of India
   Not Negotiable

(iii) Account Payee Only

Some times the lines of crossing contain the words "Accounts Payee Only." This is also a version of general crossing. The effect of such a crossing may be two-fold. It may affect, firstly, the negotiability of the cheque, and secondly, the duty of the collecting banker. For the words "Account Payee only" is a direction to the collecting banker that the contents of the cheque shall be received only for the payee and credited to his account.

(iv) "Not Negotiable" Crossing

When the lines of crossing carry the words "not negotiable" the crossing is said to be "not negotiable" crossing. Section 123 permits the use of such words and section 130 states their effect upon the negotiable character of the cheque. "A person taking a cheque crossed generally or specially, bearing in either case the words 'not negotiable', shall not have, and shall not be capable of giving, a better title to the cheque than that which the person from whom he took it had."

The words "not negotiable" are a danger signal equivalent to saying "Take care, this cheque may be stolen". This does not mean that this instrument cannot be transferred it can be transferred but, "every one who takes a cheque may be stolen." This does not mean that this instrument cannot be transferred. It can be transferred but, "every one who takes a cheque marked 'not negotiable' takes it at his own risk."

(v) Who may Cross

According to Section 125, "a cheque may be crossed by the following parties:

(i)	By Drawer	The drawer of cheque may cross it generally or specially.
(ii)	The Holder	Where the cheque is uncrossed the holder may cross it generally or specially. If the cheque is crossed generally, the holder may cross it specially. If the cheque is crossed generally or specially the holder may add the words "not negotiable".
(iii)	The Banker	Where a cheque is crossed specially, the banker to whom it is crossed may again cross it specially to another banker, or his agent for collection.

L. MATERIAL ALTERATIONS

A cheque contains a mandate of the drawer to his banker to pay a specified sum of money to the bearer or the person mentioned therein or to his order. Any alteration or correction therein, to be valid, must be made by, or with the consent of, the drawer and confirmed by his full signature. The paying banker should be very careful in this regard and should not make payment if the cheque bearer an alteration, specially a material alteration, without confirmation by the drawer.

"Any change in an instrument which causes to speak a different language in legal effect from that which it originally spoke or which changed the legal identity or character of the instrument either in its terms or in the relation of parties thereto is a material alteration.

Examples of Material Alterations

- Alteration of the date of the cheque
- Alteration of the place of payment
- Alteration of amount of the cheque
- Alteration in the name of the parties
- The substitution of the word 'bear' in place of 'order' in cheque
- Alteration of the crossing of a cheque

(a) Legal Effect of Material Alterations

According to section 87, any material alteration of a negotiable instrument renders the same void as against any one who is a party thereto at the time of making such alteration and does not consent thereto, unless it was made into carry out the common intention of the original parties. Any such alteration, if made by an endorsee, discharges his endorser from all liability to him in respect of the consideration thereof. Thus, a material alteration on a negotiable instrument shall have the following effects:

(i) The instrument becomes a void one as against all persons who were the parties to the instrument at the time the alteration was made and who did not give their consent for such alteration. The person making such alteration remains responsible on the instrument. But the liability of a person who becomes a party to the instrument after the alteration has been made is not affected.

(ii) A material alteration made with the consent of the parties to the instrument shall not become a void one.

(iii) An alteration, though material, will not vitiate the instrument if—
  (a) It is made before the execution of instrument, i.e. before it is issued to the other party,
  (b) It is made merely for the purpose of correcting a mistake, e.g., the year 1979 was wrongly written as 1969, and
  (c) It is made to carry out the common intention of the original parties to the instrument.

In *Anirudhan* v. *Thomco's Bank*[11] the court held that if the alteration is made by a stranger without the knowledge of the promisee the other party is discharged if the instrument is in the possession of the promisee or his agent but if the instrument is altered by a stranger when the instrument was not in the custody of the promisee the promisor is not discharged. But on the terms of this section such an alteration would be void as against any person who is a party to the instrument and does not consent to the alteration.

M. BURDEN OF PROOF

In case of a dispute regarding the material alteration, the question arises as to which party should prove the presence of anyone of the above mentioned circumstances which render the instrument effective in spite of the material alteration. The burden of proof, therefore, fall on the person who seeks to enforce the negotiable instrument.

N. WRONGFUL DISHONOUR VIS-A-VIS DEFICIENCY IN SERVICE

Wrongful dishonour of a cheque means refusal of a bank to pay it on an invalid ground, such as misplaced credits or wrong debits resulting in showing reduced balance of the account insufficient to honour the cheque. For wrongful dishonour of his cheque, a customer can bring action against the bank for "loss or damage" as used in Section 31 of the Negotiable Instruments Act, which includes, in addition to any pecuniary loss or damage, the loss of credit or injury to reputation for which the customer may recover

11. AIR 1963 SC 746.

substantial damage. The following are the different laws under which the customer can go against the bank.

(i) Action under breach of contract;
(ii) Action under breach of duty;
(iii) Action under libel;
(iv) Action under Consumer Protection Act;
(v) Action under ombudsman;
(vi) Action under Section 138 of the Negotiable Instruments Act.

(a) Breach of Contract

Dishonour of a cheque can lead to a pure action for breach of contract. The relationship between a banker and his customer is one of contractual and may be defined as that of debtor and creditor with the super added obligation of honouring the customer's cheques. Hence, wrongful dishonouring of the cheque of the customer amounts to be a breach of contract and is liable for damages.

(b) Breach of Duty

Wrongful acts other than a breach of contract such as negligence and fraud, included in the legal term "tort", may result in the dishonour of a cheque. A customer may sue the banker in tort for breach of duty on the part of banker likely to damage the customer's credit.

(c) Libels

This relates to the answer given for the dishonour of the cheque if the answer is defamatory, the customer may proceed against the banker in an action for libel. Libel is a statement in writing or some other permanent form causing the person concerned to be regarded with, hatred, ridicule or contempt whom the libel against is published.

(d) Consumer Protection Act

Action can be taken against the bank under Consumer Protection Act, 1986 for deficiency in service.

(e) Ombudsman

Customer can lodge a complaint against the bank, if the customer is not satisfied with bank service under ombudsman established by the law.

(f) Section 138 of Negotiable Instruments Act

From 1st April 1989, a drawer of a cheque is liable to penalties in case of dishonour of the cheque for insufficiency, etc. of funds in the account. An action can be taken against the drawer within one month of cause of action arising, after serving 15 days' notice. In *Kusum Ingots and Alloys Ltd.* v. *Pennar Peterson Securities,*[12] the Supreme Court held:

The object of bringing Section 138 on statute is to inculcate faith in the efficacy of banking operations and credibility in transacting business on negotiable instruments.

The ingredients which are to be satisfied for making out a case under Section 138 NI Act are:

(i) a person must have drawn a cheque on an account maintained by him in a bank for payment for a certain amount of money to another person from out of that account for the discharge of any debt or other liability;

(ii) that cheque has been presented to the bank within a period of six months from the date on which it is drawn or within the period of its validity, whichever is earlier;

(iii) that cheque is returned by the bank unpaid, either because the amount of money standing to the credit of the account is insufficient to that account by an agreement made with the bank;

(iv) the payee or the holder in due course of the cheque makes a demand for the payment of the said amount of money by giving a notice in writing, to the drawer of the cheque, within 15 days of the receipt of information by him from the bank regarding the return of the cheque as unpaid; and

(v) the drawer of such cheque fails to make payment of the said amount of money to the payee or the holder in due course of the cheque within 15 days of the receipt of the said notice.

If the aforementioned ingredients are satisfied then the person who has drawn the cheque shall be deemed to have committed an offence. In the present case the ingredients of Section 138 NI Act are *prima facie* established from the complaint and the documents filed with it. Therefore, no exception can be taken against the order of the Magistrate taking cognizance of the offence under Section 138 NI Act against the appellants.

O. BANK DRAFTS

For remitting money from one place to another, banks issue demand drafts on their branches at the place of destination. It is issued on request to a customer who has to make a guaranteed payment, that is, in circumstances where the payee wishes to be certain that the cheque will be paid upon presentation.

12. (2000) 2 SCC 745. Also see, Suman Sethi *v.* Ajay K. Churiwal, (2000) 2 SCC 380.

(a) Legal Status of a Draft

According to section 13(1) of the Negotiable Instruments Act, 1881, a negotiable instrument mean "a promissory note, bill of exchange or cheque." It does not make mention of a bank draft as a negotiable Instrument. There are, however, two sections in the Negotiable Instrument Act which expressly treat a bank draft at par with a bill of exchange or cheque. Section 85A States:

> "an order to pay money drawn by one office of a bank upon another office of the same bank for a sum of money payable to order or demand."

Section 131A provides that "the provisions of this chapter shall apply to any draft, as defined in section 85A, as if the draft were a cheque.

A bank draft is, thus a payment instruction similar to a cheque and is always drawn by one branch on another to pay a specified sum of money to the person named therein or his order.

3

The Transfer of Property Act, 1882

A. INTRODUCTION

The expression 'transfer of property' as defined in section 5, is wide enough to cover any transaction which has the effect of conveying, property from one living person to another, conveying of the property involves the creation of new title or interests in favour of the transferee. That is to say, if new title or interest has not been created in favour of the transferee the property is not conveyed, hence no transfer of property.[1]

B. SALE OF IMMOVABLE PROPERTY

"Sale" defined— "Sale" is a transfer of ownership in exchange for a price paid or promised or part-paid and part-promised.[2]

(a) Sale how made

Such transfer, in the case of tangible immovable property of the value of one hundred rupees and upwards, or in the case of a reversion or other tangible thing can be made only by a registered instrument.

In the case tangible immovable property of a value less than one hundred rupees, such transfer may be made either by a registered instrument or by delivery of the property.

Delivery of tangible immovable property takes place when the seller places the buyer, or such person as he directs, in possession of the property.

(b) Contract for Sale

A contract for the sale of immovable property is a contract that a sale of such property shall take place on terms settled between the parties. It does not, of itself, create any interest in or charge on, such property.

1. Quoted in S.N. Shukla, Transfer of Property Act (1999) at 29.
2. Section 54.

C. DEFINITION OF SALE

Sale is defined as being a transfer of ownership. In a sale there is an absolute transfer of all rights in the property sold. The words, "transfer of ownership" stand in contrast with the words "transfer of an interest" occurring in section 58 in the definition of mortgage and with "transfer of a right to enjoy property" in the definition of lease. In a mortgage or in a lease there is a partial transfer of rights while in a sale all the rights of ownership which the transferor has, pass to the transferee. A sale must be distinguished from a hire-purchase agreement. If the transferee has to pay entire purchase price it indicates that the transaction is sale but where the transferee is given a right to terminate the agreement, the transaction may be a hire purchase agreement.

(a) The Essential Elements of a Sale

I. the parties;
II. the subject matter;
III. the price or consideration; and
IV. the transfer or conveyance.

I. Parties to Sale

The parties to sale are the seller and the buyer. The seller must be a person competent to transfer within the meaning of section 7 of T.P.A. i.e., must be competent to contract and has right to transfer that property. The buyer may be any person who is not disqualified to be a transferee. A duly executed transfer by way of sale to a minor is valid.

II. Subject Matter of Sale

The subject matter is immovable property which may be tangible immovable property, such as land, houses, or things attached to the earth or it may be intangible immovable property, such as rights of ferry or fishery, or right to a mortgage debt, etc. But the property must be in existence at the date of transfer by way of sale and is transferable property within the meaning of section 6 of the Transfer of Property Act.

III. Price or Consideration

The transfer of ownership in exchange for a price is the essence of a Sale Price means Money Price. If the consideration of the transfer is something other than price, it is not a sale. It may be an exchange but not sale. A pre-payment of the price is not a condition precedent to the completion of the sale. Similarly, a transfer of land is satisfaction of a wife's claim for dower would not be a sale.[3]

3. Talib Ali *v.* Mst. Fatima, 2 Luck. 575 Quoted in *Supra* note 1.

IV. Transfer or Conveyance

There must be conveyance, i.e., transportation of absolute interest in the property by the seller in favour of the purchaser in the manner prescribed by law. Thus, there must be a transfer of property. The adjustment of the rights of the partners in a dissolved firm is not a transfer of property. The adjustment of the rights of the partners in a dissolved firm is not a transfer nor it is for a price.[4]

(b) Mode of Sale

A sale can be effected:

1. Where such property is tangible:
   (a) by a registered instrument if it is of the value of Rs. 100 or upwards;
   (b) by a registered instrument or delivery of the property when it is less than Rs. 100 in value;
2. Where such property is intangible or reversion only by a registered instrument.

D. TANGIBLE AND INTANGIBLE IMMOVABLE PROPERTY

The distinction between tangible and intangible property may be compared with that made by English law between corporeal and incorporeal things. Corporeal thing would be one, which are capable of being seen or touched, e.g., an undivided share in immovable property. Reversion, which is a type of immovable property, is the residue of an original estate, which is left after the grantor has granted smaller estate.

The distinction between tangible and intangible property is that one who is in physical possession of land, i.e. a present right to enjoy the possession of land is in possession of tangible property; whereas if he has the mere right over the land in the possession of another and which may be right to future possession, is said to be in possession of intangible property.

(a) Delivery of Property

Tangible immovable property of a value less than Rs. 100 can be sold either by registered instrument or by delivery of the property. Delivery takes place when the seller places the buyer, or such person as he directs, in possession of the property. Delivery of possession may be actual or constructive. Thus, possession of house may be given by delivery of the keys. Where the property sold is in the possession of tenants, the Calcutta High Court has held in *Sibendrapada* v. *Secretary of State*[5] that the sale can be effected only by a registered instrument. The Madras High Court has taken

4. Commissioner of Income Tax *v.* Ramdev Pradhan, 4 (1971) 37 CLT 114.
5. (1907) 34 Cal. 207. Quoted in *Supra* Note 1.

a contrary view.[6] The decision in Sibendrapada case is supported by an observation of the Privy Council in *Bishwanath Prasad* v. *Chandra Narayan* that for the purpose of Sec. 54 there must be a real delivery of the property.

E. RIGHTS AND LIABILITIES OF BUYER AND SELLER

In the absence of a contract to the contrary, the buyer and the seller of immovable property respectively are subject to the liabilities, and have the rights, mentioned in the rules next following, or such of them as are applicable to the property sold:

(1) The seller is bound:

(a) to disclose to the buyer and material defect in the property or in the seller's title thereto of which the seller is, and the buyer is not, aware and which the buyer could not with ordinary care discover;
(b) to produce to the buyer on his request for examination all documents of title relating to the property which are in the seller's possession or power;
(c) to answer to the best of his information all relevant questions put to him by the buyer in respect of the property or the title thereto;
(d) on payment or tender of the amount due in respect of the price, to execute a proper conveyance of the property when the buyer tenders it to him for execution at a proper time and place;
(e) between the date of the contract of sale and the delivery of the property, to take as much care of the property and all documents of title relating thereto which are in his possession, as an owner of ordinary prudence would take of such property and documents;
(f) to give, on being so required, the buyer, or such person as he directs, such possession of property as its nature admits; and
(g) to pay all public charges and rent accrued due in respect of the property up to the date of the sale, the interest on all encumbrances on such property due on such date, and, except where the property is sold subject to encumbrances, to discharge all encumbrances on the property then existing.

(2) The seller shall be deemed to contract with the buyer that the interest which the seller professes to transfer to the buyer subsists, and that he has power to transfer the same:

Provided that, where the sale is made by a person in a fiduciary character, he shall be deemed to contract with the buyer that the seller has done no act whereby the property is encumbered or whereby he is hindered from transferring it.

The benefit of the contract, mentioned in this rule shall be annexed to, and shall go with the interest of the transferee as such; and may be enforced

6. Muthukaruppan *v.* Muthusamban (1915) 38 Mad 1158. *Ibid.*

by every person in whom that interest is for the whole or any part thereof from time to time vested.

(3) Where the whole of the purchase-money has been paid to the seller, he is also bound to deliver to the buyer all documents of title relating to the property, which are in the seller's possession or power:

Provided that, (a) where the seller retains any part of the property comprised in such documents, he is entitled too retain them all, and (b) where the whole of such property is sold to different buyers, the buyers of the lot of greatest value, is entitled to such documents. But in case (a) the seller, and in case (b) the buyer, of the lot of greatest value, is bound, upon every reasonable request by the buyer, or by any of the other buyers, as the case may be, and at the cost of the person making the request, to produce the said documents and furnish such true copies thereof or extracts therefrom as he may require and in the meantime, the seller, or the buyer of the lot of greatest value, as the case may be, shall keep the said documents safe, uncancelled and undefected, unless prevented from so doing by fire or other inevitable accident.

(4) The seller is entitled:

(a) to the rents and profits of the property till the ownership thereof passes to the buyer; and
(b) where the ownership of the property has passed to the buyer before payment of the whole of the purchaser—money, to a charge, upon the property in the hands of buyer, and transferee. Without consideration or any transferee with notice of the non-payment, for the amount of purchase-money, or any part thereof remaining unpaid and for interest of such amount or part from the date on which possession has been delivered.

(5) The buyer is bound:

(a) to disclose to the seller any fact as to the nature or extent of the seller's interest in the property of which the buyer is aware, but of which he has reason to believe that the seller is not aware and which materially increases the value of such interest;
(b) to pay or tender, at the time and place of completing the sale, the purchase-money to the seller or such person as he directs: provided that, where the property is sold free from encumbrances, the buyer may retain out of the purchase-money, the amount of any encumbrances on the property existing at the date of sale, and shall pay the amount so retained to the persons entitled thereto;
(c) where the ownership of the property has passed to the buyer, to bear any loss arising from the destruction, injury or decrease in value of the property not caused by the seller.
(d) Where the ownership of the property has passed to the buyer, as between himself and the seller, to pay all public charges and rent which may become payable in respect of the property, the principal

moneys due on any encumbrances subject to which the property is sold and the interest thereon afterwards accruing due.

(6) The buyer is entitled:

(a) where the ownership of the property has passed to him to the benefit of any improvement in, or increase in value of, the property, and to the rents and profits thereof; and

(b) unless he has improperly declined at accept delivery of the property, to a charge on the property as against the seller and all persons claiming under him, to the extent of the seller's interest in the property, for the extent of the seller's interest in the property, for the amount of any purchase money properly paid by the buyer in anticipation of the delivery and for interest on such amount; and, when he properly declines to accept the delivery also for the earnest (if any) and for the costs (if any) awarded to him of a suit to compel specific performance of the contract or to obtain a decree for its recession.

A mission to make such disclosures as are mentioned in this section, Paragraph (1) clause (a), and paragraph (5) clause (a) in fraudulent.

F. RIGHTS AND LIABILITIES OF THE SELLER AND THE BUYER

In the absence of contract to the contrary, the section sets forth the rights and liabilities of the buyer and the seller. There is a clear distinction between the rights and liabilities before the completion of sale and rights and liabilities after the sale. The former are contractual; the later are regulated by the rule that property having been passed to the buyer the transaction cannot be avoided. They are as follows:

(a) Liabilities of the Seller before Completion of the Sale

The duties of the seller before completion of the sale are:

(a) to disclose material defects in the property or in the seller's title thereto [Section 55(1)(a)];
(b) to produce title deeds [Section 55(1)(b)];
(c) to answer questions as to title [Section 55(1)(c)];
(d) to execute conveyance [Section 55(1)(d)];
(e) to take care of the property [Section 55(1)(e)]; and
(f) to pay out goings [Section 55(1)(g)].

(i) Seller's Duty of Disclosure

The seller is under a duty to disclose to the buyer every material defect in the property or in his own title thereto.

This duty arises with respect to these defects of which the seller is, and the buyer is not aware and which the buyer could not with ordinary care discover. In other words, the duty is with regard to latent defects but not patent defects, which the buyer could discover for himself. For instance, the existence of an open rights of way or the ruinous state of building is an apparent defect while a defect in title is a latent defect. Similarly, an underground drain is a latent defect and if the buyer does not know of its existence, the seller is duty-bound to inform him of its existence.

The material defect, therefore, which the vendor must disclose may be either in respect of property itself or the title of the vendor, e.g., an encumbrance, as easement or a restrictive covenant. If such defects are not disclosed then the following consequence would result:

(a) If the purchaser discovers such defects the sale is completed, he may either rescind the contract or take the property and later claim damages.
(b) If such defects are discovered after the sale is completed, the buyer is entitled to claim damages and he may sue to set aside the sale. Ordinarily once the sale is complete, it cannot be avoided either by the seller or the buyer, but in the case of non-disclosure of a material defect the rule is otherwise, because an omission to make such disclosure is fraudulent.

Under the later half of clause (g) of Section 55(1) of the transfer of Property Act where the property is not sold subject to an encumbrance, the vendor is bound to discharge all encumbrances on the property then existing and effect that the said premises are free from all encumbrances, claims and demands occasioned or created by the vendor, would not be in compliance with Section 55(1)(g) of the Transfer of Property Act.

(ii) Production of Title Deeds

It is the seller's duty to produce title-deeds relating to the immovable property contracted to be sold for the inspection of the buyer in order that the buyer should satisfy himself as to title. It is the buyer's interest to inspect the title deeds for otherwise he may be fixed with constructive notice of matters, which he would have discovered if he had investigated the title. [Section 55(e)].

(iii) Seller's Duty to Answer Material Questions as to Title

The seller is further bound to answer all relevant questions put to him by the buyer in respect of the property or title. The right to put questions to the seller does not affect his duty to made disclosure as required by clause (a). The buyer's right to take objections and to insist on proof of a title free from doubt may be lost by waiver.

ILLUSTRATION

A contracts to sell a house to B. Before the execution of the deed of sale, B enters into possession and tries to raise money on a mortgage of the house B had waived his right to make objections to the title to A.

(iv) Seller's Duty to Execute Conveyance

It is the seller's duty to execute conveyance. This execution of the conveyance by the seller and the payment of the price by the buyer is to take place, in the absence of a contract to the contrary, simultaneously. If either party uses for specific performance he must show that he was ready and willing to perform his duty.

(v) Care of Property

It is the duty of the seller to take care of the property between the date of contract and the delivery of the property to the buyer. The seller is some times said to be a trustee for the buyer. His duties are, therefore, analogous to those imposed upon a trustee by Section 15 of the Indian Trust Act. If the Seller neglects his duty the buyer is entitled to compensation in the event of any loss or damage to the property.[7]

(vi) Payment of Out Goings

The last duty of the seller, is to pay public charges and rent, etc., up to the date of the completion of sale. Public charges would include Government revenue, municipal taxes, etc. The seller is also under a duty to discharge all encumbrances on the property existing at the date of the sale except where the property is sold subject to encumbrances.

(b) Liabilities of the Seller after Completion of Sale

The liabilities of the seller after the completion of the sale are:

(a) to give possession (Section 55(1)(f)];
(b) to covenant for title impedely [Section 55(2)]; and
(c) to deliver title deeds on receipt of price [Section 55(3)].

(i) Seller's Duty to Give Possession

In the absence of a contract to the contrary, the vendor is under a duty to give possession immediately on the execution of the sale-deed. The non-payment of the purchase-money does not prevent the ownership from passing from the vendor to the purchaser, and the latter, notwithstanding such non-payment, may bring a suit for possession.

The vendor is bound to give such possession of the property as its nature admits. Possession of incorporeal right such as a right to fishery cannot be its very nature take place by actual physical possession.[8]

(ii) Covenant of Title

Sub-Section (2) lays down that the seller shall be deemed to contract with the buyer that the interest which he transfers to the buyer subsists and that he has the power to transfer the same. An express covenant of title in a sale

7. *Id.*, at 184.
8. Peare Lal *v.* Hublala, AIR 1945, All. 139.

deed is not necessary. Since under this sub-section such a covenant is implied in every sale of immovable property. The legal effect of such covenant may be summarized thus:

(a) The covenant imports an absolute warranty of title.
(b) If a defect in the vendor's title is discovered after the sale is duly completed, the vendor is entitled to use for damages and claim a return of the purchase money if he is dispossessed in consequence of his vendor's defective title.[9]
(c) The liability is, however, limited to the title, which the vendor professes to transfer. Thus if he only professed to transfer occupancy rights he is not liable if he is evicted by title paramount.
(d) The covenant runs with the land. It is, therefore, enforceable the subsequent purchasers of the land.

(iii) Delivery of Title-deeds

The general rule is that the title-deeds pass with the land as incidents of the property. But the buyer is not entitled to the deeds until the whole of the purchase-money has been paid. As soon as the purchaser has paid the price the vendor is bound to deliver the title-deeds.

(c) Before the Completion—Rights of the Seller

Until ownership is passed to the purchaser, the seller is owner and the rents and profits belong to him. In case the seller refuses to execute the sale-deed as agreed, the purchaser is entitled to claim compensation from the date when the deed should have been executed.

(d) After Completion—Seller's Lien

Section 55(4) lays down a very important rule, namely, that if the sale is completed by conveyance but the price or any part of it is unpaid, the seller acquires a charge on the property for the unpaid price. If the vendor has already delivered possession of the property to the purchaser before the payment of price he is not entitled to recover possession on the ground of non-payment of the price. His only remedy is to enforce his charge against the property. This statutory charge has been described as a non-possessory for the reason that it arises when the vendor has parted with the possession of the property.

The change can be enforced under section 100 of the act by the Sale of the property. It cannot, however, be enforced against a *bonafide* purchaser for value without notice of charge.[10]

9. *Id.* at 185.
10. *Id.* at 54-55.

(e) Buyer's Liabilities before Completion

The buyer's liabilities before the completion of the sale are:

(a) to disclose facts materially increasing the value of the property [Sec. 55(a)]; and
(b) to pay the price [Sec. 55(5)(b)].

(i) Duty to Disclose Facts

The buyer is bound to disclose the seller any fact as to the nature or extent of the seller's interest in the property. This duty corresponds to the duty of the seller to disclose material defects in the property. A non-disclosure of such fact on the part of the buyer would be fraudulent just as much as a non-disclosure by the seller would be. The obligation of the buyer to disclose facts extends only to the nature and extent of the seller's interest in the property, and this obligation arises only;

(i) If the buyers know or has reason to believe that the seller does not know the nature and extent of his interest; and
(ii) If the fact materially increases the value of the property.

In the English case, *Summer* v. *Griffith*[11] an old woman of eighty-eight, being in distress and without legal assistance, was induced to sell her property at one-fourth of its face value under the impression that she could not make out a good title whereas the purchaser knew that she could, and thus concealed the fact from her, the court said: "if a person comes to me and offers to sell me a property which I know to be five times the value he offers it for, he being ignorant of his rights and in the belief that he cannot make out a good title which I know that he can; and I conceal that knowledge from him is not that a *Suppression Veri* which is one of the elements which constitute a fraud?"[12]

(ii) Payment of Price

Ordinarily, the obligation to pay the purchase-money on the one hand and the obligation to execute the conveyance or complete the sale on the other are obligations, which should be performed concurrently.

(f) Buyer's Liabilities after Completion

The buyer's liabilities after completion of the sale are two:

(i) to bear loss to the property, and
(ii) to pay the outgoings.

(g) Buyer's Liability for Loss

The ownership ordinarily passes to the buyer on execution of the sale-deed, and if any loss occurs to the property either by way of accidental destruction or deterioration, it must be borne by the buyer.

11. *Supra* Note 1 at 187.
12. *Id.* at 188.

(h) Buyer's Duty to Pay Charges etc.

Under section 55(1)(g) the seller pays charges and taxes which have accrued due up to date of the sale. After the sale, such charges and taxes must be paid by the buyer.

(i) Buyer's Right

The buyer has two rights. One of them is before the completion of the sale and other is after completion of the sale. They are as follows:

(i) Before Completion: Buyer's Lien

The buyer has, on the seller failing to complete the sale, a charge for the amount paid by him in advance on account of the purchase money. This charge is converse of the sellers charge for unpaid price. The charge, unlike the seller's charge, can be enforced against all persons holding, the property irrespective of the question of notice such a charge can even be enforced against a purchaser for consideration with or without notice of the charge.[13]

(ii) After Completion: Improvements and Profits

After the completion of the sale, the vendor has no claim to participate in any benefit, which the purchaser may derive from his purchase.

G. MORTGAGES OR IMMOVABLE PROPERTY AND CHARGES

(a) "Mortgage", "mortgagor", "mortgagee", "mortgage-money" and "mortgage-deed" defined

A mortgage is the transfer of an interest in specific immovable property for the purpose of securing the payment of money advanced or to be advanced by way of loan, an existing or future debt or the performance of an engagement which may give rise to a pecuniary liability.

The transferor is called a mortgagor, the transferee a mortgagee; the principal money and interest of which payment is secured for the time being are called the mortgage-money, and the instrument (if any) by which the transfer is effected is called a mortgage deed.

(b) Simple Mortgage

Where, without delivering possession of the mortgaged property, the mortgagor binds himself personally to pay the mortgage-money, and agrees, expressly or impliedly, that, in the event of his failing to pay according to his contract, the mortgage shall have a right to cause the mortgaged property to be sold and the proceeds of sale to be applied, so far as may be necessary,

13. *Id.* at 189.

in payment of the mortgage-money, the transaction is called a simple mortgage and the mortgagee a simple mortgagee.

(c) Mortgage by Conditional Sale

Where the mortgagor ostensibly sells the mortgaged property—

On condition that on default of payment of the mortgage money on a certain date the sale shall become absolute, or

On condition that on such payment being made the sale shall become void, or

On condition that on such payment being made the buyer shall transfer the property to the seller, the transaction is called mortgage by conditional sale and the mortgage a mortgage by conditional sale:

Provided that no such transaction shall be deemed to be a mortgage, unless the condition is embodied in the document, which effects or purports to effect the sale.

(d) Usufructuary Mortgagor

Where the mortgagor delivers possession or expressly or by implication binds himself to deliver possession of the mortgaged property to the mortgagee, and authorizes him to retain such possession until payment of the mortgage-money, and to receive the rents and profits accruing from the property or any part of such rents and profits and to appropriate the same in lieu of interest, or in payment of the mortgage-money, or partly in lieu of interest or partly in payment of the mortgage-money, the transaction is called a usufructuary mortgage and the mortgagee an unufructuary mortgagee.

(e) English Mortgage

Where the mortgagor binds himself to repay the mortgage-money on a certain date and transfer the mortgaged property absolutely to the mortgagee, but subject to a proviso that he will retransfer it to the mortgagor upon payment of the mortgage-money as agreed, the transaction is called an English mortgage.

(f) Mortgage by Deposit of Title-deeds

Where a person in any of the following towns, namely, the towns of Calcutta, Madras and Bombay, and in any other town which the State Government concerned may by notification in the Official gazette specify in this behalf, delivers to a creditor or his agent documents of title to immovable property, with intent to create a security thereon, the transaction is called a mortgage or deposit of title-deeds.

(g) Anomalous Mortgage

A mortgage which is not a simple mortgage, a mortgage by conditional sale, an usufructuary mortgage, and English mortgage or a mortgage by deposits of title deeds within the meaning of this section is called an anomalous mortgage.

Definition and Nature of Mortgage

When a person lends money to another he may be content to make the loan simply on the borrower's promise to repayment of the money. In the former case the lender has a right to sue for the money if it is not paid, but if the borrower becomes insolvent, the lender may lose part or all of his money. But if some security of value is given for repayment of the loan, the lender is protected even if the borrower becomes insolvent, for he can always realise his money from the property given by way of security.

The most important kind of security is mortgage. The essential nature of mortgage is that it is a transfer of an interest in specific immovable property to the lender, called a mortgagee. To quote Mahmood, J. in *Gopal* v. *Parsottam*,[14] mortgagee . . . cannot be better defined than by the definition adopted by the legislature in Section 58 of the transfer of Property Act. Section 58 defines mortgage as follows:

"A mortgage is the transfer of an interest in specific immovable property for the purpose of securing the payment of money advanced or to be advanced by way of loan, a pecuniary liability" (Emphasis added).

As against sale or gift, the mortgage is simply the transfer of an interest in the property mortgaged. It is not the transfer of absolute interest in the property. Again, unlike lease (which is also the transfer of an interest on payment of rent) the purpose of the transfer of an interest in the mortgaged property is to secure the payment of a loan.

A mortgage is a transfer of an interest in specific immovable property for the purpose of securing the payment of money advanced or to be advanced by way of loan, an existing or future debt, or the performance of an engagement, which may give rise to a pecuniary liability. There is necessarily a transfer of interest in specific immovable property by reason of the execution of the mortgage. That would be there irrespective of whether a debt has arisen or not because it is a necessary element of mortgage, but a mortgage is not always executed for securing debt which has already arisen. A mortgage can be executed for securing payment of money to be advanced. Money, which may be paid later, may be secured by a current mortgage. Instances are too many to need citation. Equitable mortgages executed in favour of Banks to secure overdraft accounts would operate as mortgages but the debts thereunder would arise only when liability is incurred by reason of a debit being found in the overdraft account as a result of operating the account. Execution of Mortgage by itself does not give rise to a debt.[15]

14. (1883) 5 All. 121, 137 (F.B.).

15. Janardhaba Mallan and Others *v.* Gangadharan and Other, AIR 1983 Ker. 178.

Element of a Mortgage

The following are the essential characteristics of a mortgage:

(1) There must be a transfer of an interest.
(2) There must be specific immovable property intended to be mortgaged.
(3) The transfer must be made to secure the payment of a loan or to secure the performance of a contract.

Transfer of an Interest

The word, "transfer of an interest" signify that the interest which passess, to the mortgagee is not ownership or dominion which, not with standing the mortgage is not ownership or dominion which, notwithstanding the mortgage, resides in the mortgagor.

Mortgage is simply a transfer of interest in the immovable property while the ownership still retains with the mortgagors.

Specific Immovable Property

The next requisite of a mortgage is that immovable property must be distinctly specified. The description of the property in the mortgage deed, if any, must at least be sufficient to identify the property. The word 'specific' is to be distinguished from the word "general." For instance, the word "my house and landed property" or "my house and property" have been held to be general and vague on the other hand, the words "a house situated in Ghaziabad owned and possessed by us" have been held to be sufficiently specific.[16]

Consideration of Mortgage

The third essential of a mortgage is that it must be supported by consideration. The consideration of a mortgage may be either (1) money advanced or to be advance by way of loan; (2) an existing or future debt; or (3) the performance of an engagement giving rise to pecuniary liability. A mortgage is created for the purpose of securing a debt or other obligation. A transfer, which is made by way of discharging a debt, is not a mortgage.

Forms of Mortgage

Mortgage is a transfer of an inter specific immovable property. The nature of the right transferred depends upon the form of the mortgage. It, therefore becomes necessary to consider the kinds of mortgage, which are set out in Section 58. The section enumerates following six classes of mortgage:

1. Simple mortgage.
2. Mortgage by conditional sale.

16. *Id.* at 196.

3. Usufructuary mortgage.
4. English mortgage.
5. Mortgage by deposit to title deeds.
6. Anomalous mortgage.

1. Simple Mortgage

The characteristics of a simple mortgage are: (1) that the mortgagor must have bound himself personally to repay the loan, (2) that to secure the loan he has transferred to the mortgage the right to have specific immovable property sold in the event of his having failed to repay, and (3) that possession of the property is not given to the mortgagee.

The essential characteristic of a simple mortgage, therefore is that possession is not given to the mortgagee of the mortgaged property. That is expressly provided in the definition itself. All the rights, which the mortgagee has, are these: First to recover the money, which he has loaned. His second right is that in the event of non-payment, "the mortgagee shall have a right to cause the mortgaged property to be sold and the proceeds of sale to be applied . . . in payment of the mortgage money." Therefore, the mortgagee under a simple mortgage has no right whatsoever to actual possession of the crucial difference between a simple mortgage and usufructuary mortgage. In a Usufructuary mortgage possession is given to the mortgagee [clause (d) of Section 58] whereas in a simple mortgage the possession of the mortgaged property remains with the mortgagor.[17]

Personal Undertaking

A personal undertaking to pay is essential element of a simple mortgage. The covenant to pay may be express or implied from the terms of a particular transaction. The promise to pay is implicit in the borrowing transaction, itself but it may be displaced by the terms of the mortgage transaction as, for example, in the case of usufructuary mortgage.

Right to have the Mortgaged Property Sold

It is also necessary to constitute a simple mortgage that the mortgage must be given the right to cause the property to be sold for the purpose of realising the mortgage-debt. The words "cause the property to be sold" indicate that the power of sale is not to be exercised without the intervention of the court.[18]

No Delivery of Possession

The outstanding feature of a simple mortgage is that possession is not delivered to the mortgagee, but remains with the mortgagor. Since the mortgagee is not put into possession of the property, he has no right to

17. Anaji Thamaji Patil *v.* Rabho Bhivraja Patil and Anothers, AIR 1973 Bom. 75.
18. Krishanlal *v.* Gangaram, (1891) 13, All. 28.

satisfy the debt out of the rents and profits, nor can he acquire the absolute ownership of mortgaged property by foreclosure.

2. Mortgage by Conditional Sale

A simple mortgage usually carried interest, for the mortgagee being out of possession, interest is the only benefit which he derives in such transaction. But the Mohammedan Law forbids the taking of interest and therefore in order of evade the prohibition of interest, a kind of mortgage, known as *byebil wafa* was devised. The mortgagor purported to make over the property to the mortgagee, by way of an absolute sale, and the mortgagee (the ostensible buyer) agreed to resell the property, at the expiry of a certain stipulated time, on being repaid the money advanced by him. This kind of mortgage came into vogue in India during the Muslim rule. It was given a legal recognition in the Bengal Regulation Act (1 of 1978).

Mortgage by conditional sale as defined in the Act, is an ostensible sale on condition that upon repayment the buyer shall transfer the property to the seller.

Essentials of a Mortgage by Conditional Sale

In a mortgage by conditional sale:

(1) The mortgagor must ostensibly sell the immovable property.

(2) There must be a condition that either,

  (a) on the repayment of the money due under the mortgage on a certain date, the sale shall become void or the buyer shall retransfer the property to the seller, or

  (b) in default of payment on that date the sale shall become absolute.

(3) The condition must be embodied in the document which effects of purports to effect the sale.

3. Usufructuary Mortgage

The characteristics of a usufructuary mortgage are:

(1) possession of the property is delivered to the mortgagee;

(2) the mortgagee is to get rents and profits in lieu of interest or principal or both;

(3) no personal liability is incurred by the mortgagor; and

(4) the mortgagee cannot foreclose or sue for sale.

Possession

The essence of the transaction is that the mortgagor is bound to put the mortgagee in possession of the property. If the possession is not delivered, the mortgagee may sue for possession or for the recovery of the mortgage money under Section 68(d). In *Pratap Bahadur* v. *Gujadhar,*[19] the mortgagor

19. (1902) 24, All. 521.

covenanted to put the mortgagee in possession of a certain village on a subsequent date, and to pay interest at 24 percent, until possession was delivered. It was held that the mortgage was usufructuary mortgage. On the other hand, in *Yashwani* v. *Vithal*[20], where there was a covenant that the interest, the mortgagee could take possession, and would appropriate the rents and profits towards interest, it was held that the transaction was a simple mortgage.

Where a usufructuary mortgage is executed in respect of a lease or other property and the same is leased out by the mortgagee to the mortgagor to secure his interest in the property, it is always open to the mortgagee to sue the mortgagor and take possession of the property or to induce some other tenant.

Rents and Profits

The method by which the rents and profits are to be appropriated depends upon the terms of the mortgage-deed. The rents and profits or part of the rents and profits may be appropriated,—

(i) in lieu of interest,
(ii) in lieu of principal, or
(iii) in lieu of principal and interest.

In the first case, the mortgagor recovers possession when he pays the principal. In the second case, the mortgagor continues to pay interest and is entitled to recover possession when the rents and profits received by the mortgagee equal the amount of the principal. In the last case, the mortgagor is not to recover possession until the principal and interest are paid out of the rents and profits.

No Personal Liability

The mortgagor cannot be sued personally for the debt. The mortgagee is only entitled to remain in possession of the mortgaged property till the principal and interest are defrayed according to the terms of the agreement. Since a usufructuary mortgagee is entitled to remains in possession until the debt is paid-off, no time limit can be fixed expressly during which the mortgage is to subsist.

4. English Mortgage

An English mortgage is a transaction in which the mortgagor binds himself to repay the mortgage money on a certain date, and transfers the mortgaged property absolutely to the mortgagee, but subject to a proviso that he will retransfer it to the mortgagor upon payment of the department. Thus, the main features of this mortgage are—

(i) that the mortgagor should bind himself to repay the mortgage money on a certain day;

20. (1897) Bom. 267.

(ii) that the mortgaged property should be transferred absolutely to the mortgagee; and

(iii) that such absolute transfer should be made subject to a proviso that the mortgagee will reconvey the property to the mortgagor, upon payment by him of the mortgage money on the appointed day.

5. Mortgage by Deposit of Title-deeds

In England, a mortgage of this kind is called an "equitable mortgage" as opposed to a "mortgage" because in this type of mortgage, there is simply a deposit of document of title without anything more, without writing or without any other formalities. The object of the Legislature in providing for this kind of mortgage is to give facility to the mercantile community in cases where it may be necessary to raise money all of a sudden before an opportunity call be afforded or preparing the mortgage-deed. This mortgage, therefore, does not require any writing and being an oral transaction is not affected by the Law of Registration. In India, equitable mortgages have been recognized since the decision of the Privy Council in *Verdu Seth Sam* v. *Luckputty*[21]. The term equitable mortgage and being inappropriate in India on account of the absence of classification or division of estates or rights into legal and equitable, it is called a mortgage by deposit of title-deeds.

A mortgage by deposit of title-deeds is form a mortgage recognized by Section 58(f) of the Transfer of Property Act which provides that it may be effected in certain town, where a person delivers to a creditor or his agent, the documents of title to immovable property with intent to create a security thereon.

Under the definition of mortgage by deposit by Section 58(f) of the Transfer of Property Act, the essential requisites of such a mortgage are:

(i) a debt;

(ii) deposit of the title deeds; and

(iii) an intention that the deeds shall be security for the debt.

6. Anomalous Mortgage

The classification of mortgages contained in Section 58 is not exhaustive. It only describes certain forms of mortgages which are in common use in India. Several other kinds of mortgages are in use in various parts of India which are in the nature of usufructuary mortgage. These and other types of mortgages have been given the name of 'anomalous' mortgage. Anomalous mortgage has been defined as a mortgage which does not fall under any of the live classes mentioned above.

An anomalous mortgage includes: (1) a simple mortgage usufructuary, and (2) a mortgage usufructuary by conditional sale, which are described below:

(1) A simple mortgage usufructuary is combination of a simple mortgage and a usufructuary mortgage and consequently an anomalous

21. (1862) 8 MIA 307.

mortgage. In this transaction, the mortgagee is in possession and pays himself the debt out of the rents and profits and there is also personal undertaking as well as a right to cause the property to be sold on the expiry of the date fixed for payment.

(2) A mortgage usufructuary by conditional sale is another instance of an anomalous mortgage. Here the mortgagee is in possession as a usufructuary mortgagee for a fixed period and if the debt is not discharged at the expiry of the period, he gets all the rights of a mortgagee by conditional sale. In case the debt is not paid within the time fixed, the mortgagee gets the right of foreclosure, that is a right to deprive the mortgagor's right of redemption.

H. MODE OF TRANSFER IN A MORTGAGE

There are three ways in which property may be transferred by way of mortgage:

(a) Registered instrument;
(b) Delivery of possession; and
(c) Deposit of title-deeds.

Registered Instrument

In the case of mortgage other than a mortgage by deposit of title-deeds if the principal money secured in Rs. 100 or upwards, a registered instrument is compulsory. A combined reading of Section 59 of the Transfer of Property Act and Section 17(1)(b) of the Indian Registration Act, so far as mortgages are concerned, makes it absolutely clear that the value of Rs. 100 contemplated must have reference only to the principal amount secured under the mortgage and not to the interest that may accrue.

Registration of Mortgage by Deposit of Title-deeds

When the debtor deposits with the creditor the title-deeds of his property with an intent to create a security, the law implies a contract between the parties to create a mortgage, and no registered instrument is required under Section 9 of the Transfer of Property Act as in other classes of mortgage. It is essential to bear in mind that the essence of a mortgage by deposit of title-deeds in the actual handing over by a borrower to the lender of documents of title to immovable property with the intention that those documents shall constitute a security which will enable the creditor ultimately to recover the money which he has lent but if the parties chose to reduce the contract to writing this implication of law is excluded by their express bargain, and the document will be the sole evidence of its terms. In such a case, the deposit and the document both from integral parts of the transaction and are essential ingredients in the creation of the mortgage. It follows that, in such a case, the document which constitute the bargain regarding security, requires registration under section 17 of the Indian Registration Act as non-testamentary instrument creating an interest in immovable property, where the value of such property is Rs. 100 and upwards. If a document of this character is not registered, it cannot be used in the evidence at all and the transaction itself cannot be proved by oral evidence either.

In *Pranjivandes Metha* v. *Chan Ma Pkee*,[22] the Privy Council observed as follows:

(a) Where titles are handed over with nothing said expect that they are to be security, the law supposes that the scope of the security is the scope of the title.
(b) Where, however, titles are handed over accompanied by a bargain that bargain must rule.
(c) When the bargain is a written bargain, it and it alone must determine what is the scope and extent of security.

Delivery of Possession

When the Principal money secured is less than Rs. 100, a mortgage may be effected either by registered instrument or by delivering of possession.

In the case of a simple mortgage as there is no delivery of possession, the rule is that it must be effected by registered instrument irrespective of the amount secured by such mortgage.

Deposit of Title-deeds

This is a mortgage by deposit of title-deeds and it is not necessary that it should be in writing, but this type of mortgage can be effected only in certain towns specified in section 58(f). Accordingly, whatever the amount secured might be, it can be made in those specified towns without any formalities.

Rights of the Mortgagee

As provided in several sections of the Act, the rights of a mortgagee are:[23]

(1) Right of foreclosure or sale (Sec. 67)
(2) Right to sue for mortgage money (Sec. 68)
(3) Right to exercise power of sale, if any (Sec. 69)
(4) Right to have a receiver, appointed (Sec. 69-A)
(5) Right to accession to mortgaged property (Sec. 70)
(6) Right to the benefit of the renewed lease (Sec. 71)
(7) Right to spend money in certain cases (Sec. 72)
(8) Right to proceeds of revenue sale or compensation on acquisition of the mortgaged property. (Sec. 73)

22. AIR 1916 PC 115, 431A, 122.
23. S.P. Padhi, Allied Laws for Co-operatives (1968) at 68.

Rights of the Mortgagor

The rights of the mortgagor are as follows:

(1) Right of redeem (Sec. 60)
(2) Right to require the mortgagee to transfer the property to a third person on redemption (Sec. 60-A)
(3) Right of inspection on production of documents (Sec. 60-B)
(4) Right of usufructuary mortgage or to recover possession (Sec. 62)
(5) Right to redeem separately or simultaneously (Sec. 61)
(6) Right to accession (Sec. 63)
(7) Right to improvements to mortgaged property (Sec. 63)
(8) Right to the benefits of renewal or mortgage leased (Sec. 64)
(9) Right to make leases. (Sec. 65-A)

Liabilities of the Mortgagee in Possession

The liabilities of the mortgagee in possession can be stated as follows:

(i) To manage the property.
(ii) To collect the rents and profits thereof.
(iii) To pay Government revenue and all other charges of a public nature in the absence of a contract to the contrary during continuance of possession.
(iv) To make necessary repair to the property.
(v) He must not commit any act, which is destructive to the property.
(vi) To keep clear, full and accurate accounts of all sums received and spent by him as mortgagee.

Liabilities of the Mortgagor

The liabilities of the mortgagor are as under:

1. To pay for acquired accession which are separable and which he wants to make. (Sec. 63)
2. To pay costs or improvements that were necessary to preserve the property. (Sec. 63-A)
3. Implied contracts by mortgagor, which he is deemed to undertake, and which run with the land. (Sec. 63)
4. Not to commit acts of waste. (Sec. 66)

I. DOCTRINE OF CLOG ON REDEMPTION

The doctrine is expressed in the maxim: "Once a mortgage always a mortgage and nothing but a mortgage."

It means that the mortgagee shall not make any stipulation which will prevent a mortgagor who has paid principal, interest and costs from getting back his mortgaged property. The discharge of the mortgage must restore the mortgagor to the same position to which he would have been placed had there been no mortgage at all.

Contracts entered into as a part of the mortgage transaction which are repugnant to the mortgagor's contractual or equitable right to redeem cannot be enforced by the mortgagee. The law requires that there shall be a right of redemption. Since a mortgage is only a security for the repayment of the debt or a performance of obligation, on payment, the mortgagor is entitled to receive back the hypothecia. Any stipulation to prevent redemption on payment, is a clog or a fetter on the equity of redemption and, therefore, void.

Remedies of the Mortgagee

(l) On the personal covenant:

- (a) Suit for mortgagee money—
  - (i) to obtain a personal decree if there is an undertaking to that effect or the hypothecia is lost on account of destruction or fire; and
  - (ii) by bringing the hypothecia to sale.
- (b) *Suit for damages*—The mortgagee is entitled to claim damages when the mortgagor commits waste or a breach of the covenant for quite enjoyment. In case of the hypothec, damages can be claimed against strangers responsible for the waste.

1. *Remedies against hypotheca:* The remedies against the hypotheca are—

- (a) Judicial Sale (i.e. through Court)
- (b) Foreclosure
- (c) Possession
- (d) Private sale
- (e) Appointment of a receiver.

In the Transfer of Property Act, remedies (a) and (b) mentioned above are dealt with in Section 67 and remedies (c) and (d) in sections 69 and 69-A respectively. The possessory remedies are available to the usufructuary mortgagee.

J. CHARGE

Where immovable property of one person is by the act of parties or by operation of law made security for payment of money to another and the transaction does not amount to a mortgage, the latter person is said to have a charge on the property and all the provisions herein before contained which apply to a simple mortgage, shall, so far as may be apply to such a charge.

Creation of Charge

It is almost a settled law that no particular form of words is necessary to create a charge.

Formalities of Charge

Charge created by decree—(1) A decree creating a charge on property other than the one compromised in the suit should be registered. When a charge arising under a compromise is embodied in a decree, no registration or attestation is necessary.

(2) An award creating a charge requires registration.

(3) Charge by act of parties—In relation to a charge created by act of parties the formalities of simple mortgage should be complied with.

Distinction between Charge and Mortgage

(1) In mortgage, there is a transfer of interest in a property for security for a debt to the mortgagee; whereas there is no such transfer in a charge.

(2) A charge can be created by the act of parties.

(3) Section 59 of The Transfer of Property Act requires a mortgage deed to be attested by two witnesses while a charge need not be made in writing and even if it is in writing. It need not be attested.

(4) In certain mortgages (mortgage by conditional sale and anomalous mortgage), the mortgagee has a right of foreclosure, while a charge holder has no such right, and his right is only to bring the property to sale.

(5) A charge cannot be enforced against transferee for consideration without notice; whereas a transferee of property subject to a mortgage takes the property subject to the said encumbrance and he takes only the remaining interest in the property minus the interest transferred.

(6) In a charge, the charge holder has to proceed against the property charged and it negatives a personal liability. But, a right of sale of a specified property to support the personal covenant to pay indicates that the transaction is a mortgage. The absence of personal liability of a person whose property is charged is the principal test that distinguishes a charge from a simple mortgage.

Instances of Creation of Charge

(i) By act of parties:

(a) Where 'M' has executed a Promissory Note in favour of 'P' and on the same date a "Bechiq" was sent by 'M' to 'P', in which it was stipulated what the amount due under the Promissory Note should come out from the timber in the jungle, held that 'P' was entitled to a charge on 'M's timber in the jungle.[24]

(b) A document described as Zimanama containing a condition that the loss arising out of the Zimanama is to be paid from out of specific property, held, the instrument amounts to a charge.[25]

24. M. Ram *v.* Lal, A.I.R. (1929) Lah. 274.
25. Virbhan *v.* Saligram (1937) Lah. 35.

(ii) By operation of law:

(a) An unpaid vendor has a charge over his property sold.
(b) A co-mortgagor by repayment of the mortgaged debt is entitled to claim contribution and acquires a charge in respect thereof over the property.

Instances of Charges by Operation of Law

(c) A co-sharer paying entire appears of rent is entitled to a charge on the other co-sharer's portion of the holding.
(d) A trustee is entitled under Section 32 of the Trust Act to a charge on the income as well as the corpus of the trust-estate for all monies properly expended in performing the obligations of the trust.
(e) Vendor's charge for unpaid purchase money under Section 55 (Clause 4) of the transfer of Property Act.
(f) Vendor's charge for prepaid purchase money under Section 55 (Clause 6) of the Transfer of Property Act.
(g) Charge in favour of a person entitled to contribution under section 82 of the Transfer of Property Act.
(h) Charge created by decree of Court. But, it is one created by the judicial decree. It was held that a decree is in a category by itself and is not created by act of parties or by operation of law.

Instances where no Charge is Created

(1) Where the parties do not intend that there should be a present right to have the security made available, but, only there should be a right in the future by agreement, such as, a license to seize goods, there will be no charge.
(2) A covenant that the oblige can recover from the 'person and property' of the debtor is too vague to create a charge on any of his properties.
(3) A Declaration that 'our properties at Delhi and Ludhiana will be responsible for the debt does not create a charge over the property.'[26]

Remedies of a Charge Holder

(1) Remedy by judicial sale as is exercised by a simple mortgage.
(2) Additional remedy given by contract.

In *Renuko Bai* v. *Bhooson*[27], a charge-holder was given by contract between the parties the remedy of taking possession of the property. It was held that charge was not thereby invalidated. Decree passed was that the possession should be delivered to the charge-holder unless the property was redeemed within a time fixed by the Court.

26. Puran Chand *v.* Puran Chand, A.I.R. (1923), Lah., p. 625.
27. A.I.R. (1939) Nag. 132.

(3) A maintenance charge-holder has also a right to execute the decree personally against the judgment-debtor.

K. LEASE

A lease of immovable property is a right to enjoy such property made for a certain time, express or implied, in consideration of a price paid or promised, of money, a share in the crops, service or any other thing of value, to be rendered, periodically or, on specified occasions to the transfer or by the transferee, who expects the transfer on such terms. The transferor is called the lesser (landlord), the transferee is called the lassee (tenant), the price is called the premium (Salami) and the money, share or service or other thing is called the rent.

Essential Elements of a Lease

(1) A lease involves the transfer of a right to enjoy the property.

(2) The term of the lease should be certain, i.e., the period of its commencement and termination should be fixed.

The consideration for the lease should be a periodical payment, known as rent or premium or rent in addition to premium.

Types of Leases

(1) Perpetual lease, (2) Tenancy at will, (3) Tenancy by sufferance, (4) Tenancy by holding over, (5) Periodical lease, and (6) Lease for a fixed term.

(1) *Perpetual Lease*—A permanent lease where the tenant is not liable for ejectment.

(2) *Tenancy at Will*—Here the lesser and the lessee reserve the right to put an end to, the lease at the will of either party.

(3) *Tenancy by Sufferance*—When a person, who comes into possession by a lawful title, continues in possession after his title has been determined, without obtaining the consent of the person then entitled, he is said to be a tenant by sufferance. The tenancy requires no notice for its determination. The landlord may enter or the tenant may give up the lease at any time without notice.[28]

The Distinction between Tenancy at will and Tenancy by Sufferance

(i) The former requires a notice for its determination whereas the latter does not so require.

(ii) The latter is not entitled to embezzlements, whereas the former is entitled to it.

---

28. Moorse *v.* Makham Singh, (53), IC 180 (Pat).

(iii) Tenancy at will may arise by implication of law in cases of permissive possession, whereas a tenancy at sufferance is merely a fiction to avoid continuance in possession operating as a tresspass.

(4) *Tenancy by Holding Over*—There is a distinction between a tenant continuing in possession after the determination of his lease without the consent of the landlord and a tenant doing so with the landlord's consent. The former is a tenant by sufferance while the latter is a tenant holding over. The latter's rights are governed by Section 116 of the Transfer of Property Act which provides that acceptance of rent or otherwise giving consent for continuance of the lease after the termination of the period of lease given rise to the presumption that the lease is allowed to be renewed from year to year or from month to month according to the purpose for which the property is leased. If it is a lease of a house, the renewal is presumed to be from month to month. If it is a lease for agricultural or manufacturing purposes, the lease is presumed to be from year to year.

(5) *Periodical Lease*—A lease from month to month is an illustration of a periodical lease. Such a lease is not to be regarded as expiring at the end of the first month or at the end of each succeeding month, nor is there a re-letting at the commencement of each month of tenancy. It is a letting for a period of time which is determinable by the notice to quit.

(6) *Lease for a fixed Term*—A lease for a fixed period is one granted for any period irrespective of the length of its duration. However, it was held in a notable case that tenancy granted during war time 'for the duration of the war,' does not satisfy this definition.

L. DURATION OF LEASE

In the absence of a contract to the contrary, a lease of immovable property for agricultural and manufacturing purposes shall be deemed to be a lease from year to year and is terminable by six-month's notice on either side, expiring with the end of a year of the tenancy and a lease from month to month, terminable by fifteen days' notice, expiring with the end of the month of the tenancy.

Termination of Leases

According to Section III of the Transfer of Property Act, a lease is determined by the following methods:

(a) by the expiry of the time-limit;
(b) by express surrender if there is a mutual agreement between the lessor and the lessee; and
(c) by implied surrender.

ILLUSTRATION

A lessee accepts from his lesser a new lease of the property leased to take effect during the continuance of the existing lease. This is an implied surrender of the former lease.

(d) By forfeiture, i.e.,
  (i) in case of breach of express condition by lessee;
  (ii) if the lessee renounces his character as such by setting up a title in himself or in a third person; and
  (iii) if the lessee is adjudicated as insolvent, provided that in all the above cases, a lesser gives notice of his intention to determine the lease.

(e) On the expiration of time of a proper notice to determine the lease.

(f) In case the interests of the lessee and the lessor become vested in one and the same person.

(g) Where the interest of the lessor in the property terminates or extinguishes due to the happening of such event.

Notice to Quit

A tenancy at will is terminated by a demand for possessions. A tenancy for a fixed term determines on the expiration of the term. A periodical tenancy, however, is determined only by a proper notice to quit.

Requirements of a Valid Notice to Quit

There are two conditions for the validity of a notice of ejectment:

1. A tenancy from month to month requires fifteen days' notice expiring with the end of the tenancy and a tenancy from year to year requires six months' notice ending with the year of the tenancy.
2. It should terminate the tenancy at the end of the year or month of the tenancy as the case may be.

To see whether a notice complies with the second requirement in the case of a lease from month to month or year to year arising by virtue of a holding over after the expiry of the term of a lease, the date of expiry of the lease should be ascertained. The expiry of fifteen days or six months notice, as the case may be, should coincide with the expiry of the tenancy. In *Binaya Krishna Das* v. *Salsiccioni*[29], a lease for four years, commenced from the 1st of June, 1921. Under Section 110 of the Transfer of Property Act, that day was excluded in computing the duration of the lease. The lease, therefore, ended at mid-night of 1st June, 1925.

The tenant held over and became a tenant from month to month. Since the tenancy commenced from 2nd June, 1925, to terminate it, a notice to quit should expire with the month ending at mid-night on the first day of any month.

29. AIR (1942) P.C. 299.

M. FORM OF LEASE

A lease of immovable property from year to year or any term exceeding one year or reserving a yearly rent, can be made only by a registered instrument. All other leases of immovable property may be made either by a registered instrument or by oral agreement accompanied by delivery of possession. When a lease of immovable property is made by a registered instrument or where there are more instruments than one, each such instrument shall be executed by both lessor and the lessee.

A lease being a contract, the parties must be competent to enter into a contract.

Remedies of the Lessee

The lessee who has been evicted by title paramount can recover from the lessor the consideration for the lease and the pecuniary loss suffered by him, e.g., the cost of defending the suit for ejectment as well as any amount recovered by him as cost and mesne profits. Likewise, a sub-lease is entitled to recover from the lessee the extra amount paid by him to secure a fresh lease from the proprietor who has put an end to the head-lease. The remedies of specific performance are available equally to the lessor and lessee.

Remedies of the Lesser

The following remedies are available for a lessor:

(1) Action for rent

An action for arrears of rent may be brought either on the express term or a term implied by the reservation of right.

(2) Action for use and occupation

A tenant at will is not liable to pay rent after expiry of the term, as there is liability to pay. Further, he is not a tress-passer and, therefore, not liable for mesne profits. The landlord can, however, recover from him compensation for use and occupation.

(3) Distress

This is the right of the landlord to distrain for arrears of rent upon all goods including immovable fund on the premises. This may be done even without legal process as security for the payment of rent.

(4) Mesne profits

This remedy is available if the tenant becomes a tress-passer:

(1) *Suit for Injunction:* The lesser is entitled to an injunction if, the lessee is putting the demised land to an unauthorized due. A mandatory injunction was granted to demolish a building unauthorisedly constructed.

4

Banking Regulation Act, 1949

A. INTRODUCTION

The provisions of Banking Regulation Act, as in force for the time being shall be applicable to co-operative societies subject to certain modifications.

According to section 5 of the Banking Regulation Act, "Cooperative Bank" means a State Co-operative Bank, a Central Co-operative Bank and a Primary Co-operative Bank.

B. FORMS OF BUSINESS IN WHICH BANKING COMPANIES MAY ENGAGE (S. 6)

(1) In addition to the business of banking, or banking company may engage in any one or more of the following forms of business, namely:

(a) the borrowing, raising, or taking up of money; the lending or advancing of money either upon or without security; the drawing, making, accepting, discounting, buying, selling, collecting and dealing in bills of exchange, hundis, promissory notes, coupons, drafts, bills of lading, railway receipt, warrants, debentures, certificates, scripts and other instruments, and issuing of letters of credit, traveller's cheques and circular selling, on commission, underwriting and dealing in stock, funds, shares, debentures, debenture stock, bonds, obligations, securities and investments of all kinds; the purchasing and selling of bonds, scrip's or other forms of advances; the receiving of all kinds of bonds, scripts or other forms of securities on behalf of constituents or others, the negotiating of loans and advances; the receiving of all kinds of bonds, scripts or valuables on deposit or for safe custody or otherwise; the providing of safe deposit vaults; the collecting and transmitting of money and securities;

(b) acting as agents for any Government or local authority or any other person or persons; the carrying on of agency business of any description including the clearing and forwarding of goods, giving of receipts and discharges and otherwise acting as an attorney on behalf of customers, but excluding the business of a managing agent or secretary and treasurer of a company;

(c) contracting for public and private loans and negotiating and issuing the same;
(d) the effecting, insuring, guaranteeing, underwriting, participating in managing and carrying out of any issue; public or private, of State, municipal or other loans or of shares, stock, debentures, or debenture stock of any company, corporation or association and the lending of money for the purpose of any such issue;
(e) carrying on and transacting every kind of guarantee and indemnity business;
(f) managing, selling and realizing any property which may come into the possession of the company in satisfaction or past satisfaction of any of its claims;
(g) acquiring and holding and generally dealing with any property or any right, title or interest in any such property which may form the security or part of the security for any loans or advances or which may be connected with any such security;
(h) undertaking and executing trusts;
(i) undertaking the administration or estates as executor, trustee or otherwise;
(j) establishing and supporting or aiding in the establishment and support of association, instructions, funds, trusts and conveniences calculated to benefit employees or ex-employees of the company or the dependents or connections of such person; granting pensions and allowances and making payments towards insurance, subscribing to or guaranteeing money for charitable or benevolent objects or for any exhibition or for any public, general or useful object;
(k) the acquisition, construction, maintenance and alteration of any building or works necessary or convenient for the purposes of the company;
(l) selling, improving, managing, developing, exchanging, leasing, mortgaging, depositing of or turning into account or otherwise dealing with all or any part of the property and rights of the company;
(m) acquiring and undertaking whole or any part of the business of any person or company, when such business is of nature enumerated or described in this sub-section;
(n) doing all such other things as are incidental or conducive to the promotion or advancement of the business of the company; and
(o) any other forms of business, which the Central Government may by notification in the official Gazette, specify as a form of business in which it is lawful for a banking company to engage.

(2) No banking company shall engage in any form of business other than those referred to in sub-section (1).

Section 6 of the Act provides elaborately for a wide variety of business, which a banking company may engage itself in. A fair consideration of this section as well as the definition of "banking" in the Banking Regulation Act, 1949, would have no doubt in any one's mind that chit fund transaction indulged in by a banking company at any rate partakes the character of a banking activity.

C. USE OF WORDS "BANK", "BANKER" OR "BANKING"

A cooperative bank shall use as part of its name or in connection with its business any of the words "bank", "banker" or "banking".
This section shall not apply to—

(a) Primary credit society.
(b) A cooperative society formed for the protection of mutual interest of cooperative banks or cooperative Land Mortgage Banks.
(c) Any co-operative society formed by the employers of a banking company or State Bank of India or a corresponding new bank.

Banker: The relationship of the banker with his customer is that of debtor and creditor. A depositor who deposits money in bank in his current account is nothing more than a creditor and it cannot be said that there has been any entrustment to the bank for any particular purpose. The bank is of course liable to refund the money to deposit when the depositor calls for it, but the money deposited belongs to the bank and the bank is entitled to deal with it as it likes.

D. CASH RESERVE

(1) Every banking company, not being a scheduled bank, shall maintain in India by way of Cash Reserve with itself or by way of balance in a current account with the Reserve Bank or by way of net balance in current account or in one or more of the aforesaid ways, a sum equivalent, to at least three percent of the total of its demand and time liabilities in India as on the last Friday of the second preceding fortnight and shall submit to the Reserve Bank before the twentieth day of every month a return showing the amount so held on alternative Fridays during a month with particulars of its demand and time liabilities in India on such Fridays or if any such Friday is a public holiday under the Negotiable Instrument Act, 1881 (26 of 1881), at the close of business on the preceding working day.

Explanation: In this section, and Sec. 24,—

(a) "liabilities in India" shall not include—

(i) the paid-up capital or the Reserves or any credit balance in the profit and loss account of the banking company;
(ii) any advance taken from the Reserve Bank or from the Development Bank or from the Exim Bank or from the Reconstruction Bank or from the National Bank by the banking company;
(iii) in the case of a Regional Rural Bank, also any loan taken by such bank from its sponsor bank;
   (a) "fortnight" shall mean the period from Saturday to the second following Friday, both days inclusive;
   (b) "net balance in current accounts" shall, in relation to a banking company, mean the excess, if any, of the aggregate of the credit balances in current account maintained by that banking company

with the State Bank of India or a subsidiary bank or a corresponding new bank over the aggregate of the credit balance in current account held by the said banks with such banking company;

(c) for the purpose of computation of liabilities, the aggregate of the liabilities of a banking company to the State Bank of India, a subsidiary bank, a corresponding new bank, a regional rural bank, another banking company, a co-operative bank or any other financial institution notified by the Central Government in this behalf, shall be reduced by the aggregate of the liabilities of all such banks' institutions to the banking company; and

(d) The expression "co-operative bank" shall have the meaning assigned to it in Cl. (cci) of Sec. 56.

(2) The Reserve Bank may, for the purposes of this section and Sec. 24, specify from time to time, with reference to any transaction or class of transaction, that such transaction or transaction shall be regarded as liability in India of a banking company and, if any question arises as to whether any transaction or class of transaction shall be regarded for the purposes of this section and section 24 as liability in India of a banking company, the decision of the Reserve Bank thereon shall be final.

E. MAINTENANCE OF A PERCENTAGE OF ASSETS

(1) After the expiry of two years from the commencement of this Act, every banking shall maintain in India in cash, gold or unencumbered approved securities, value at a price not exceeding the current market price, an amount which shall not at the close of business on any day be less than 20 percent of the total of its demand and time liabilities in India.

Explanation—For the purposes of this section, "unencumbered approved securities" of banking company shall include its approved securities lodged with another institution from advance or any other credit arrangement to the extent to which such securities have not been drawn against or availed of.

(2) In computing the amount for the purposes of sub-section (1) the deposit required under sub-section (2) of Sec. 11 to be made with the Reserve Bank by a banking company incorporated outside India and any balance maintained in India by a banking company in current account with the Reserve Bank or the State Bank of India or with any other bank which may be notified in this behalf by the Central Government, including in the case of a scheduled bank the balance required under Sec. 42 of the Reserve Bank of India Act, 1934 (2 of 1934), to be so maintained, shall be deemed to be cash maintained in India.

(2-A) (a) Notwithstanding anything contained in sub-section (1) or in sub-section (2) after expiry of two years from the commencement of the Banking Companies (Amendment) Act, 1962 (36 of 1962),—

(1) a Scheduled bank, in addition to the average daily balance which it is, or may be required to maintain under Sec. 42 of the Reserve Bank of India Act, 1934 (2 of 1934), and

(2) every other banking company, in addition to the Cash Reserve which it is required to maintain under Sec. 18 shall maintain in India—

(a) In cash, or

(b) In gold valued at a price not exceeding the current market price or in unencumbered approved securities valued at a price, determined in accordance with such one or more of, or combination of, the following methods of valuation, namely, valuation with reference to cost price, market price, book value or face value, as may be specified by the Reserve Bank from time to time, amount which shall not, at the close of business on any day, be less than twenty-five percents, or such other percentage not exceeding forty percent as the Reserve Bank may, from time to time, by notification in the official Gazette, specify, of the total of its demand and time liabilities in India, as on the last Friday of the second preceding fortnight,

(b) In computing the amount for the purpose of Cl. (a)—

(i) the deposit required under sub-section (2) of Sec. 11 to be made with the Reserve Bank by the banking company incorporated outside India;

(ii) any cash or balances maintained in India by a banking company other than a scheduled bank with itself or with the Reserve Bank or by way of net balance in current account in excess of the aggregate of the cash or balance or net balance required to be maintained under Sec. 18;

(iii) any balance maintained by a scheduled bank with the Reserve Bank in excess of the balance required to be maintained by it under Sec. 42 of the Reserve Bank of India Act, 1934 (2 of 1934);

(iv) the net balance in current accounts maintained in India by a scheduled bank; and

(v) any balances maintained by a Regional Rural Bank in call or fixed shall be deemed to be cash maintained in India.

Explanation—For the purpose of Cl. (a) of this sub-section, the market price of an approved security shall be the price as on the date of the issue of the notification or as on any earlier or later date as may be notified from time to time by the Reserve Bank in respect of any class or classes of securities.

(2-B) the Reserve Bank may, by notification in the official Gazette, vary the percentage referred to in sub-section (2-A) in respect of a Regional Rural Bank.

(3) For the purpose of ensuring compliance with the provisions of this section, every banking company, shall not later than twenty days after the end of the month to which it relates, furnish to the Reserve Bank in the prescribed form and manner a monthly return showing particulars of its assets maintained in accordance with this section, and its demand and time and liabilities in India at the close of business on each alternative Friday during the month, or if any such, is a public holiday, at the close of business on the preceding working day:

Provided that every regional Rural bank shall also furnish a copy of the said return to the National Bank.

(4) (a) If on any alternate Friday or, if such Friday is a public holiday, on the preceding working day, the amount maintained by a banking company at the close of business on that day falls below the minimum prescribed by of under Cl. (a) of sub-section (2-A), such banking company shall be liable to pay to the Reserve Bank in respect of that day's default, penal interest for that day at the rate of three percent per annum above the bank rate on the amount by which the amount actually maintained falls short of the prescribed minimum on that day; and

(b) If the default occurs again on the next succeeding alternate Friday, or if such Friday is a public holiday, on the preceding working day, and continues on succeeding alternate Fridays or preceding working days, as the case may be, the rate of penal interest shall be increased to a rate of five percent, per annum above, the bank rate on each such shortfall in respect of that alternate Friday and each succeeding alternate Friday or preceding working day, if such Friday is a public holiday, on which the default continues.

(5) (a) Without prejudice to the provisions of sub-section (3) Reserve Bank may require a banking company to furnish to it return in the form and manner specified by it showing particulars of its assets maintained in accordance with business on each day of a month; and

(b) Without prejudice to the provisions of sub-section (4) on the failure of a banking company to maintain as on any day, the amount so required to be maintained by or under Cl. (a) of sub-section (2-A) the Reserve Bank may, in respect of such default, require the banking company to pay penal interest for that day, as provided in Cl. (a) of sub-section (4) and if the default continues on the next succeeding working day, the penal interest may be increased as provided in Cl. (b) of sub-section (4) or the concerned days.

(6) (a) The penalty payable under sub-section (4) and sub-section (5) shall be paid within a period of fourteen days from the date on which a notice issued by the Reserve Bank demanding payment of the same is served on the banking company and in the event of failure of the banking company to pay the same within such period, the penalty may be levied by a direction of the principal Civil Court having jurisdiction in the area where an office of the defaulting banking company is situated, such direction to be made only upon an application made by the Reserve Bank in this behalf to the Court; and

(b) Where the Court makes a direction under Cl. (a), it shall issue a certificate specifying the sum payable by the banking company and every such certificate shall be enforceable in the same manner as if it were a decree made by the Court in a suit.

(7) When under the provisions of Cl. (b) of sub-section (4) penal interest at the increased rate of five percent, above the bank rate has become payable by the banking company, if thereafter amount required to be maintained on the next succeeding alternative Friday, or if such Friday is a public holiday

the next preceding working day is still below the prescribed minimum, every director, a manager or secretary of the banking company, who is knowingly and wilfully a party to the default shall be punishable with fine which may extend to five hundred rupees and with a further fine which may extend to five hundred rupees for each subsequent alternate Friday or the preceding working day, as the case may be, on which the default continues.

(8) Notwithstanding anything contained in this section, if the Reserve Bank is satisfied, on an application in writing by the defaulting banking company, that the banking company had sufficient cause for its failure to comply with the provisions of Cl. (a) of sub-section (2-A), the Reserve Bank may not demand the payment of the penal interest.

Explanation: In this section, the expression "public holiday", means a day which is a public holiday under the Negotiable Instruments Act, 1881 (26 of 1881).

F. SUBMISSION OF RETURNS

The accounts and balance sheet referred to in section 29 together with auditor report shall be published in the prescribed manner and three copies thereof shall be furnished as returns to the Reserve Bank within six months from the end of the period to which that refers:

Provided that the Reserve bank may in any case extend the said period of six months for the furnishing of such returns by a further period not exceeding three months:

Provided further that a Co-operative bank, other than a Primary Co-operative Bank shall furnish such returns also to the National Bank for Agriculture and Rural Development (NABARD).

G. INSPECTION

(1) Notwithstanding anything to the contrary contained in [Sec. 235 of the Companies Act, 1956 (1 of 1956)], the Reserve bank at any time may, and on being directed so to do by the Central Government shall cause an inspection to be made by one or more of its officers of any banking company and its books and accounts; and the Reserve Bank shall apply to the banking company for a copy of its report on such inspection.

(1-A) (a) Notwithstanding anything to the contrary contained in any law for the time being in force and without prejudice to the provisions of sub-section (1), the Reserve Bank, at any time, may also cause a scrutiny to be made by any one or more of its officers, of the affairs of any banking company and its books and accounts; and

(b) A copy of the report of the scrutiny shall be furnished to the banking company if the banking company makes a request for the same or if any adverse action is contemplated against the banking company on the basis of the scrutiny.

(2) It shall be the duty of every director or other officer or employee of the banking company to produce to any officer making an inspection under sub-section (1) or a scrutiny under sub-section (1-A). All such books, accounts and other documents in his custody or power and to furnish him with any statements and informations relating to the affairs of the banking company as the said officer may require of him within such time as the said officer may specify.

(3) Any person making an inspection under sub-section (1) [or a scrutiny under sub-section (1-A)] may examine on oath any director or other officer [or employee] of the banking company in relation to its business, and may administer an oath accordingly.

(4) The Reserve Bank shall, if it has been directed by the Central Government to cause an inspection to be made, and may, in any other case report to the Central Government on the inspection [or scrutiny] made under this section, and the Central Government, if it is of opinion after considering the report that the affairs of the banking company are being conducted to the detriment of the interests of its depositors, may after giving such opportunity to the banking company to make a representation in connection with the report as, in the opinion of the Central Government, seems reasonable by order in writing—

(a) prohibit the banking company from receiving fresh deposits; and
(b) prohibit the Reserve Bank to apply under Sec. 38 for the winding up of the banking company:

Provided that the Central Government may defer, for such period as it may think fit, the passing of an order under this sub-section, or cancel or modify any such order, upon such terms and conditions as it may think fit to impose.

(5) The Central Government may, after giving reasonable notice the banking company, publish the report submitted by Reserve Bank or such portion thereof as may appear necessary.

(6) The powers exercisable by the Reserve Bank under this section in relation to regional rural banks may (without prejudice to the exercise of such powers by the Reserve Bank in relation to any regional rural bank whenever it considers necessary so to do) be exercised by the National Bank in relation to the regional rural banks, and accordingly, sub-sections (1) to (5) shall apply in relation to regional rural banks as if every reference therein to the Reserve Bank included also a reference to the National Bank.]

Explanation: For the purpose of this section, the expression "banking company" shall include—

(i) in the case of a banking company incorporated outside India, all its branches in India; and
(ii) in the case of a banking company incorporated outside India—
  (a) all its subsidiaries formed for the purpose of carrying on the business of banking exclusively outside India; and
  (b) all its branches whether situated in India or outside India.

H. POWER TO THE RESERVE BANK TO GIVE DIRECTIONS

(1) Where the Reserve Bank is satisfied that—

(a) in the public interest; or

(b) in the interest of banking policy; or

(c) to prevent the affairs of any banking company being conducted in a manner detrimental to the interests of the depositors or in a manner prejudicial to the interests to the banking company; or

(d) to secure the proper management of any banking company generally.

It is necessary to issue directions to banking companies generally or to any banking company in particular, it may, from time to time, issue such directions as it deems fit, and the banking companies or the banking company as the case may be, shall be bound to comply with such directions.

(2) The Reserve Bank may, on representation made to it or on its own motion, modify or cancel any direction issued under sub-section (1) and in so modifying or cancelling any direction may impose such conditions as it thinks fit, subject to which the modification or cancellation shall have effect.

I. PENALTIES

(1) Whoever in any return, balance-sheet or other document [or any information required or furnished] by or under or for the purposes of any provision of this Act, wilfully makes a statement which is false in any material particular, knowing it to be false, or wilfully omits to make a material statement shall be punishable with imprisonment for a term which may extend to three years and shall also be liable to fine.

(2) If any person falls to produce any book, account or other document or to furnish any statement or information which under sub-section (2) of Sec. 35 it is his duty to produce or furnish, or to answer any question relating to the business of a banking company which he is asked by [an officer making an inspection or scrutiny under that section] he shall be punishable with a fine which may extend to [two thousand rupees] in respect of each offence, and if he persists in such refusal, to a further fine which may extend to [one hundred rupees] for every day during which offence continues.

(3) If any deposits are received by a banking company in contravention of an order under Cl. (a) of sub-section (4) of Sec. 35, every director or other officer of the banking company, unless he proves that the contravention took place without his knowledge or that he exercised all due diligence to prevent it, shall be deemed to be guilty of such contravention shall be punishable with a fine which may extend to twice the amount of the deposits so received.

(4) If any other provision of this Act is contravened or if any default is made in—

(i) complying with any requirement of this Act or of any order, rules or direction made or condition imposed thereunder; or

(ii) carrying out the terms of, or the obligations under a scheme sanctioned under sub-section (7) of Sec. 45;

by any person, such person shall be punishable with fine which may extend to two thousand rupees, and where a contravention or default is a continuing one, with a further fine which may extend to one hundred rupees for every day, during which the contravention or default continues.

(5) Where a contravention or default has been committed by a company every person who, at the time contravention or default was committed, was in change of, and was responsible to, the company for the conduct of the business of the company, as well as the company, shall be deemed to be quality business of the company, as well as the company, shall be liable to be proceeded against and punished accordingly:

Provided that nothing contained in this sub-section shall render, any such person liable to any punishment provided in this Act if he proves that the contravention or default was committed without his knowledge or that he exercised all due diligence to prevent the contravention or default.

(6) Notwithstanding anything contained in sub-section (5) where contravention or default has been committed by a company, and it is proved that the same was committed with the consent or connivance of, or is attributable to any gross negligence on the part of, director, manager, secretary or other officer of the company, such director, manager, secretary or other officer shall also be deemed to be guilty of that contravention or default and shall be liable to be proceeded against and punished accordingly.

Explanation: For the purposes of this section—

(a) "Company" means any body corporate and includes a firm or other association of individuals; and
(b) "Director" in relation to a firm, means a partner in the firm.

J. ACT TO APPLY TO CO-OPERATIVE SOCIETIES SUBJECT TO MODIFICATIONS

The provisions of this Act, as in force for the time being, shall apply to, or in relation to, co-operative societies as they apply to, or in relation to, banking companies to the following modifications, namely:

(a) Throughout this Act, unless the context otherwise requires,

(i) references to a "banking company" or "the company", "such company" shall be construed as references to a cooperative bank;
(ii) references to "commencement of this Act" shall be construed as references to commencement of the Banking Laws (Application to Co-operative Societies Act), 1965 (23 of 1965);
   (a) in Sec. 2, the words and figures "the Companies Act, 1956 (I of 1956) and" shall be omitted;

(b) in Sec. 5,—

(i) after Cl. (cc), the following clauses shall be inserted, namely:

(cci) "co-operative bank" means a State Co-operative bank, a central co-operative bank and a primary co-operative bank;

(ccii) "co-operative credit society" means a co-operative society, the primary object to which is to provide financial accommodation to its members and includes a primary co-operative land mortgage bank; cooperative bank, central cooperative bank and a primary cooperative bank;

(cciii) "director", in relation to a co-operative society, includes a member of any committee or body for the time being vested with the management of the affairs of that society;

(cciv) "primary agricultural credit society" means a co-operative society,—

(1) the primary object or principal business of which is to provide financial accommodation to its members for agricultural purposes or for purposes connected with agricultural activities including the marketing of crops; and
(2) the bye-laws of which do not permit admission of any other co-operative society as a member:

Provided that this sub-clause shall not apply to the admission of a co-operative bank as a member by reason of such co-operative society out of funds provided by the State Government for the purpose;

(ccv) "primary co-operative bank" means a co-operative society, other than a primary agricultural credit society,—

(1) the primary object or principal business of which is the transaction of banking business;
(2) the paid-up share capital and Reserve of which are not less than one lakh of rupees; and
(3) the bye-law of which do not permit admission of any other co-operative society as a member:

Provided that this sub-clause shall not apply to the admission of a co-operative bank as a member by reason of such co-operative bank subscribing to the share capital of such co-operative society out of funds provided by the State Government for the purpose;

(ccvi) "primary credit society" means a co-operative society, other than a primary agricultural credit society—

(1) the primary object or principal business of which is the transaction of banking business;
(2) the paid-up share capital and Reserves of which are less than one lakh of rupees; and
(3) the bye-laws of which do not permit admission of any other co-operative society as a member:

Provided that this sub-clause shall not apply to the admission of a co-operative bank as a member by reason of such co-operative bank subscribing to the share capital of such co-operative society out of funds provided by the State Government for the purpose.

Explanation: "If any dispute arises as to the primary object or principal business of any co-operative society referred to in Cls. (cciv), (ccv) and (ccvi), a determination thereof by the Reserve Bank shall be a final;

(ccvii) "Central co-operative bank", "co-operative bank", "co-operative society", "primary rural credit society" and "State co-operative bank" shall have the meanings respectively assigned to them in the National Bank for Agriculture and Rural Development Act, 1981;

(d) for Sec 5-A, the following section shall be substituted, namely: "5-A, Act to override bye-law, etc.—(1) The provisions of this Act shall have effect, notwithstanding anything to the contrary contained in the bye-law of a co-operative society or in any agreement executed by it, or in any resolution passed by it in general meeting, or by its board of directors or other body entrusted with the management of its affairs, whether the same be registered, executed by it, or in any resolution passed by it in general meeting, or by its board of directors or other body entrusted with the management of its affairs, whether the same be registered, executed or passed, as the case may be, before or after commencement of the Banking Laws (Application to Co-operative Societies) Act, 1965 (23 of 1965).

(2) Any provision contained in the bye-law, agreement or resolution aforesaid shall, to the extent to which it is repugnant to the provisions of this Act, become or be void, as the case may be."

(e) In Sec. 6, in sub-section (1),—

(i) in Cl. (b), the words "but excluding the business of a managing agent of secretary and treasurer of a company" shall be omitted;
(ii) in Cl. (d), after the word "company", the words "co-operative society" shall be inserted;
(iii) in Cl. (m), after the word "company", the words "or co-operative society" shall be inserted;

[(f) for Sec. 7., the following section shall be substituted, namely;

"7, Use of words 'bank', 'banker' or 'banking'—(1) No co-operative society other than a co-operative bank shall use as part of its name or in connection with its business any of the words 'bank', 'banker', or 'banking' and no co-operative society shall carry on the least on of such words.

(2) Nothing in this section shall apply to—

(a) a primary credit society, or
(b) a co-operative society formed for the protection of the mutual interest of Co-operative Banks or co-operative land mortgage banks, or
(c) any co-operative society, not being a primary credit society, formed by the employees of—
    (i) a banking company or the State Bank of India or a corresponding new bank or a subsidiary bank of such banking company, State Bank of India or a corresponding new bank, or

(ii) a co-operative bank or a primary credit society or a co-operative land mortgage bank.

Insofar as the word 'bank', banker' or 'banking' appears as part of the name of the employer bank, or as the case may be, of the bank, whose subsidiary the employer bank is;

[(fi) In Sec. 8, for the proviso, the following proviso shall be substituted, namely:

"Provided that this section shall not apply,—

(a) to any such business as aforesaid which was in the course of being transacted on the commencement of Cl. (iii) of Sec. 42 of the Banking Laws (Amendment) Act, 1983, so, however, the said business shall be completed before the expiry of one year from such commencement, or

(b) to any business as is specified in pursuance of Cl. (o) of sub-section (1) of Sec. 6;"

(fii) In Sec. 9, for the second proviso, the following proviso shall be substituted, namely:

Provided further that in the case of a primary credit society which becomes a primary co-operative bank after the commencement of Cl. (iii) of Sec. 42 of the Banking Laws (Amendment) Act, 1983, the period of seven years shall commence from the day it so becomes a primary co-operative bank:

Provided also that the Reserve Bank may, in any particular case, extend the aforesaid period of seven years by such period as it may consider necessary where it is satisfied that, such extension would be in the interests of the depositors of the co-operative bank.]

(h) For Sec. 11, the following section shall be substituted namely:

11. Requirement as to minimum paid-up capital and Reserves.—

(1) Notwithstanding any law relating to co-operative societies for the time being in force, no co-operative bank shall commence or carry on the business of banking in India unless the aggregate value of its paid up capital and Reserves is not less than one lakh rupees:

Provided that nothing in this sub-section shall apply to—

(a) any such bank which is carrying on such business at the commencement of the Banking Laws (Application to Co-operative Societies) Act, 1965 (23 of 1965), for a period of three years from such commencement; or

(b) to a primary credit society which becomes a primary co-operative bank after such commencement, for a period of two years from the date it so becomes a primary co-operative bank or for such further period not exceeding one year as the Reserve Bank, having regard to the interests of the depositors of the primary co-operative bank may think fit in any particular case to allow.

(2) For the purposes of this section, *'value'* means the real or exchangeable value and the nominal value, which may be shown in the books of the co-operative bank concerned.

(3) If any dispute arises in computing the aggregate value of the paid-up capital and Reserves of any such co-operative bank, a determination thereof by the Reserve Bank shall be final for the purpose of this section.";

(j) [(j) For Sec. 18, the following section shall be substituted, namely:

18. *Cash Reserves:* (l) Every co-operative bank, not being a State co-operative bank for the time being included in the Second Schedule to the Reserve Bank of India Act, 1934 (2 of 1934), (hereinafter referred to as a Scheduled State Co-operative Bank), shall maintain in India by way of Cash Reserve with itself of balance in a current account with the Central Co-operative Bank of the district concerned, or in one or more of the aforesaid ways, a sum equivalent to at least three percent. Of the total of its demand and time liabilities in India, as on the last Friday of the second preceding fortnight and shall submit to the Reserve Bank before the fifteenth day of every month a return showing the amount so held on liabilities in India on such Friday or if any such Friday is a public holiday under the Negotiable Instruments Act, 1881 (26 of 1881) at the close of business on the preceding working day.

Explanation: In this section and in Sec. 24—

(a) 'liabilities in India' shall not include—
   (i) the paid up capital or the Reserves or any credit balance in the profit and loss account of the co-operative bank;
   (ii) any advance taken from a State Government, the Reserve Bank, the Development Bank, the Exim Bank, the Reconstruction Bank, the National Bank or from the National Co-operative Development Corporation established under Sec. 3 of the National Co-operative Development Corporation Act, 1962 (26 of 1962), by the co-operative bank;
   (iii) in the case of a State or Central Co-operative bank, also any deposit of money with it representing the Reserve fund or any part thereof maintained with it by any other co-operative society within its area of operation, and in the case of a Central Co-operative bank, also an advance taken by it from the State Co-operative bank of the State concerned;
   (iv) in the case of a primary co-operative bank, also any advance taken by it from the State co-operative bank of the State concerned or the Central Co-operative bank of the district concerned; and
   (v) in the case of any co-operative bank, which has granted an advance against any balance maintained with it, such balance to the extent of the amount outstanding in respect to such advance and; in case of any co-operative bank the amount of any advance or other credit arrangement drawn and availed or against approved securities;

(b) fortnight shall mean the period from Saturday to the second following Friday, both days inclusive;

(c) net balance in current accounts shall in relation to a co-operative bank, mean the excess, if any, of the aggregate of the credit balances in current account maintained by that co-operative bank with the State Bank of India or a subsidiary bank or a corresponding new bank, over the aggregate of the credit balances in current accounts held by the said banks with such co-operative bank;

(d) for the purpose of computation of liabilities, the aggregate of the liabilities of a co-operative bank to the State Bank of India, a subsidiary bank, a corresponding new bank, a Regional Rural Bank, a banking company, or any other financial Institution notified by the Central Government in this behalf shall be reduced by the aggregate of the liabilities of all such banks and institutions to the co-operative bank; and

(e) any cash with a co-operative bank or any balance held by a co-operative bank with another bank, shall not, to the extent such cash or such balances represents the balance in, or investment of, agricultural credit Stabilization Fund of such co-operative bank, be deemed to be cash maintained in India.

(2) The Reserve Bank may, for the purposes of this section and Sec. 24, specify from time to time, with reference to any transaction or class of transactions, that such transaction or transaction shall be regarded as liability in India of a co-operative bank, and if any question arises as to whether any transaction or class of transactions shall be regarded for the purposes of this section and Sec. 24, as liability in India of a co-operative bank, the decision of the Reserve Bank thereon shall be final.

(k) For Sec. 19, the following section shall be substituted, namely;

"19. Restriction on holding shares in other co-operative societies—No co-operative bank shall hold shares in any other co-operative society except to such extent and subject to such conditions as the Reserve Bank may specify in that behalf:

Provided that nothing contained in this section shall apply to—

(i) shares acquired through funds provided by the State Government for that purpose;

(ii) in the case of a Central Co-operative Bank, the holding of shares in the State Co-operative Bank to which it is affiliated; and

(iii) in the case of a primary co-operative bank, the holding of shares in the Central Co-operative Bank of the State in which it is registered:

Provided further that where any shares are held by a co-operative bank in contravention of this section at the commencement of the Banking Laws (Application to Co-operative Societies) Act, 1965 (23 of 1965), the co-operative bank shall without delay report the matter to the Reserve Bank and shall, notwithstanding any thing contained in this section be entitled to hold the shares for such period and on such conditions as the Reserve Bank may specify."

[(1) For Sec. 20 of the principal Act, the following section shall be substituted, namely:

"20. Restrictions on loans and advances.—(1) No. of co-operative banks shall—

(a) make any loans or advances on the security of its own shares; or

(b) grant unsecured loans or advances—

(i) to any of its directors; or

(ii) to firms or private companies in which any of its directors is interested as partner or managing agent or guarantor or to individuals in cases where any of its directors is a guarantor; or

(iii) to any company in which the chairman of the board of directors of the co-operative bank (where the appointment of a chairman is for a fixed term) is interested as its managing agent, or where there is no managing agent, as its chairman or managing director:

Provided that nothing in Cl. (b) shall apply to the grant of unsecured loans or advances—

(a) made by a co-operative bank—

(i) against bills for supplies or services made or rendered to Government or bills of exchange arising out of *bona fide* commercial or trade transactions, or

(ii) in respect whereof trust-receipts are furnished to the co-operative bank;

(b) made by a primary co-operative bank to any of its directors or to any other person within such limits and on such terms and conditions as may be approved by the Reserve Bank in this behalf.

(2) Every co-operative bank shall, before the close of the month succeeding that to which the return relates, submit to the Reserve Bank an advances granted by it to companies in cases other than those in which the co-operative bank is prohibited under sub-section (1) to make unsecured loans and advances in which any of its directors is interested as director or managing agent or guarantor.

(3) If, on examination of any return submitted under sub-section (2) it is appears to the Reserve Bank that any loans or advances referred to in that sub-section are being granted to the detriment to the interests of the depositors of the co-operative bank, the Reserve Bank may, by order in writing, prohibit the co-operative bank from granting any such further loans or advances or impose such restrictions on the grant thereof as it thinks fit, and may by like order direct the co-operative bank to secure the re-payment of such loans or advance within such time as may be specified in order.";

(m) In Sec. 20-A, in sub-section (1),

(i) the words and figures "notwithstanding anything to the contrary contained in Sec. 293 of the Companies Act, 1956 (I of 1956) shall be omitted;

(ii) in Cl. (a), for the words "any of its directors", the words "any of its past or present directors" shall be substituted];

(n) In Sec. 21, in sub-section (2), in Cls. (c) and (d), for the words "any one company, firm, association of persons or individual", the words "any one party" shall be substituted;

(o) In Sec. 22—

(i) for sub-sections (1) and (2), the following sub-sections shall be substituted, namely:

(1) Save as hereinafter should provided, no co-operative society carry on banking business in India unless—

(a) it is a primary credit society, or

(b) it is a co-operative bank and holds a licence issued in that behalf by the Reserve Bank, subject to such conditions, if any, as the Reserve Bank may deem fit to impose:

Provided that nothing in this sub-section shall apply to a co-operative society, not being a primary credit society or a co-operative bank carrying on banking business at the commencement of the Banking Laws (Application to Co-operative Societies) Act, 1965 (23 of 1965), for a period of one year from such commencement.

(2) Every Co-operative Society carrying on business as a co-operative bank at the commencement of the Banking Laws (Application to Co-operative Societies) Act, 1965 (23 of 1965), shall before the expiry of three months from such commencement, every co-operative bank which comes into existence as a result of the division of any other co-operative society carrying on business as a co-operative bank, or the amalgamation of two or more co-operative societies carrying on banking business shall before the expiry of three months from its so coming into existence, every primary credit society which becomes a primary co-operative bank after such commencement shall before the expiry of three months from the date on which it so becomes a primary co-operative bank and every co-operative societies other than a primary credit society shall before commencing banking business in India, apply, in writing to the Reserve Bank for a licence under this section:

Provided that nothing in Cl. (b) of sub-section (1) shall be deemed to prohibit—

(i) a co-operative society carrying on business as co-operative bank at the commencement of the Banking Laws (Application to Co-operative Societies) Act, 1965 (23 of 1965), or

(ii) a co-operative bank which has come into existence as a result of the division of any other co-operative society carrying on business as a co-operative bank, or the amalgamation of two or more co-operative societies carrying on banking business at the commencement of the Banking Laws (Application to Co-operative Societies) Act, 1965 (23 of 1965), or at any time thereafter; or

(iii) a primary credit society which becomes a primary co-operative bank after such commencement, from carrying on banking business until it is granted a licence in pursuance of this that the licence cannot be granted to it.

(iv) in sub-section (4) in Cl. (iii), the words, brackets, figure and letter and sub-section (3-A) shall omitted";]

(p) in Sec. 23, [(i) for sub-section (1), the following sub-section shall be substituated, namely:

(1) Without obtaining the prior permission of the Reserve Bank, no co-operative bank shall open a new place of business or change otherwise than within the same city, town or village, the location of an existing place of business:

Provided that nothing in this sub-section shall apply to—

(a) the opening for a period not exceeding one month of a temporary place of business within a city, town or village or the environs thereof within which the co-operative bank already has a place of business, for the purpose of affording facilities to the public on the occasion of an exhibition, a conference or a mela or other like occasion;

(b) the opening or changing the location of branches by Central co-operative bank within the area of its operation;"

(2) After sub-section the following sub-section shall be inserted, namely:

(4-A) any co-operative bank other than a co-operative bank requiring the permission of the Reserve Bank under this section shall forward its application to the Reserve Bank through the National Bank which shall give its comments on the merits of application and send to the Reserve Bank:

Provided that the co-operative bank shall also send an advance copy of the application directly to the Reserve Bank.

(q) In Sec. 24;—

(i) In sub-section (1) the words "after the expiry of two years from the commencement of this act shall be omitted;

(ii) for sub-section (2) and (2-A) the following sub-sections shall be substituted, namely:

(2) In computing the amount for the purposes of sub-section (1)—

(a) any balances maintained in India by a co-operative bank in current account with the Reserve Bank or by way of net balance in current accounts and in the case of the scheduled State co-operative bank, also the balance required under section 42 of the Reserve Bank of India Act, 1934 (2 of 1934) to be so maintained,

(b) any balances maintained by a primary co-operative bank with Central Co-operative Bank with the State co-operative bank of the State concerned, and

(c) any balances maintained by a primary co-operative bank of the district concerned or with the State shall be deemed to be cash maintained in India.

(2-A) (a) Notwithstanding anything contained in sub-section (1) in sub-section (2), after the expiry of two years from the commencement of the Banking Laws (Application to Co-operative Societies) Act, 1965, Reserve Bank, having regard to the interests of the co-operative bank concerned, may think fit in any particular case to allow:

(i) a scheduled State co-operative bank, in addition to the average daily balance which it is or may be, required to maintain under Sec. 42 of the Reserve Bank of India Act, 1934 (2 of 1934), and

(ii) every other co-operative bank, in addition to the cash Reserve which it is required to maintain under Sec. 18, shall maintain in India, in cash, or in gold valued at a price not exceeding the current market price or in unencumbered approved securities valued at a price determined in accordance with such one or more of, or combination of, the following methods of valuation, namely, valuation with reference to cost price, market price, book value, or face value as may be specified by the Reserve Bank from time to time, an amount which shall not, at the close of business on any day, be less than twenty-five per cent, or, such other percentage not exceeding forty per cent. As the Reserve Bank may, from time to time, by notification in the Official Gazette, specify, of the total of its demand and time liabilities in India, as on the last Friday of the second preceding fortnight.

(b) In computing the amount for the purpose of Cl. (a) the following shall be deemed to be cash maintained in India, namely:

(i) any balance maintained by a scheduled State Co-operative Bank with the Reserve Bank in excess of the balance required to be maintained by it under Sec. 42 of the Reserve Bank of India Act, 1934 (2 of 1934),

(ii) any cash or balances maintained in India by a co-operative Bank, other than a scheduled State co-operative bank with itself or with the State Co-operative Bank or the state concerned, or in current accounts with Reserve Bank or by way of net balance in current accounts and in the case of a primary co-operative bank, also any balance maintained with the Central co-operative bank of the district concerned, in excess of the aggregate of the cash or balances required to be maintained under Sec. 18, and

(iii) any net balance in current accounts.

Explanation: For the purposes of this sub-section,—

(a) approved securities, or a portion thereof, representing investment of moneys of Agricultural Credit Stabilization Fund of a co-operative bank shall not be deemed to be unencumbered approved securities,

(b) in case a co-operative bank has taken an advance against any balance maintained with the State Co-operative Bank of the State concerned or with the Central co-operative bank of the district concerned, such balance to the extent to which it has been drawn against or availed or shall not be deemed to be cash maintained in India;

(c) for the purpose of Cl. (a) the market price of an approved security shall be the price as on the date of the issue of the notification or as on any earlier or later date, as may be notified from time to time by the Reserve Bank in respect of any class or classes of securities;

(d) in sub-section (3), for the proviso, the following proviso shall be substituted, namely:

(iv) In sub-section (3), for the proviso the following proviso shall be sub-section, namely:
"Provided that every co-operative bank, other than a primary co-operative bank, shall also furnish within the said period, a copy of the said return to the National Bank."

(v) in sub-section (6), in Cl. (a) for the words "fourteen days", the words "thirty days" shall be substituted;]

[(qq) After Sec. 24, the following section shall be inserted, namely: 24-A. Power to exempt—without prejudice to the provisions of Sec. 53, the Reserve Bank may, by notification in the official Gazette, declare that, for such period and subject to such conditions as may be specified in such notification the whole or any part of the provisions of Sec. 18 or Sec. 24, as may be specified therein, shall not apply to any co-operative bank or class of Co-operative Banks, with reference to all or any of the offices of such co-operative bank or banks, or with reference of the whole or any part of the assets and liabilities of such co-operative bank or banks."

[(ri) in the second proviso to Sec. 26, for the expression "regional rural bank", the expression "co-operative bank, other than a primary co-operative bank" shall be substituted;

(rii) in Sec. 27, for sub-section (3), the following sub-section shall be substituted, namely:

(3) Every co-operative bank, other than a primary co-operative bank, shall submit a copy of there turn which it submits to the Reserve Bank under sub-section (1) also to National Bank and the powers, exercisable by the Reserve Bank under sub-section (2) may also be exercised by the National Bank in relation to Co-operative Banks, other than primary Co-operative Banks";

(s) for Secs. 29 and 30 the following section shall be substituted, namely.

29. *Accounts and balance-sheet:* (1) At the expiration of each year ending with the 30th day of June, every co-operative bank, in respect of all business transacted by it, shall prepare with reference to that year a balance-sheet and profit and loss account as on the last working day of the year in the forms set out in the Third Schedule or is near thereto as circumstances admit.

(1) The balance-sheet and profit and loss account shall be signed by the manager or the principal officer of the bank and where there are more than three directors of the bank, by at least three of those directors, or where there are not more than three directors, by all the directors.

(2) The Central Government, after giving not less than three months' notice of its intention so to do by a notification in the official Gazette may from time to time by a like notification amend the forms set out in the Third Schedule";

[(t) In Sec. 31,—

(i) for the words "within three months" and "of three months", the words "within six months" and "of six months" shall, respectively, be substituted; and

(ii) for the second proviso, the following proviso shall substituted, namely:

Provided further that a co-operative bank other than a primary co-operative bank shall furnish such returns also to the national Bank";]

(w) In Sec. 35,—

(i) in sub-section (1),—

(a) for the words and figures "Sec. 235 of the Companies Act, 1956 (1 of 1956)", the words "any law relating to co-operative societies for the time being in force" shall be substituted;

(b) the following proviso shall be inserted at the end, namely: "Provided that the Reserve Bank may, if it considers it necessary or expedient so to do, cause an inspection to be made of a primary co-operative bank under this sub-section by one or more officers of a State co-operative bank in the State in which such primary co-operative bank is registered";]

(iii) after sub-section (4), the following sub-Section shall be inserted, namely:

(4-A) Without prejudice to the provisions of sub-sections (4) the Reserve Bank may, if it considers it necessary or expedient so to do supply a copy of the report on any inspection or scrutiny to the state co-operative bank and the Registrar of Co-operative Societies of the State in which the bank which has been inspected or whose affairs have been scrutinised is registered.

[(iv)] in sub-section (6), for the expressions "Regional rural banks" and "regional rural bank" wherever they occur, the expressions "co-operative bank other than primary Co-operative Banks" and "co-operative bank other than a primary co-operative bank" shall, respectively be substituted,];

(x) In Sec. 35-A in sub-section (1) in Cl. (c), for the words "any banking company", the words "the banking business of any co-operative bank" shall be substituted;

[(z) In Sec. 36 in sub-section (1),—

(b) for Cl. (d), the following clause shall be substituted, namely: "(d) at any time, if it is satisfied that for the reorganisation of expansion of co-operative credit on sound lines it is necessary so to do, by an order in writing and on such terms and conditions as may be specified therein:

(i) depute one or more of its officers to which the proceedings at any meeting of the Board of directors of the co-operative bank or of any other body constituted by it and require the co-operative bank to give an opportunity to the officer so deputed to be heard at such meetings and to offer such advice on such matters as the officer may consider necessary or proper of the reorganization and expansion of co-operative credit on sound lines, and also require such officer to send a report of such proceedings to the Reserve Bank; and

(ii) appoint one or more of its officers to observe the manner in which the affairs of the co-operative bank or its offices or branches are conducted and made a report thereon."]

(z-a) In Sec. 36-A,—

(i) for sub-section (1), the following sub-section shall be substituted, namely:

"(1) The provisions of Sec. 11, Sec. 18 and Sec. 24 shall not apply to a co-operative bank which has been refused a licence under Sec. 22 or whose licence has been cancelled under that section or which is or has been prohibited or precluded from accepting alteration made in its bye-laws,";

(ii) after sub-section (2), the following sub-section shall be inserted, namely:

"(2) Subject to the provisions of sub-sections (1) and (2), a co-operative society carrying on business as a primary co-operative bank at the commencement of the Banking Laws (Application to Co-operative Societies) Act, 1965 (23 of 1965), or a co-operative society which becomes a primary co-operative bank after such commencement shall, notwithstanding that it does not at any time thereafter satisfy the requirements of the definition of primary co-operative bank [(in Cl. (ccv) of Sec. 5] continue to be a primary co-operative bank within the meaning of this Act, and may, with the approval of the Reserve Bank and subject to such terms and conditions as the Reserve Bank may specify in that behalf, continue to carry on the business of banking."

[(z-aa) In Sec. 36-AD, sub-section (3) shall be omitted].

(z-b) Part II-A, [Pt. II-C], Pt. III, except sub-sections (1), (2) and

(z-c) In Sec. 46,—

(i) in sub-section (4), the word "or" occurring at the end of Cl. (i) and Cl. (ii) shall be omitted;

(ii) in Cl. (a) of the Explanation, after the words "includes A", the words "co-operative society" shall be inserted;

(z-f) In Sec. 49-A, for the proviso, the following proviso shall be substituted, namely:

"Provided that nothing contained in this section shall apply to—

(a) a primary credit society,

(b) any other co-operative society accepting such deposits at the commencement of the Banking Laws (Application to Co-operative Societies) Act, 1965 (23 of 1965), for a period of one year from the date of such commencement; and

(c) any savings bank scheme run by the Government";

(z-j) In Sec. 52,—

(i) in sub-section (2), the words, figures and letter "and the form in which the official liquidator may file lists of debtors to the Court having jurisdiction under Part III, Part III-A and the particulars which such lists may contain" shall be omitted;

(ii) [(z-ji) in Sec. 54, after the expression "Reserve Bank" wherever it occurs, the expression "or the national bank" shall be inserted.]

(iii) (z-k) for Sec. 55 and the First Schedule, the following section shall be substituted, namely:

"55. Act 18 of 1891 and Act 46 of 1949 to apply in relation to Co-operative Banks.—

(1) The Bankers' Book Evidence Act, 1891, shall apply in relation to a co-operative bank as it applies in relation to a bank as defined in Sec. 2 of that Act.

(2) The Banking Companies (Legal Practitioners' Clients' Accounts) Act, 1949, shall apply in relation to a co-operative bank as it applies in relation to a banking company as defined in Sec. 2 of that Act.";

(z-i) for the Third Schedule and the Fourth Schedule, the following Schedule shall be substituted, namely:

"THE THIRD SCHEDULE"
(See Sec. 29)
FORM A
Form of Balance-Sheet

Capital and Liabilities		*Property and Assets*	
1. Capital:	**Rs. P.**	**1. Cash:**	**Rs. P.**
(i) Authorised capital		In hand and with Reserve Bank (the National Bank), State Bank of India, State Co-operative Bank and Central Co-operative Bank...........	
....Shares of Rs. ....each			
....Shares of Rs. ....each			
....			
(ii) Subscribed capital		**2. Balances with other Banks:**	
Shares of Rs. ....each		(i) Current deposits	
Shares of Rs. ....each		(ii) Savings bank deposits	
....		(iii) Fixed deposits	
(iii) Amount called up		**3. Money at call and short Notices:**	
On ....Shares at Rs.		**4. Investments:**	
Each less calls unpaid		(i) In Central and State Government Securities (at Book value)	
On ....Shares at Rs. ......each less calls unpaid....................................		Face value Rs.	
Of (iii) above held by		Market value Rs.	
(a) Individuals.........		(ii) Other trustee securities.	
(b) Co-operative Institutions.		(iii) Shares in co-operative institutions other than in items below	
(c) State Government			
2. Reserve Fund and other Reserves:			
(i) Statutory Reserve.		(iv) Other investments (to be specified)...	
(ii) Agricultural (Credit Stabilization Fund).			

(Contd.)

(Contd.)

Capital and Liabilities	*Property and Assets*
(iii) Building Fund…….	**5. Investments out of the Principal/ Subsidiary State Partnership Fund.**
(iv) Dividend Equalization Fund …….	
(v) Special Bad Debts Reserve……..	
(vi) Bad and Doubtful Debts Reserve …….	
(vii) Investment Depreciation Reserve……..	
(viii) Other funds and Reserve (to be specified)	

5

Consumer Protection Act, 1986

A. INTRODUCTION

According to the preamble the purpose of the Act is to provide for the better protection of the interests of consumers and for that purpose to make provision for the establishment of consumer councils and other authorities for the settlement of consumer disputes and for matters connected therewith.

For providing cheaper and speedier Justice to a consumer the Act provides for the setting up of Consumer Protection Councils both at the Central and State level and also establishment of 'Consumer Disputes Redressal Agencies' for the purpose. Such agencies are:

(i) Consumer Disputes Redressal Forum to be known as "District Forum";
(ii) Consumer Disputes Redressal Commission to be known as "State Commission"; and
(iii) National Consumer Disputes Redressal Commission.

B. DEFINITION OF COMPLAINANT (S. 2b)

Complaint means,

(i) a consumer; or
(ii) any voluntary consumer association registered under the Companies Act, 1956 or under any other law for the time being in force; or
(iii) the Central Government or any State Government, who or which makes a complaint; and
(iv) to the various forums provided under the act.

(a) Complaint (S. 2(c))

Complaint means any allegation in writing made by a complainant with a view to obtaining any relief provided by or under this act that the services mentioned in the complaint suffer from deficiency in any respect.

(b) Consumer (S. 2(d))

Consumer means any person who—

(a) buys any goods for a consideration which has been paid or promised or partly paid and partly promised, or under any system of deferred payment and includes any user of such goods other than the person who buys such goods for consideration paid or promised or partly paid or partly promised or under any system of deferred payment when such use is made with the approval of such person, but does not include a person who obtains of such person, but does not include a person who obtains such goods for resale or for any commercial purpose; or

(b) hires or avails of any services for a consideration which has been paid or promised or partly paid and partly promised or under any system of deferred payment and includes any beneficiary of such services other than the person who hires the services for consideration paid or promised, or partly paid and partly promised, or under any system of deferred payment, when such services are availed of with the approval of the first mentioned person. Thus if any person:

Either: (i) buys any goods for consideration, or (ii) hires or avails of any services for a consideration, he is a consumer. A person who is allotted a house by a State Housing Board is a Consumer under the Act.[1]

(c) Consumer Dispute (S. 2(c))

'Consumer Dispute' means a dispute where the person against whom a complaint has been made, denies or disputes the allegation contained in the complaint.

(d) Deficiency (S. 2(g))

"Deficiency" means any fault, imperfection, shortcoming or inadequacy in the quality, nature and manner of performance which is required to be maintained by or under any law for the time being in force or has been undertaken to be performed by a person in pursuance of a contract or otherwise in relation to any service. Irregular supply of electricity is deficiency in service but there must be a clear finding on the point before responsibility is fixed an account of such deficiency in service.[2]

(e) Service (S. 2(d)(ii))

Any person who hires services for a consideration is a consumer. According to section 2(1)(0): "Service" means Service of any description which is made available to potential users and includes the provision of facilities in connection with banking, financing, insurance, transport, processing, supply of electrical or other energy, board or lodging or both, entertainment, amusement or the purveying a news or there information,

1. Prio Ranjan Roy *v.* Bihar State Housing Board and Others, 11(1994) SPJ 1330.
2. Chairman, Orissa State Electricity Board *v.* Dibakar Mohanty, (1993) (2) (PR 367), Quoted in R.K. Bangia. *"A Hand Book of Consumer Protection Laws and Procedure"* (1997) at 146.

but does not include the rendering of any service free of charge or under a contract of personal service.

(f) Consideration for Service Necessary

To enable a consumer to bring an action he must have availed the services for a consideration. The consideration may be either paid or promised or partly paid and partly promised or under any system of deferred payment.

A person hiring banking services for consideration is a consumer. Thus, if the depositor of a Fixed Deposit Receipt in a bank applied for a premature encashment and the same was delayed, the depositor was a consumer entitled to file a complaint as such.[3]

(g) Service without Consideration (S. 2(d)(ii))

The consumer must hire any Services "for a consideration", Section 2(1) also stipulates that service does not include the rendering of any service free of charge. When the services are rendered without consideration, the complaint cannot be entertained in a consumer forum.

(h) Person [S. 2 (m]: "Person" includes

(i) a firm whether registered or not;
(ii) a Hindu undivided family;
(iii) a Co-operative society;
(iv) every other association of persons whether registered under the Societies Registration Act, 1860 or not.

C. SERVICE OF SUMMONS

If the plaint is properly presented, it is admitted as per 0_4, R_2. After the plaint being admitted, summons to the defendant be sent as per 0_5, $R_{7,8}$.

(a) Definition

Summons is a document issued from the office of a Court of Justice, calling upon the person to whom it is directed to attend before a judge or office of the court on the day mentioned therein.

(b) Summons to Defendants (S. 27)

Where a suit has been duly instituted, a summon may be issued to the defendant to appear and answer the claim and may be served in the manner prescribed.

3. P. Nagabhushana Rao *v.* Union of India, (1991) CPJ 352.

Where a suit has been duly instituted by filing a plaint, the first duty of the court is to issue a summon calling on the defendant to appear and answer the claim on a day specified therein either in person or by a pleader duly instructed or accompanied by some person able to answer all material questions. A Summon mentioning wrong date for appearance or appearance on a day when the court is closed, is not a summon as required under 0_5, R_1. The date is essential ingredient of the summon[4].

(c) Essentials of a Summon

Every Summon shall:

(i) Intimate to the defendant of the date of hearing and whether he is to appear in person or by a pleader;
(ii) Contain a direction whether the date is fixed for settlement of issues only or final disposal of the suit; and
(iii) Order the defendant to produce all documents in his possession or power upon which he intends to rely in support of his case.

(d) Modes of Service of Summons (O_5, R_{10})

Service of the summons shall be made by delivering or tendering a copy thereof signed by the Judge or such officer as he appoints in this behalf, and sealed with the seal of the court.

(i) Personal or Direct Service

The Summon should be handed over in person to the defendant or adult male or female member of his family. Such personal service is also called direct service because service is made by delivering a copy thereof to the defendant personally, or to an agent or other person on his behalf and the signature of the person to whom the copy is so handed over must be obtained[5].

(ii) Service by affixing a copy of summons on defendant's house with an order of the court

(a) Where the defendant or his agent or in their absence an adult member of the family refuses to sign the acknowledgement, or

(b) Where the service officer after using all due and reasonable diligence, cannot find the defendant who is absent from his residence at the time when service is sought to be effected on him at his residence and there is no likelihood of his being found at the residence, within a reasonable time and there is no other such person on whom service can be effected, the serving officer shall affix a copy of the summons on the outer door. If the court is satisfied, it declares the service to have been duly effected[6].

4. AIR 1964 MP 261.
5. See. O_5 $R_{11\text{-}15}$.
6. See, O_5 R_{17}

(iii) Service by registered post in addition to Personal Service

The Summons can also be served to the defendant by registered post also. The acknowledgement of the registered post summon is essential. The court issuing the summons shall declare that the summons had been duly served on the defendant; provided that where the summons was properly addressed, prepaid and duly sent by registered post.[7]

(iv) Substituted Service

Where the court is satisfied that the defendant is avoiding service, or the defendant cannot be served. In any way, the court shall order the summons to be served by affixing a copy thereof in some conspicuous part of the house. Such service is valid. Service may be ordered to be effected by publication in a local newspaper also.[8]

Penalties (S. 27)

Where a trader or a person against whom a complaint is made or the complainant fails or omits to comply with any order made by the District Forum, the State Commission or the National Commission, as the case may be, such trader or person or complainant shall be punishable with imprisonment for a term which shall not be less than one month but which may extend to three years, or with fine which shall not be less than two thousand rupees but which may extend to ten thousand rupees, or with both:

Provided that the District form, the State Commission or the National Commission, as the case may be, may, if it is satisfied that the circumstances of any case so require, impose a sentence of imprisonment or fine, or both for a term lesser than the minimum term and the amount lesser than the minimum amount, specified in this section.[9]

No consumer court can grant a relief either final or in term which is not enumerated under section 14 of the consumer Protection Act and hence no proceedings Under Section 27 can be initiated for non-compliance of such order.[10]

D. CONSUMER PROTECTION COUNCILS

(a) The Central Consumer Protection Council (S. 4)

(1) The Central Government may, by notification, establish effect from such date as it may specify in such notification, a Council to be known at the Central Consumer Protection Council (hereinafter referred to as the Central Council).

7. See, O_5 $R_{19\text{-}A}$.
8. See, O_5 R_{20}.
9. *Supra* Note 2 at 164.
10. Anant Prasad Chaudhary *v.* Madan Sah and Others, 1993(1) CPR 385.

(2) The Central Council shall consist of the following members, namely:

(a) the Minister-in-charge of the consumer affairs in the Central Government, who shall be its chairman, and

(b) such number of other official or non-official members representing such interests as may be prescribed.

(b) Procedure for Meetings of the Central Council (S. 5)

(1) The Central Council shall meet as and when necessary, at least one meeting of the Council shall be held every year.

(2) The Central Council shall meet at such time and place as the Chairman may think fit and shall observe such procedure in regard to the transaction of its business as may be prescribed.

(c) Objects of the Central Council (S. 6)

The objects of the Central Council shall be to promote and protect the rights of the consumer such as—

(a) the right to be protected against the marketing of goods and services which are hazardous to life and property;

(b) the right to be informed about the quality, quantity, potency, purity, standard and price of goods or services, as the case may be so as to protect the consumer against unfair trade practices;

(c) the right to be assured, wherever possible, access to a variety of goods and service at competitive prices;

(d) the right to be heard and to be assured that consumer's interests will receive due consideration at appropriate forums;

(e) the right to seek redressal against unfair trade practices for restrictive trade practices or unscrupulous exploitation of consumers; and

(f) the right to consumer education.

E. THE STATE CONSUMER PROTECTION COUNCIL (S. 7)

(1) The State Government may, by notification, establish with effect from such date as it may specify in such notification, a council to be known as the Consumer Protection Council for . . .(hereinafter referred to as the State Council).

(2) The State Council shall consist of the following members, namely:

(a) the Minister Incharge of consumer affairs in the State Government who shall be its Chairman;

(b) such number of other official or non-official members representing such interests and may be prescribed by the State Government.

(3) The State Council shall meet as and when necessary but not less than two meetings shall be held every year.

(4) The State Council shall meet at such time and place as the Chairman may think fit and shall observe such procedure in regard to the transaction of its business as may be prescribed by the State Government.

(a) Object of the State Council (S. 8)

The objects of every State Council shall be to promote and protect within the State the right of the consumers laid down in clauses (a) to (f) of Section 6.

F. CONSUMER DISPUTES REDRESSAL AGENCIES

(a) Establishment of Consumer Disputes Redressal Agencies (S. 9)

There shall be established for the purposes of this Act, the following agencies, namely:

(a) a Consumer Dispute Redressal Forum to be known as the "District Forum" established by the State Government in each district of the State by notification;

(b) a Consumer Disputes Redressal Commission to be known as the "State Commission" established by the State Government in the State by notification; and

(c) a National Consumer Disputes Redressal Commission established by the Central Government by notification.

In *T.P. Dobhal v. Chairman, U.P. State Electricity Board,*[11] the Court held that the Consumer Protection Act, 1986 has a retrospective operation. A consumer has a right to seek relief before the Rederessal Forums even if the cause of action arose before the enforcement of the Act, provided the Act is not barred under the Law of Limitation.

(b) Composition of the District Forum (S. 10)

(1) Each District Forum shall consists of—

(a) a person who is or who has been, or is qualified to be a District Judge, who shall be its President;

(b) two other members who shall be persons of ability, integrity and standing, and have adequate knowledge or experience of, or have shown capacity in dealing with, problems relating to economics, law, commerce, accountancy, industry, public affairs or administration, one of whom shall be a woman.

(2) Every appointment under sub-section (1) shall be made by the State Government on the recommendation of a selection committee consisting of the following, namely:

(i) the President of the State Commission—Chairman.

(ii) Secretary, Law Department of the State—Member

11. (1994) CPJ 132: 194(1) (PR 252).

(iii) Secretary incharge of the Department dealing with consumer affairs in the State—Member.

(3) Every member of the District Forum shall hold office for a term of five years or up to the age of 65 years, whichever is earlier, and shall not be eligible for re-appointment:

Provided that a member may resign his office in writing under his hand addressed to the State Government and on such resignation being accepted, his office shall become vacant and may be filled by the appointment of a person possessing and of the qualifications mentioned in sub-section (1) in relation to the category of the member who has resigned.

(4) The salary or honorarium and other allowances payable to, and the other terms and conditions of service of the members of the District Forum shall be such as may be prescribed by the State Government.

(c) Jurisdiction of the District Forum (S. 11)

(1) Subject to the other provisions of this Act, the District Forum shall have jurisdiction to entertain complaints where the value of the goods or services and the compensation, if any, claimed does not exceed rupees twenty lakhs.

(2) A complaint shall be instituted in a District Forum within the local limits of whose jurisdiction—

(a) the opposite party or each of the opposite parties, where there are more than one, at the time of the institution of the complaint, actually and voluntarily resides or carries on business or has a branch office or personally work for gain, or

(b) any of the opposite parties, where there are more than one, at the time of the institution of the complaint, actually and voluntarily resides, or carries on business or has a branch office, or personally works for gain, provided that in such case either the permission of the District Forum is given, or the opposite parties who do not reside, or carry on business or have a branch office, or personally work for gain, as the case may be, acquiesce in such institution; or

(c) the cause of action, wholly or in part, arises.

In *Smt. Kulwant Kaur v. Punjab State Electricity Board and another,*[12] the court held that a person cannot move two Forums simultaneously for the same relief. Thus, when a complaint under the workmen's compensation Act is subjudice the Redressal Forum cannot entertain complaint for the same relief.

In *Smti. Gurvinder Bedi v. Delhi Development Authority,*[13] the Court held that charging of escalated price of a flat by DDA does not constitute deficiency in service and pricing is not a factor which falls within the purview of the Consumer Disputes Redresal Forum.

12. 1993 (2) CPR 400 (SCDRC), Punjab.
13. 1995 (3) CPR 695 (INCDRC), New Delhi.

In *Doctor Sumrita Nursing Home v. Ms G.N. Sales and others,*[14] the court held that the disputes regarding goods including machinery used in business where purpose is to make profit, fall outside the jurisdiction of the Redressal Forum.

(d) Manner in which Complaint shall be made

A complaint in relation to any goods sold or delivered or agreed to be sold or delivered or any service provided or agreed to be provided may be filed with a District Forum by—

(a) the consumer to whom such goods are sold or delivered or agreed to be delivered or such service provided or agreed to be provided;
(b) any recognized consumer association whether the consumer to whom the goods sold or delivered or agreed to be sold or delivered or service provided or agreed to be provided is a member of such association or not;
(c) one or more consumers, where there are numerous consumers having the same interest, with the permission of the District Forum, on behalf of, or for the benefit of, all consumers so interested; or
(d) the Central or the State Government.

An Electricity Board has been ordered to pay compensation on account of excess voltage of electricity.[15]

In *Ashok Kumar Singh v. Union of India through General Manager, N.E. Railway,*[16] the court held that the Railway Authorities have been held responsible for not taking care to advertise change in timings of express train well in time.

In Dayanand A. Avasare v. Bharat Petroleum Corporation Ltd. and Others,[17] the court held that a LPG cylinder containing excessive gas above the permissible limit is defective goods and there is deficiency in service on the part of it dealer and the manufacturer in supplying such a gas cylinder to the consumer without keeping a view the safety precaution provided under the gas cylinder rules.

(e) Procedure on Receipt of Complaint

(1) The District Forum shall, on receipt of a complaint, if it relates to any goods—

(a) refer a copy of the complaint to the opposite party mentioned in the complaint directing him to give his version of the case within a period of thirty days or such extended period not exceeding fifteen days as may be granted by the District Forum;

14. 1993 (2) CPR 164 (SCDRC), Punjab.
15. *Gujarat Electricity Board v. Smt. Sharda Madhusudan Desai,* 1992(11) CPR 692.
16. 1993(1) CPR 292.
17. 1993(1) CPR 279.

(b) where the opposite party on receipt of a complaint referred to him under clause (a) denies or disputes the allegations contained in the complaint, or omits or fails to take any action to represent his case, within the time given by the District Forum, the District Forum shall proceed to settle the consumer dispute in the manner specified in clauses (c) to (g);

(c) where the complaint alleges a defect in the goods which can not be determined without proper analysis or test of the goods, the District Forum shall obtain a sample of the goods from the complainant, seal it and authenticate it in the manner prescribed and refer the sample so sealed to the appropriate laboratory along with a direction that such laboratory make an analysis or test, whichever may be necessary, with a view to finding out whether such goods suffer from any defect alleged in the complaint or from any other defect and to report its findings thereon to the District Forum within a period of forty-five days of the receipt of the reference or within such extended period as may be granted by the District Forum;

(d) before any sample of the goods is referred to any appropriate laboratory under clause (c), the District Forum may require the complainant to deposit to the credit of the Forum such fees as may be specified, for payment to the appropriate laboratory for carrying out the necessary analysis or test in relation to the goods in question;

(e) the District Forum shall remit the amount deposited to its credit under clause (d) to the appropriate laboratory to enable it to carry out the analysis or test mentioned in clause (c) and on receipt of the report from the appropriate laboratory, the District Forum shall forward a copy of the report along with such remarks as the District Forum may feel appropriate to the opposite party;

(f) if any of the parties disputes the correctness of the findings of the appropriate laboratory, or dispute the correctness of the methods of analysis or test adopted by the appropriate laboratory, the District Forum shall require the opposite party or the complainant to submit in writing his objections in regards to the report made by the appropriate laboratory; and

(g) the District Forum shall thereafter give a reasonable opportunity to the complainant as well as the opposite party of being heard as to the correctness or otherwise of the report made by the appropriate laboratory and also as to the objection made in relation thereto under clause (f) and issue an appropriate order under section 14.

(2) The District Forum shall, if the complaint received by it under section 12 relates to goods in respect of which the procedure specified in sub-section (1) cannot be followed, or if the complaint relates to any services;—

(a) refer a copy of such complaint to the opposite party directing him to give his version of the case within a period of thirty days or such extended period not exceeding fifteen days as may be granted by the District Forum;

(b) where the opposite party, on receipt of a copy of the complaint, referred to him under clause (a) denies or disputes the allegations contained in the complaint, or omits or fails to take any action to represent his case within the time given by the District Forum, the District Forum shall proceed to settle the consumer dispute—

(i) on the basis of evidence brought to its notice by the complainant and the opposite party, where the opposite party denies or disputes the allegations contained in the complaint, or

(ii) on the basis of evidence brought to its notice by the complainant where the opposite party omits or fails to take any action to represent his case within the time given by the Forum.

(3) No proceedings, complying with the procedure laid down in sub-sections (1) and (2) shall be called in question in any court on the ground that the principles of natural justice have not been complied with.

(4) For the purposes of this section, the District Forum shall have the same powers as are vested in a civil court under Code of Civil Procedure, 1908 while trying a suit in respect of the following matters, namely:

(i) the summoning and enforcing the attendance of any defendant or witness and examining the witness on oath;
(ii) the discovery and production of any document or other material object producible as evidence;
(iii) the reception of evidence on affidavits;
(iv) the requisitioning of the report of the concerned analysis or test from the appropriate laboratory or from any other relevant source;
(v) issuing of any commission for the examination of any witness; and
(vi) any other matter which may be prescribed.

(g) Every proceeding before the District Forum shall be deemed to be a judicial proceeding within the meaning of sections 193 and 228 of the Indian Penal Code, and the District Forum shall be deemed to be a civil court for the purposes of section 195, and Chapter XXVI of the Code of Criminal Procedure, 1973.

(5) Where the complainant is a consumer referred to in sub-clause (iv) of clause (b) of sub-section (1) of section 2, the provisions of Rule 8 of Order 1 of the First Schedule to the Code of Civil Procedure, 1908 shall apply subject to the modification that every reference therein to a suit or decree shall be construed as a reference to a complaint or the order of the District Forum thereon.

In *Rajinder Singh v. Varinder,*[18] the court held that where a complainant alleges a defect in the goods which cannot be determined without proper analysis or test it is mandatory for the District Forum to have the goods analysed in an appropriate laboratory.

In *Narayan Vyankatrishnan Iyengar v. Shaki Foods & Another,*[19] the court held that simply became the report of analysis of the sample was published

18. 11 (1994) CPJ 127
19. IJ (1994) CPJ 652.

in the newspaper does not mean that the report of analysis be discarded by the District Forum outrightly.

(f) Finding of the District Forum (S. 14)

(1) If, after the proceeding conducted under section 13, District Forum is satisfied that the goods complained against suffer from any of the defects specified in the complaint of that any for allegations contained in the complaint about the services are proved. It shall still issue an order to the opposite party directing him to do one or more of the following things, namely;

(a) to remove the defect pointed out by the appropriate laboratory from the goods in question;
(b) to replace the goods with new goods of similar description which shall be free from any defect;
(c) to return to the complainant the price, or, as the case may be the charges paid by the complaint;
(d) to pay such amount as may be awarded by it as compensation to the consumer for any loss or injury suffered by the consumer due to the negligence of the opposite party.
(e) to remove the defects or deficiencies in the services in question;
(f) to discontinue the unfair trade practice or the restrictive trade practice or not to repeat them;
(g) not to offer the hazardous goods for sale;
(h) to withdraw the hazardous goods from being offered for scale;
(i) to provide for adequate costs to parties.

(2) Every proceeding referred to in sub-section (1) shall be conducted by the President of the District Forum and at least one member thereof sitting together:

Provided that where the member, for any reason, is unable to conduct the proceeding till it is completed, the President and the other member shall conduct such proceeding *de nova*.

(2A) Every order made by the District Forum under Sub-section (1) shall be signed by its President and the member or members who conducted the proceedings:

Provided that where the proceeding is conducted by the President and one member and they differ on any point or points, they shall state the point or points on which they differ and refer the same to the other member for hearing on such point or points and the opinion of the majority shall be the order of the District Forum.

(3) Subject to the foregoing provisions, the procedure relating to the conduct of the meetings of the District Forum, its sittings and other matters shall be such as may be prescribed by the State Government.

In *P. Durga Prasad v. The Corporation of Madras,*[20] the court held that a consumer is entitled to compensation for a building plan not sanctioned within the statutory period on account of deficiency in service and negligence of the opposite party.

In *Bhoj Lal Dalmia v. General Manager, Calcutta Telephones,*[21] the court held that the Telephone Department must pay compensation to the consumer for causing harassment, torture and mental agony by charging incorrect and excessive bills.

(g) Appeal

Any person aggrieved by an order made by the District Forum may prefer an appeal against such order to the State Commission within a period of thirty days from the date of the order, in such form and manner as may be prescribed:

Provided that the State Commission may entertain an appeal after the expiry of the said period of thirty days if it is satisfied that there was sufficient cause for not finding it within that period.

Where the legislature has expressly provided for an appeal and prescribed the period of limitation the same has to be honoured by conformance, and not in its breach.[22]

In *Miss S. Srivastava v. Classic Motors*[23], the State Commission has held that where there was no direction in the original order of the Forum that interest on interest would be paid by the complainant the same cannot be claimed by the consumer by making an application for amendment of the order.

G. COMPOSITION OF THE STATE COMMISSON (S.16)

(1) Each State Composition shall consist of—

(a) a person who is or has been a Judge of a High Court, appointed by the state government, who shall be its President:
Provided that no appointment under this clause shall be made except after consultation with the Chief Justice of the High Court;

(b) two other members, who shall be persons of ability, integrity and standing and have adequate knowledge or experience of, or have shown capacity in dealing with, problems relating to economics, law, commerce, accountancy, industry, public affairs or administration, one of whom shall be a woman:

Provided that every appointment made under this clause shall be made by the State Government on the recommendation of a selection committee consisting of the following, namely—

20. 11 (1994) CPJ 538.
21. 11 (1994) CPJ 559.
22. *Dynamic Machines (P) Ltd. v. Jai Koran Medicine,* 11 (1994) CPJ 226.
23. 11 (1994) CPI 433.

(i) President of the State Commission—Chairman.
(ii) Secretary of the Law Department of the State—Member.
(iii) Secretary, incharge of Department dealing with consumer affairs in the State—Member.

(2) The salary or honorarium and other allowance payable to, and the other terms and conditions of service of the members of the State Commission shall be such as may be prescribed by the State Government.

(3) Every member of the State Commission shall hold office for a term of five year or up to the age of sixty-seven years, whichever is earlier and shall not be eligible for re-appointment.

(4) Notwithstanding anything contained in sub-section (3), a person appointed as a President or as a member before the commencement of the Consumer Protection (Amendment) Act, 1993, shall continue to hold such office as President or member, as the case may be, till the completion of his term.

(a) Jurisdiction of the State Commission (S. 17)

Subject to the other provisions of this Act, the State Commission shall have jurisdiction—

(a) to entertain
  (i) complaints where the value of the goods or services and compensation, if any, claimed exceeds rupees (twenty lakhs but does not exceed rupees one crore); and
  (ii) appeals against the order of any District Forum within the State; and
(b) to call for the records and pass appropriate orders in any consumer dispute which is pending before or has been decided by any District Forum within the State, where it appears to the State Commission that such District Forum has exercised a jurisdiction not vested in it by law, or has failed to exercise a jurisdiction so vested or has acted in exercise of its jurisdiction illegally or with material irregularity.

In *Punjab State Electricity Board v. M/s Anand Aggarwal Oils (Pvt.) Ltd.*,[24] the court held that Redressal Fora under Consumer Protection Act do not have jurisdiction to pass any injunction order interim injunction orders.

In *Sumangla Steel Ltd. v. The Oriental Insurance Co. Ltd.*[25], the Sate Commission has held that the determination of the question of the reasonability of compensation fixed by an insurer is a matter which falls within the jurisdiction of the Consumer Protection Act.

24. 1993 (2) CPR 157 (SCDRC) Punjab.
25. 11(1994) CP 192.

(b) Procedure Applicable to State Commissions (S.18)

The provisions of Sections 12, 13 and 14 and the rules made thereunder for the disposal of complaints by the District Forum shall, with such modifications as may be necessary, be applicable to the disposal of disputes by the State Commission.

In *Dr. M.S. Shenay* v. *M/S Hindustan Engineering Company and another,*[26] the court held that Section 11 of the Consumer Protection Act applies only to District Forum. Therefore, Jurisdiction of State Forum will be governed by the provision contained in the Code of Civil Procedure.

(c) Vacancy in the Office of the President (S. 18A)

When the office of the President of the District Forum or of the State Commission, as the case may be, is vacant or when any such President is, by reason of absence or otherwise, unable to perform the duties of his office, the duties of the office shall be performed by such person, who is qualified to be appointed as President of the District Forum or, as the case may be, of the State Commission, as the State Government may appoint for the purpose.

(d) Appeals (S. 19)

Any person aggrieved by an order made by the State Commission in exercise of its powers conferred by sub-clause (1) of Clause (a) of Section 17 may prefer an appeal against such order to the National Commission within a period of thirty days from the date of the order in such form and manner as may be prescribed:

Provided that the National Commission may entertain an appeal after the expiry of the said period of thirty days if it is satisfied that there was sufficient cause for not filing it within that period.

In *Krishna Devi Kedia* v. *Chairman, L.I.C. of India and others,*[27] the National Commission has held that the complaint is entitled to be paid not merely the amount insured under her husband's policy of life Insurance and Interest thereon but is also entitled to the accrued bonus as per the scheme applicable to the Insurance policy in question.

H. COMPOSITION OF THE NATIONAL COMMISSION (S. 20)

(l) The National Commission shall consist of—

(a) A person who is or has been a Judge of the Supreme Court, to be appointed by the Central Government, who shall be its President:

26. 1993(1) CPR 316.
27. 11(1994) CPJ 114 (N.C.).

Provided that no appointment under this clause shall be made except after consultation with the Chief Justice of India.

(b) Four other members who shall be persons of ability, integrity and standing and have adequate knowledge or experience of, or have shown capacity in dealing with, problems relating to economics, law, commerce, accountancy, industry, public affairs or administration, one of whom shall be a woman:

Provided that every appointment under this clause shall be made by the Central Government on the recommendation of a selection committee consisting of the following, namely:

(a) a person who is a Judge of the Supreme Court, to be nominated by the Chief Justice of India—Chairman.
(b) The Secretary in the Department of Legal Affairs in the Government of India—Member.
(c) Secretary of the Department dealing with consumer affairs in the Government of India—Member.

(2) The salary or honorarium and other allowances payable to and the other terms and conditions of service of the members of the National Commission shall be such as may be prescribed by the Central Government.

(3) Every member of the National Commission shall hold office for a term of five years or up to the age of seventy years, whichever is earlier and shall not be eligible for re-appointment.

(4) Notwithstanding anything contained in sub-section (3) a person appointed as a President or a member before the commencement of the Consumer Protection (Amendment) Act, 1993, shall continue to hold such office as President or member, as the case may be, till the completion of his term.

(a) Jurisdiction of the National Commission (S. 21)

Subject to the other provisions of this Act, the National Commission shall have jurisdiction—

(a) to entertain—
  (i) complaints where the value of the goods or services and compensation, if any, claimed exceeds rupees one crore; and
  (ii) appeals against the order of any State Commission; and

(b) to call for the records and pass appropriate orders in any consumer dispute which is pending before or has been decided by any State Commission where it appears to the National Commission that such State Commission has exercised a jurisdiction not vested in it by law, or has failed to exercise a jurisdiction so vested, or has acted in the exercise of its jurisdiction so vested, or has acted in the services of its jurisdiction illegally or with material irregularity.

In *Telecom District Manager, Patna* v. *Kalyanpur Cement Ltd*,[28] the court held that justification of the National Commission is limited to dispute where there has been wrongful, illegal and improper exercise of jurisdiction.

(b) Power and Procedure Applicable to the National Commission (S. 22)

The National Commission shall in the disposal of any complaints or any proceedings before it, have—

(a) the powers of a civil court as specified in sub-sections (4), (5) and (6) of section 13; and

(b) the power to issue an order to the opposite party directing him to do any one or more of the things referred to in clauses (a) to (i) of sub-section (I) of sub-section 14, and follow such procedure as may be prescribed by the Central Government.

(c) Appeal (S. 23)

Any person, aggrieved by an order made by the National Commission in exercise of its powers conferred by sub-clause (i) of clause (a) of section 21, may prefer an appeal against such order to the Supreme Court within a period of thirty days from the date of the order:

Provided that the Supreme Court may entertain an appeal after the expiry of the said period of thirty days if it is satisfied that there was sufficient cause for not filing it within that period.

(d) Finality of Orders (S. 24)

(i) Every order or a District Forum, the State Commission or the National Commission shall not admit a complaint unless it is filed within two years from the date on which the cause of action has arisen.

(ii) Notwithstanding anything contained in sub-section (1), a complaint may be entertained after the period specified in sub-section (1), if the complainant satisfies the District Forum, the State Commission or the National Commission, as the case may be, that he had sufficient cause for not filing the complaint within such period:

Provided that no such complaint shall be entertained unless the National Commission, the State Commission or the District Forum, as the case may be, records its reasons for condoning such delay.

The section provides limitation period for admitting complaints. The Forum cannot admit a complaint unless it is filed within two years from the date on which the cause of action has arisen.[29]

28. 1991 C. S. 54.

29. Shind Engineering Industries *v.* J.S. Birdi and Sons, 11(1994) CPJ 439.

I. LIMITATION PERIOD (S. 24A)

(1) The District Forum, the State Commission or the National Commission shall not admit a complaint unless it is filed within two years from the date on which the cause of action has arisen.

(2) Notwithstanding anything contained in sub-section (1), a complaint may be entertained after the period specified in sub-section (1), if the complaint satisfies the District Forum, the State Commission or the National Commission, as the case may be, that he had sufficient cause for not filing the complaint within such period:

Provided that no such complaint shall be entertained unless the National Commission, the State Commission or the District Forum, as the case may be, records its reasons for condoning such delay.

J. ADMINISTRATIVE CONTROL (S. 24B)

The National Commission shall have administrative control over all the State Commissions in the following matters, namely:

(i) calling for periodical return regarding the institution, disposal, pendency of cases;

(ii) issuance of instructions regarding adoption of uniform procedure in the hearing of matters. Prior service of copies of documents produced by one party to the opposite parties, furnishing of English translation of judgements written in any language, speed, grant of copies of documents; and

(iii) generally overseeing the functioning of the State Commissions or the District Forum to ensure that the objects and purpose of the Act are best served without in any way interfering with their quasi-judicial freedom.

(2) The State Commission shall have administrative control over all the District Fora within its jurisdiction in all matter referred to in sub-section (1).

K. ENFORCEMENT OF ORDERS BY THE FORUM, THE STATE COMMISSION OR THE NATIONAL COMMISSION (S. 25)

Every order made by the District Forum, the State Commission or the National Commission may be enforced by the District Forum, the State Commission or the National Commission, as the case may be, in the same manner as if it were decree or order made by a court in a suit pending therein and it shall be lawful for the District Forum, the State Commission or the National Commission to send, in the event of its inability to execute it, such order to the court within the local limits of whose jurisdiction—

(c) in the case of an order against a company, the registered office of the company is situated, or

(d) in the case of an order against any other person, the place where the person concerned voluntarily resides or carries on business or personally works for gain, is situated, and thereupon, the court to which the order is so sent, shall execute the order as if it were a decree or order sent to it for execution.

L. DISMISSAL OF FRIVOLOUS OR VEXATIOUS COMPLAINTS (S. 26)

Where a complaint instituted before the District Forum, the State Commission or the National Commission, as the case may be, is found to be frivolous or vexatious, it shall, for reasons to be recorded in writing, dismiss the complaint and make an order that the complainant shall pay to the opposite party such cost, not exceeding ten thousand rupees.

6

Indian Evidence Act, 1872

A. INTRODUCTION

A fact may be proved either by oral evidence of the fact or by documentary evidence, if any. This means that there are two methods of proving a fact. One is by producing witnesses of fact, which is called oral evidence, and the other, by producing a document which records the fact in question and this is called documentary evidence. All statements which the court permits or requires to be made before it by witnesses in relation to the matters of fact under inquiry; such statements are called oral evidenced.[1]

B. ORAL EVIDENCE MUST BE DIRECT (S. 60)

Oral evidence must, in all cases, whatever, be direct; that is to say—if it refers to a fact which could be seen, it must be the evidence of a witness who says he saw it; if it refers to a fact which could be heard, it must be the evidence of a witness who says he heard it; if it refers to a fact which could be perceived by any other sense or in any other manner, it must be the evidence of a witness who says he perceived it by that sense or in that manner; if it refers to an opinion or to the grounds on which that opinion is held, it must be the evidence of the person who holds that opinion on those grounds:

Provided that the opinions of experts expressed in any treatise commonly offered for sale, and the grounds on such opinions are held, may be provided by the production of such treatise if the author is dead or cannot be found, or has become incapable of giving evidence, or cannot be called as a witness without an amount of delay or expense which the court regards as unreasonable:

Provided also that, if oral evidence refers to the existence or condition of any material thing other than a document, the court may, if it thinks fit, require the production of such material thing for its inspection.

(a) Direct Oral Evidences

Oral evidence must be direct. This means that a witness can tell the court of only a fact of which he has the first hand personal knowledge in the sense

1. Sec. 59 of Indian Evidence Act.

that he received the fact by any of the senses.[2] If, on the other hand, the statement was not made in his presence or hearing and he subsequently came to know of it through some other source, he cannot appear as a witness, for his knowledge is a derived knowledge and is nothing but hearsay and it is a maxim of law that hearsay evidence is not relevant. In *Kishore v. Narayan Chandra*[3], the court observed that "No one ever conceived that an agreement could be proved by a witness swearing that he heard another say that such an agreement was made," in the stated case where a person appeared to give evidence of a benami transaction, the fact of which he had heard from other. That is why Section 60 requires that oral evidence must be direct, and then gives the meaning of direct oral evidence.

(b) Grounds of Exclusion of Hearsay Evidence

The following are the grounds of exclusion of hearsay evidence:

(i) Irresponsibility of the original declarant because he is not subject to oath or cross-examination or for penalty for perjury.
(ii) It presupposes better testimony and is a substitution of weaker for stronger proof.

The general rule is, that hearsay evidence is not admissible in proof of a fact, which has been stated by a third person. This rule has been long established as a fundamental principle.[4] In *Jaddoo Singh* v. *Malti Devi*,[5] a police officer testified that he was informed by a person about the movement of a truck carrying liquor, the informant was not examined, the evidence held to be not admissible.[6]

C. PROOF OF CONTENTS OF DOCUMENTS (S. 61)

The contents of document may be provided either by primary or by secondary evidence.

The contents of a document can be proved either by the primary evidence of the document or by its secondary evidence. Where entries in account books were sought to be proved and no body appeared, and no base vouchers etc. were produced, to support the entries, the evidence was not allowed.[7] There is no third method of proving the contents of a document.

2. See, Avtar Singh, '*Principles of Law of Evidence*' (1996).
3. AIR 1982 Cal. 142.
4. *Id.* at 214-15.
5. AIR 1983, All. 87.
6. Bhugdomal Gangaram *v.* State of Gujarat, AIR 1983 SC 906.
7. Chandrakanta Ben *v.* Vadilal Bapalal, AIR 1989 SC 1269.

D. PRIMARY EVIDENCE (S. 62)

Primary evidence means the document itself produced for the inspection of the court.

Explanation 1: Where a document is executed in several parts, each part is primary evidence of the document.

Where a document is executed in counterpart, each counterpart being executed by one or some of the parties only, each counterpart is primary evidence as against the parties executing it.

Explanation 2: Where a number of documents are all made by one uniform process, as in the case of printing lithography, or photography each is primary evidence of the contents of the rest; but, where they are all copies of a common original, they are not primary evidence of the contents of the original.

ILLUSTRATION

A person is shown to have been in possession of a number of placards, all printed at one time from one original. Any one of the placards is primary evidence of the contents of any other, but no one of them is primary evidence of the contents of the original.

The expression evidence of a document is defined in section 62, the following four are included in the expression "primary evidence":

1. The original document itself produced for the inspection of the court.
2. Where a document is executed in several parts, each part is primary evidence of the document.
3. Where a document is executed in counterparts, each counterpart is primary evidence against the party signing it. *For example,* in the case of a cheque, the drawer signs the main cheque so that it is a primary evidence against him and the counterfoil may be signed by the payee of the cheque so that it will be a primary evidence against the payee.
4. Where a number of documents are all made by one uniform process, as, for example, by printing, lithography or photography, each is primary evidence of the contents of document.

The section is based upon the principle that the "best evidence in the possession of power of the party must be produced. What the best evidence is, it must depend upon circumstances. Generally speaking, the original document is the best evidence." This is the general and ordinary rule; the contents can only be proved by the writing itself.

There is probably no rule of evidence that is better known than this that secondary evidence of the contents of written document is, in general, not relevant. "The contents of every written paper are, according to the ordinary and well established rules of evidence, to be proved by the paper itself, and by that alone, if the paper be in existence.[8]

Where the writer of a letter was not examined as a witness and no opportunity was given to the opposite party to cross-examine him, the letter was held by the Supreme Court to be not reliable evidence.[9] The truth of the contents of a document can, however, be also proved by any other evidence and not necessarily by the evidence of the author of the document.[10]

E. SECONDARY EVIDENCE (S. 63)

Secondary evidence means and includes:

(1) Certified copies given under the provisions hereinafter contained;
(2) Copies made from the original by mechanical process which in themselves insure the accuracy of the copy, and copies compared with such copies;
(3) Copies made from or compared with the original;
(4) Counterparts of documents as against the parties who did not execute them; and
(5) Oral accounts of the contents of a document given by some person who has himself seen it.

ILLUSTRATION

(a) A photography of an original is secondary evidence of its contents—though the two have not been compared, if it is proved that the thing photographed was the original.
(b) A copy compared with a copy of a letter made by a copying machine is secondary evidence of the contents of the letter, if it is shown that the copy made by the copying machine was made from the original.
(c) A copy transcribed from a copy, but afterwards compared with the original, is secondary evidence, but the copy not so compared is not secondary evidence of the original, although the copy from which it was transcribed was compared with the original.
(d) Neither an oral account of a copy compared with the original, nor an oral account of a photograph or machine-copy of the original, is secondary evidence of the original.

---

8. Prithichand *v.* State of H.P. (1989) ISCC 1932 the case arising out of the rape of a minor girl, the medical report was that of a lady doctor who being on maternity leave was not able to appear, the report was allowed to be proved by another lady doctor who was conversant with her handwriting and signature.
9. Vinod Chaturvedi *v.* State of M.P., AIR 1984 SC 911.
10. Ramji Dayawala *v.* Invest. Import, AIR 1981 SC 2085.

F. PROOF OF DOCUMENTS BY PRIMARY EVIDENCE (S. 64)

Documents must be proved by primary evidence except in the cases hereinafter mentioned.

The section embodies one of the underlying principles which is that a document must be proved by its primary evidence. The meaning of the expression "Primary evidence" has been explained in Section 62.

It has been held in several decisions that objections, if any, as to the mode of proving a document should be at the trial stage itself. If no objection is taken at that stage, subsequently at the stage of appeal, it would be too late and would not be allowed.[11] Where, however, a copy of the insurance policy and not the original document was produced before the Tribunal, the other party making no objection than, an objection before the appellate court was allowed so as to exclude the evidence.[12]

G. CASES IN WHICH SECONDARY EVIDENCE RELATING TO DOCUMENTS MAY BE GIVEN (S. 65)

Secondary evidence may be given to the existence, condition or contents of a document in the following cases:

(a) When the original is shown or appears to be in the possession or power of the person against whom the document is sought to be proved; or of any person out of reach of or not subject to the process of the Court, or of any person legally bound to produce it, and when after the notice mentioned in section 66, such person does not produce it;

(b) When the existence, condition or contents of the original have been proved to be admitted in writing by the person against whom it is to be proved or by his representative in interest;

(c) When the original has been destroyed or lost, or when the party offering evidence of its contents cannot, for any other reason not arising from his own default or neglect, produce it in reasonable time;

(d) When the original is of such a nature as not to be easily movable;

(e) When the original is a public document within the meaning of section 74;

(f) When the original is a public document of which a certified copy is permitted by this Act, or by any other law in force in India, to be given in evidence; and

(g) When the original consists of numerous accounts or other documents which cannot conveniently be examined in Court, and the fact to be proved is the general result of the whole collection.

11. S.A. Khan *v.* Bhajan Lal, AIR 1993 SC 13348.
12. State of Haryana *v.* Chanji, AIR 1982 P&H 282.

In case (a), (c) and (d) any secondary evidence of the contents of the document is admissible.

In case (b), the written admission is admissible.

In cases (e) or (f), a certified copy of the document, but no other kind of secondary evidence, is admissible.

In case (g), evidence may be given as to the general result of the documents by any person who has examined them, and who is skilled in the examination of such documents.

(a) When Secondary Evidence can be given

The circumstances in which secondary evidence can be given are strictly regulated by the Act. Such circumstances are listed in section 65.

In substance, the section provides that secondary evidence can be given in the following cases:

1. When the original is shown or appears to be in the possession or power—
   (a) of a person against whom the document is sought to be proved, or
   (b) any person out of reach of, or not subject to the process of, the court, or
   (c) any person legally bound to produce it, and although due notice has been given to him in accordance with the terms of section 66, he does not produce it.
2. When the existence, condition or contents have been proved to be admitted in writing by the party against whom the document is to be proved or by his representative-in-interest.
3. When the original has been destroyed or lost, or when the party offering evidence of its contents, cannot for any other reason not arising from his own default or neglect, produce it in reasonable time.
4. When the original is of such a nature as not to be easily movable. This would include cases of bulky documents.
5. When the original is a public document within the meaning of section 74.
6. When the original is a document of which the Evidence Act or any other law of the country permits certified copies to be given in evidence.
7. When the original consists of numerous accounts of other documents which cannot be conveniently examined in the court and the fact to be provided is the general result of the whole collection.

(b) Types of Secondary Evidence in Different Situations

Where the document is in the possession of a party who does not even after notice produce it, or when the original has been lost or destroyed or when it is not easily movable, any kind of secondary evidence of the contents can be given.

When the contents of the document have been admitted by the party against whom it has to be proved, his written admission can be given as a secondary evidence of the document.

Where the original is public document or is a document of which the law permits certified copies, the only secondary evidence admissible is that of certified copies, and no other secondary evidence can be given.

Where the original is a bulky document which cannot be conveniently examined in the court, the only kind of secondary evidence allowed is the evidence of the general result of the document given by a person who has himself examined it and is an expert or is skilled in the examination of such documents.

(c) Rules as to Notice to Produce (S. 66)

Secondary evidence of the contents of the documents referred to in section 65, clause (a), shall not be given unless the party proposing to give such secondary evidence has previously given to the party in whose possession or power the document is, or to his attorney or pleader, such notice to produce as is prescribed by law; and if no notice is prescribed by law, then such notice as the Court considers reasonable under the circumstances of the case.

Provided that such notice shall not be required in order to render secondary evidence admissible in any of the following cases, or in any other case in which the court thinks fit to dispense with it.

H. BURDEN OF PROOF AS TO PARTICULAR FACT (S. 103)

The burden of proof as to any particular fact lies on that person who wishes the Court to believe in its existence, unless it is provided by any law that the proof of that fact shall lie on any particular person.

ILLUSTRATION

A prosecutes B for theft, and wishes the Court to believe that B admitted the theft to C. A must prove the admission.

B wishes the Court to believe that, at the time, in question, he was elsewhere. He must prove it.

(a) Burden of Proving a Particular Fact

The principle of the section is that whenever a party wishes the court to believe and to act upon the existence of a fact, burden lies upon him to prove that fact. If a party wishes the court to believe that his opponent has admitted a fact, burden lies upon him to prove the fact of admission. In an action for damages for wrongful dismissal, the plaintiff has to prove that the dismissal was wrongful and to what damages he is entitled. The principle will not be affected by the fact whether the particular fact in question is negative or affirmative. In an action, for example, for damages for malicious prosecution the plaintiff wants the court to believe upon the fact that he was prosecuted without reasonable and probable cause, and although this is the negative of the issue, the plaintiff has to prove it.[13]

The following passage from the judgement of Bowen, L.J. is particularly important:

Whenever litigation exists somebody must go on with it; the plaintiff is the first to begin; if he does nothing he fails; if he makes a *prima facie* case and nothing is done to answer it, the defendant fails. The test, therefore, as to the burden of proof or onus of proof is simply: to ask oneself which party will be successful if no evidence is given, or if no more evidence is given than has been given at a particular point of the case, for it is obvious that as the controversy involved in the litigation travels on the parties from moment to moment may reach points at which the onus of proof shifts, and at which the tribunal would have to say that if the case stops there, it must be decided in a particular manner. It is not a burden that goes on forever, resting on the shoulders of the person upon whom it is first cast. As soon as he brings evidence, which, until it is answered, rebuts the evidence against which he is contending, then the evidence, which once more turns the scale. That being so, the question of onus of proof is only a rule for deciding on whom the obligation of going further, if he wishes to win, rests.

Dealing with the effect of "negative" or "affirmative" nature of the matter upon the burden of proof, his Lordship said:

Now in an action for malicious prosecution the plaintiff has the burden throughout of establishing that circumstances of the prosecution were such that a judge can see no reasonable or probable cause for instituting it. In one sense this is the assertion of a negative and we have been pressed with the proposition that when a negative is to be made out, the onus of proof shifts. That is not so, if the assertion of a negative is an essential part of the plaintiff. The terms "negative" and "affirmative" are after all relative and not absolute. In dealing with a question of negligence that term may be considered either as negative or affirmative according to the definition adopted in measuring the duty which is neglected. Wherever a person asserts affirmatively as part of his case that a certain state of things is present or is absent, or that a particular thing is insufficient for a particular purpose, that is an averment which he is bound to prove affirmatively.

13. For more details pl. See, *Supra* Note 278-79.

7

Banker's Book Evidence Act, 1891

A. INTRODUCTION

The banking system as it exists today is the outcome of many centuries and is not a development of air particular period. In all the countries, banking has been in existence in one form or the other. India was not a stranger to the concept of banking. Traces of the banking system may be found out in the Manu Smriti. During the last two centuries the banking system started taking concrete shape. During the British rule in India the banking system was moulded as per the system prevalent in Britain. All the intricacies of the banking system, naturally, crept-up in India as well. Due to complexity of the system, many problems were brought before the courts and with the passage of time involvement of courts become a regular feature. A time came when it became necessary to enact a legislation on Banker's Books. In the year 1891 a bill was introduced in the legislation to apply to British India the provision of the English Banking Books Evidence Act, 1879.[1]

B. "BANK" AND "BANKER" MEANS [S. 2(2)]

(a) any company or corporation carrying on the business of banking;
(b) any partnership or individual to whose books the provisions of this Act shall have been extended as hereinafter provided; and
(c) any post office savings bank or a money order office.

(1) "Banker's books" include ledgers, day-books, cash-books, account-books and all other books used in the ordinary business of a bank;

(2) "Legal proceeding" means—

(i) any proceeding or inquiry in which evidence is or may be given;
(ii) an arbitration; and
(iii) any investigation or inquiry under the Code of Criminal Procedure, 1973 (2 of 1974), or under any other law for the time being in force for the collection of evidence, conducted by a police officer or by any

1. The Banker's Book Evidence Act (1997) at 2.

other person (not being a magistrate) authorized in this behalf by a magistrate or by any law for the time being in force.

(3) "The Court" means the person or persons before whom a legal proceeding is held or taken;

(4) "Judge" means a Judge of a High Court;

(5) "Trial" means any hearing before the Court at which evidence is taken; and

(6) "Certified copy" means a copy of an entry in the books of a bank together with a certificate written at the foot of such copy that it is a true copy of such entry, that such entry is contained in one of the ordinary books of the bank and was made in the usual and ordinary course of business, and that such book is still in the custody of the bank, and where the copy was obtained by a mechanical or other process which in itself ensure the accuracy of the copy, a further certificate to that effect. But where the book from which such copy was prepared has been destroyed in the usual course of the bank's business after the date on which the copy had been so prepare, a further certificate to that effect, each such certificate being dated and subscribed by the principal accountant or manager of the bank with his name and official title.

In *Radhey Shyam v. Safiyabai Ibrahim*,[2] the court held that the detailed ingredients mentioned in the defining clause 8 of Section 2 of the Act for qualifying to be "certified copy" are not mandatory but merely directory. Sufficient compliance depending upon facts and circumstances of each case is enough to qualify a document to be 'certified copy'.

C. POWER TO EXTEND PROVISIONS OF ACT (S. 3)

The State Government may, from time to time, by notification in the Official Gazette, extend the provisions of this Act to the books of any partnership or individual carrying on the business of bankers within the territories under its administration, and keeping a set of not less than three ordinary account books, namely, a cash book, a day-book or journal, and a ledger, and may in like manner rescind any such notification.

D. MODE OF PROOF OF ENTRIES IN BANKER'S ACT (S. 4)

Subject to the provisions of this Act, a certified copy of any entry in a banker's book shall in all legal proceedings be received as *prima facie* evidence of the existence of such entry, and shall be admitted as evidence of the matters, transactions and accounts therein recorded in every case where, and to the same extent as, the original entry itself is now by law admissible, but not further or otherwise.

2. AIR 1988, Bom. 361.

In *State Bank of India v. Yumnam Gouramani Singh*,[3] the court held that if Branch Manager and other bank officials corroborate the entries on the books of account produced by bank, it is sufficient proof of loan transaction.

E. CASE IN WHICH OFFICER OF BANK NOT COMPELLABLE TO PRODUCE BOOKS (S. 5)

No officer of a bank shall in any legal proceeding to which the bank is not a party be compellable to produce any banker's book the contents of which can be proved under this Act, or to appear as a witness to prove the matters, transactions and accounts therein recorded, unless by order of the Court or a Judge made for special cause.

F. INSPECTION OF BOOKS BY ORDER OF COURT OR JUDGE (S. 6)

(1) On the application of any party to a legal proceeding the Court or a Judge may order that such party be at liberty to inspect and take copies of any entries in a banker's book for any of the purposes of such proceeding, or may order the bank to prepare and produce, within a time to be specified in the order, certified copies of all such entries accompanied by a further certificate that no other entries are to be found in the books of the bank relevant to the matters in issue in such proceeding, and such further certificate shall be dated and subscribed in manner hereinbefore directed in reference to certified copies.

(2) An order under this or the preceding section may be made either with or without summoning the bank, and shall be served on the bank three clear days (exclusive of bank holidays) before the same is to be obeyed, unless the Court or Judge shall otherwise direct.

(3) The bank may at any time before the time limited for obedience to any such order as aforesaid either offer to produce their books at the trial or give notice of their intention to show cause against such order, and thereupon the same shall not be enforced without further order.

In *Central Bank of India v. Shamdasani*,[4] the Court held that the bank has a statutory right under section 6 of the Act to object to any order directing inspection of their books though the order is made under Sec. 91 of the Code of Criminal Procedure, 1973.

In *Kattabomman Transport Corpn. Ltd. v. State Bank of Travancore*,[5] the word "party to a legal proceeding" would enable inspection to be made only if such inspection was necessary for the "purpose of such proceeding." In other words, there should be a main proceeding in which the Court might come to the conclusion that such inspection was necessary and it would only in such a proceeding that order could be passed for inspection.

3. AIR 1994 SC 1644.
4. AIR 1938 Bom. 33.
5. AIR 1992 Ker. 351.

G. COSTS (S. 7)

(1) The cost of any application to the Court or a Judge under or for the purposes of this Act and the costs of anything done or to be done under and order of the Court or a Judge made under or for the purposes of this Act shall be in the discretion of the Court or Judge, who may further order such costs or any part thereof to be paid to any party by the bank if they have been incurred in consequence of any fault or improper delay on the part of the bank.

(2) Any order made under this section for the payment of costs to or by a bank may be enforced as if the bank were a party to the proceeding.

(3) Any order under this section awarding costs may, on application to any Court to Civil Judicature designated in the order, be executed by such Court as if the order were a decree for money passed by itself:

Provided that nothing in this sub-section shall be construed to derogate from any power which the Court or Judge making the order may possess for the enforcement of its or his directions with respect to the payment of costs.

H. ORDER OF COURT TO BE CONSTRUED TO BE ORDER MADE BY SPECIFIED OFFICER (S. 8)

In the application of sections 5, 6 and 7 to any investigation or inquiry referred to in sub-clause (iii) of clause (4) of section 2, the order of a court or a Judge referred to in the said sections shall be construed as referring to an order made by an officer of a rank not lower than the rank of a Superintendent of Police as may be specified in this behalf by the appropriate Government.

8

Income Tax Act, 1961

A. INTRODUCTION

Income tax in its modern form was introduced in India in 1860. In 1866 the first Income Tax Act was enacted. The Income Tax Act, 1961 contains the present law of income tax. The Income Tax Act, 1961 extends to the whole of India.

B. COMPUTATION OF TOTAL INCOME

The entire income is classified and grouped under five heads[1] as follows:

(1) Income from salary.
(2) Income from house property.
(3) Income from business of profession.
(4) Income from capital gains.
(5) Income from other sources.

Income from interest on securities was grouped with income from other sources. If a person derives income from more than one head, the income should be grouped with relevant head and aggregated with other heads to calculate the gross total income and taxable income.

C. SCOPE

The scope of this study is to know about this legislation in generally and to study the provisions relating to the co-operative societies, in specific.

D. STATUS

The status of a person may be any one of the following:

(1) Resident;
(2) Not ordinarily resident; and
(3) Non-resident.

1. See, Kailash Rai, *Law of Income Tax* (1977) at 1. Also see Bihar State Co-operative Bank Ltd., *v.* CIT (1960), 391 TR 114 (SC).

The Income Tax is chargeable on the basis of status. Also for example, for non-residents certain incomes are tax free.

However, it is to be noted that the taxable entities are divided in three categories only in the case of determination of residential status of an individual or a Hindu Undivided Family but in all other cases the taxable entities are divided into two divisions only: (a) Resident, and (b) Non-resident.

According to section 6(1), an individual will be resident in India in any previous year, if he fulfils any one of the following conditions:

(a) He is in India in that year (i.e. in the previous year in respect of which the residence of the individual is being determined) for the period or periods amounting in all to 182 days or more; or
(b) During the 4 years preceding that year, he has been in India for a period or periods amounting in all to 365 days or more and has been in India in that year for a period or periods amounting in all to 60 days or more.

Each of the above conditions requires the physical presence of the individual in India in the previous year in question for sometime.

If an individual satisfies one or more of the above conditions, he will be a resident in India and if he satisfies none of the above conditions, he will be treated as a non-resident. A person will be a 'resident but not ordinarily resident in India' if he satisfies one or more of the above conditions and, also satisfies the following conditions:

(i) He has not been a resident in India in 9 out of 10 previous years preceding the previous year in question (here resident means a person who has become resident by satisfying any one of the above conditions);
(ii) He has not, during the 7 previous years preceding the previous years in question, been in India for a period or periods amounting in all to 730 days or more.

E. PERSON

Person means any one of the following:

(1) Individual;
(2) Hindu undivided family;
(3) Firm;
(4) Association of persons;
(5) Companies;
(6) Any other juridical person; and
(7) Local authority.

These are seven categories of persons chargeable to tax under the act. The aforesaid definition is inclusive, and not exclusive. Therefore, any person, not falling in the above mentioned categories, may still fall in the four corners of the term "Person" and accordingly may be liable to tax under section 4.

All the co-operative societies are assessed as Association of Persons.

F. ASSOCIATION OF PERSONS

An association of persons will be taken as resident in India in a previous year if the control and management of its affairs is situated in India either partly or wholly and it will be treated as non-resident, if the control and management of its affairs is situated wholly outside India.[2]

G. ASSESSMENT YEAR AND PREVIOUS YEAR

(a) Assessment Year

Assessment year[3] means the period of twelve months starting from April 1 of every year and ending on March 31 of the next year. It is also known as "Income Tax Year" or "financial year." For instance, the assessment year 1999-2000 which commenced on April 1, 1999 will end on March 31, 2000. The period of assessment year is fixed by Statute. Income of previous year of an assess is taxed during the following assessment year at the rates prescribed for such assessment year by the relevant Finance Act.

(b) Previous Year

Income earned in a year is taxable in the next year. The year in which income is earned is known as previous year and the next year in which income is taxable is known as assessment year. In other words, it can be said that income earned during the previous[4] year 1998-99 is taxable in the immediately following assessment year (i.e. 1999-2000) at the rate applicable for the assessment year 1999-2000.

H. CAPITAL AND REVENUE

The distinction between capital receipt and revenue (or Income) receipt or capital expenditure and revenue (or Income) expenditure is important for the purpose of any tax statue. Its reason is this that it is the revenue or income receipt and not capital receipt that is taxed. Similarly, revenue or income expenditure is deducted from the total income of the assessee but the capital expenditure is not deducted.

All the Revenue receipts are treated as Income and all the revenue expenses are treated as expenses for the purpose of all Income Tax Act. This

2. Section 6(2).
3. Section 2(9).
4. Section 3.

being the General rule, capital gains are also subjected to taxation as per the provisions of the Act. All times, capital expenditure are also allowed under a few occasions.

ILLUSTRATION

Revenue Expenses:	Salary, Rent, Interest, etc.
Capital Expenses:	Purchase of land, machine, etc.
Revenue Income:	Rental receipt, Sale, proceeds, etc.
Capital receipts:	Sale of business as a going concern, compensation received, etc.

I. INCOME WHICH DO NOT FORM PART OF TOTAL INCOME (S. 10)

There are certain categories of Income which are totally exempted from Income Tax and therefore they are not included in the total income of the assessee. Thus, these incomes are not to be taken into computation for the purpose of determining either the taxable income or the rate of tax. However, under the Finance Act, 1973 and the subsequent Finance Acts the agricultural income exempted under section 10(1) from Income tax is taken into account for the purpose of determining the rate of tax applicable to the non-agricultural income of the assessee. The onus to prove that a particular income falls under any of these categories of income and therefore not taxable lies on the assessee.[5] Hence, following income need not to be taken as income at all:

(i) Agricultural Income.
(ii) Casual and non-agricultural receipts.
(iii) Leave travel concession to an Indian citizen.
(iv) Gratuity.
(v) Pension and leave salary.
(vi) Retrenchment compensation.
(vii) Payment from provident fund.
(viii) House rent allowance.
(ix) Educational scholarship.
(x) Income of Housing Authority.
(xi) Income of marketing authority, etc.

J. INCOME CHARGEABLE TO INCOME TAX UNDER THE HEAD SALARIES (S. 15)

According to section 15 the following income shall be chargeable to income tax under the head "salaries":

5. *Supra* Note 1 at 1947; P. Seetharamma *v.* CIT, (1965) 57 T.R. 532 (SC).

(a) Any salary due from an employer or a former employer to an assessee in the previous year, whether paid or not;
(b) Any salary paid or allowed to him in the previous year by or on behalf of an employer or a former employer, though not due or before it became due to him; and
(c) Any arrears of salary paid or allowed to him in the previous year by or on behalf of an employer or a former employer, if not charged to Income tax for any earlier previous year.

Salary has been defined under section 17(1). Salary is taxable whether received or receivable, which means even if salary is not received during a particular year but accrued even then the salary is taxable. Salary includes, Basic Salary, DA, ADA, CCA, HRA [subject to sec. 10(13A)], medical allowance, interim allowance, etc. Standard deduction at 33-1/3% subject to a maximum of Rs. 20,000 is allowed. Perquisites etc. are also dealt under this head.[6]

K. INCOME FROM HOUSE PROPERTY (Ss. 22-27)

Sections 22 to 27 deal with the income from house property. The provisions of section 22 indicate that income will be chargeable to income tax under the head "Income from house property," if the following conditions exist:

(a) There is a House Property

Under Section 22 'house property' means buildings and lands appurtenant thereto. The property other than buildings and land appurtenant to the buildings have been excluded from the operation of the section. The term "building" means a structure possessing some "annual value."

It is to be noted that where the assessee is a resident in India and he owns certain house property situated outside India, the income derived by him from such house property will also be included in his total income[7] but if the assessee is non-resident, the income derived by him from the house property situated outside India cannot be assessed.

(b) The Assessee must be Owner of the House Property

Owner of the house property (not the occupier or possessor) is liable to pay tax in respect of the income from the house property.[8] "Owner" means the person who can exercise the right of the owner, not on behalf of the owner but in his own right.[9]

6. For employer-employee relationship please see, Silver Jubilee Tailoring House *v.* Chief Inspector, AIR 1974 SC 37.
7. CIT *v.* R. Venugopala Reddiar (1965) 58 ITR 439 (Mad).
8. S.G. Mercantile Corportaion Ltd. *v.* CIT (1972) 831 TR 700 (SC).
9. B. Lodha Mal Kuthiala *v.* CIT (1971) 821 TR 570 (SC).

The house property must not be occupied by the assessee for the purpose of any business or profession carried on by him the profits of which are chargeable to Income Tax.

Section 22 does not apply to a case where:

(a) the owner occupies the house property for the purpose of any business or profession carried on by him, and
(b) the profits of such business or profession are chargeable to Income Tax.[10]

The notional value of the property treated as NIL, if self occupied. If let out, the fair rental value or actual receipt whichever is higher is treated as income from house property. Out of this, the municipal taxes paid is deducted. From this, statutory allowance is also deducted as per rules. This is net annual value. Net Annual Value reduced by all expenses enlisted under section 25 is Income from House property.

Section 24(b)

The second proviso to section 24(b) has been modified w.e.f. assessment year 2003-04 to provide that at where a self-occupied property (where the annual value of property is taken to be nil) is acquired or constructed with borrowed capital on or after 1.4.1999 the deduction of interest upto Rs. 1.50 lakh will be allowed if such acquisition of construction is completed within three years from the end of the financial year in which the capital was borrowed. Prior to this amendment acquisition of construction is to be completed before 1.4.2003 to get the higher deduction of interest.

Further, no such deduction shall be allowed in respect of such interest unless the person extending the loan certifies that such interest was payable in respect of the amount advanced for acquisition or construction of the house or as refinance of the principal amount outstanding under an earlier loan taken for such acquisition or construction. This is applicable only in case of a self-occupied property.

L. INCOME FROM BUSINESS (SECTIONS 28 TO 44-D & 68 TO 69-D)

The word "Business" includes any trade, commerce or manufacture or any adventure or concern in the nature of trade, commerce or manufacture."[11]

Any Income earned by running a business or carrying on of any manufacture, trade, etc. is taxed income from business. The expenses relating to the business, subject to the provisions of the Act can be deducted. The following are the important deductions:

(i) Depreciation;
(ii) Investment Allowance;
(iii) Investment Deposit Scheme;

10. Sec. 23.
11. Sec. 2 (13), Indiramani Bai *v.* Addl. CIT, (1993) 200 ITR 594 (SC).

(iv) Expenditure on Scientific Research;
(v) Insurance premium paid by a Federal Milk Coop. Society; and
(vi) Travelling expenses, Sec. 37(3).

Some expenses are specifically not excluded, viz. payment to relatives, contribution to non-statutory provident fund, etc.

M. INCOME FROM CAPITAL GAINS (SECTIONS 45 TO 55-A)

Capital gains should be taken to mean profits or gains arising to the assessee from the transfer of a capital asset. Such capital gain is added to the total income of the previous year in which the transfers of the assets took place.[12]

According to section 45(1) any profits or gains arising from the transfer of a capital asset effected in the previous year shall, save as otherwise provided in Ss. 54, 54B, 54D, 54E, 54EA, 54EB, 54F, 54G and 54H be chargeable to Income tax under the head "Capital gains" and shall be deemed to be the income of the previous year in which the transfer took place.[13]

If any capital asset is transferred by one persons to another (subject to the definitions of capital asset and transfer as per this Act) and any gain is derived in such transaction the entire income is taxable. Provisions are differently made for short-term and long-term capital gains. Concessions are available when the gains are long-term.

Special Provision for Computation of Capital Gains in Real Estate Transactions

Section 50C has been inserted w.e.f. assessment year 2003-2004 to provide for the following:

(1) The said section is applicable in case of only transfer of land or building or both.
(2) Where as a result of transfer of land, building or both the consideration declared to be received or accruing as a result of such transfer, is less than the value adopted or assessed by any authority of a State Government for the purpose of payment of stamp duty in respect of such transfer, the value so adopted or assessed shall be deemed to be the full value of the consideration, and capital gains shall be computed accordingly.
(3) Where the assessee claims before any assessing officer that the value adopted or assessed for stamp duty exceeds the fair market value of the property as on the date of transfer and the value so adopted or assessed for stamp duty authority has not been disputed in any appeal or revision or no reference has been made before any other authority, Court or High Court, the assessing officer may refer the valuation of the capital asset to a valuation officer.

12. Sec. 45.
13. Section 45(1) as amended by the Finance Act, 1992.

(4) The provisions contained in Wealth Tax Act, 1957 relating to valuation of property shall with the necessary modifications, apply in relation to such reference as they apply in relation to a reference made by the assessing officer under section 16A(1) of the Wealth Tax Act.

(5) If the fair market value adopted by the valuation officer is the less than the value adopted for stamp duty purposes the assessing officer may take such fair market value to be the full value of the consideration. However, the assessing officer shall take the value adopted for stamp duty purposes where the fair market value exceeds the same.

(6) If the value adopted for the stamp duty purposes is revised in any appeal, revision or reference the assessment made shall be amended to re-compute the capital gains by taking the revised value as the full consideration.

Provisions Relating to Set-off and Carry Forward of Long-Term Capital Loss (under the section 70 & 74)

From the assessment year 2003-04, losses arising from a tranfer of long-term capital asset will be allowed to be set-off only against long-term capital gains in the previous year. Further, long term capital loss shall be carried forward for eight years to be set up only against long-term capital gains.

Prior to the amendment long-term capital losses could be set-off against any capital gains (whether short-term or long-term).

N. INCOME FROM OTHER SOURCES (SECTIONS 56 TO 59)

Section 56 deals with the residuary head of income and includes within its scope all the taxable income, profits and gains which fall outside the preceding five heads. In other words, it includes within its ambit all those taxable incomes which do not fall within the following heads:

(a) Salaries;
(b) Interest on Securities;
(c) Income from house property;
(d) Profits and gains of business or profession; and
(e) Capital gains.

However, it is to be noted that Section 56 does not apply to income which is not includable in the total income of the assessee at all. These incomes exempted from tax under the residuary head "Income from other sources."[14]

In *CIT* v. *Govinda Choudhary*, [15] the Supreme Court has held that income by way of interest can be assessed as income from other sources only which it does not fall under any other head of income. Income from speculation, Card-games, horse races, etc. are taxed under this head.

14. *Supra* Note 1 at 176; CIT *v.* New India Investment Corporation Ltd., 1978 Tax LR. 832 (Cal).
15. (1993) 203 ITR 881 (SC).

O. GROSS TOTAL INCOME

The income derived from all the above said sources are called as gross total income.

(a) Rates of Income Tax: Assessment year 2003-04 Individuals

The tax rates applicable to individuals are also applicable to a Hindu undivided family, an association of persons, body of individuals and artificials juridical person. The rates applicable for the assessment year 2003-04 are as follows:

	Rates of income-tax
1. where the total income does not exceed Rs. 50,000	*Nil;*
2. where the total income exceeds Rs. 50,000 but does not exceed Rs. 60,000	10 per cent of the amount by which the total income exceeds Rs. 50,000;
3. where the total income exceeds Rs. 60,000 but does not exceed Rs. 1,50,000	Rs. 1,000 *plus* 20 per cent of the amount by which the total income exceeds Rs. 60,000;
4. where the total income exceeds Rs. 1,50,000	Rs. 19,000 *plus* 30 per cent of the amount by which the total income exceeds Rs. 1,50,000.

Paragraph A

In the case of every individual or Hindu undivided family or association of persons or body of individuals, whether incorporated or not, or every artificial juridical person referred to in sub-clause (*vii*) of clause (*31*) of section 2 of the Income-tax Act, not being a case to which any other Paragraph of this Part applies—

Surcharge on income-tax

The amount of income-tax computed in accordance with the preceding provisions of this Paragraph or in section 112 shall—

(i) in the case of every individual or Hindu undivided family or association of persons or body of individuals having a total income exceeding eight hundred and fifty thousand rupees, be reduced by the amount of rebate of income-tax calculated under Chapter VIIIA, and the income-tax as so reduced, be increased by a surcharge for purposes of the Union calculated at the rate of ten per cent, of such income-tax;

(ii) in the case of every person, other than those mentioned in item (i), be increased by a surcharge for purposes of the Union calculated at the rate of ten per cent, of such income-tax:

Provided that in case of persons mentioned in item (i) above having a total income exceeding eight hundred and fifty thousand rupees, the total amount payable as income-tax and surcharge on such income shall not exceed the total amount payable as income-tax on a total income of eight hundred and fifty thousand rupees by more than the amount of income that exceeds eight hundred and fifty thousand rupees.

	Rates of income-tax
1. where the total income does not exceed Rs. 10,000	10 per cent of the total income;
2. where the total income exceeds Rs. 10,000 but does not exceed Rs. 20,000	Rs. 1,000 *plus* 20 per cent of the amount by which the total income exceeds Rs. 10,000;
3. where the total income exceeds Rs. 20,000	Rs. 3,000 *plus* 30 per cent of the amount by which the total income exceeds Rs. 20,000.

Surcharge on income-tax

The amount of income-tax computed in accordance with the preceding provisions of this Paragraph, or in section 112, shall, in the case of every co-operative society, by increased by a surcharge for purposes of the Union calculated at the rate of two and one-half per cent of such income-tax.

Paragraph C

In the case of every firm—

	Rate of income-tax
On the whole of the total income	35 per cent.

Surcharge on income-tax

The amount of income-tax computed at the rate hereinbefore specified, or in section 112, shall, in the case of every firm, be increased by a surcharge for purposes of the Union calculated at the rate of two and one-half per cent of such income-tax.

Paragraph D

In the case of every local authority—

	Rate of income-tax
On the whole of the total income	30 per cent.

Surcharge on income-tax

The amount of income-tax computed at the rate hereinbefore specified, or in section 112, shall, in the case of every local authority, be increased by a surcharge for purposes of the Union calculated at the rate of two and one-half per cent of such income-tax.

Paragraph E

In the case of a company—

Rates of income-tax

I. In the case of a domestic company — 35 per cent of the total income;

II. In the case of a company other than a domestic company—
   (i) on so much of the total income as consists of—
      (a) royalties received from Government or an Indian concern in pursuance of an agreement made by it with the Government or the Indian concern after the 31st day of March, 1961 but before the 1st day of April, 1976; or
      (b) fees for rendering technical services received from Government or an Indian concern in pursuance of an agreement made by it with the Government or the Indian concern after the 29th day of February, 1964 but before the 1st day of April, 1976, and where such agreement has, in either case, been approved by the Central Government — 50 per cent;
   (ii) on the balance, if any, of the total income — 40 per cent;

Surcharge on income-tax

The amount of income-tax computed in accordance with the preceding provisions of this Paragraph, or in section 112, shall, in case of every company, be increased by a surcharge for purposes of the Union calculated at the rate of two and one-half per cent, of such income-tax

P. Return of Income

Every person whose total income (or the total income of any other person in respect of which he is assessable) of the previous year has exceeded the maximum tax free amount prescribed in his case, is required to furnish a return of income assessable in his hands in the prescribed manner and form (Rule 12 and forms 1, 2, 3 and 3A). The return must be furnished on or before the due date.[16] Failure to do so will invite penalty by way of interest.

(a) Due date for Furnishing of Return

S.N.	*Classes of assesses*	*Due date*
1.	If the assesses is a company	30 November of the assessment of the year.
2.	If the assessee is not a company	
	(i) If his accounts are required to be audited under Income Tax Act or under any other law,	31st October of assessment year.
	(ii) If the report of an accountant is required to be furnished under Section 80 HHC, 80 HHD, or	31st October of assessment year.
	(iii) If the assessee is a co-operative society.	31st October of assessment year.
3.	If the total income of any non-company assessee included any income from business profession (other than cases falling under (2) above.)	31st August of assessment year.
4.	In any other case.	30th June of assessment year.

Q. ADVANCED PAYMENT OF TAX

Advanced Tax is payable during any financial year on the total income which would be chargeable to tax in the assessment year immediately following that financial year.

R. CONDITIONS

No advance tax is to be paid if the amount of advance tax payable is less than Rs. 1,500. Thus, the liability to pay advance tax arises only in a case where the amount of advance tax payable is Rs. 15,000 or more due dates for payment of advance tax.

	Financial Year
Due date of instalments	*Amount payable*
On or before 15th September	Minimum of 30% of Advance tax.
On or before 15th December	Minimum of 60% of advance tax.
On or before 15th March	Advance 100% of advance tax.

16. National Council for Cooperative Training of NCUI, Legal Aspects at 28.

9

Limitation Act, 1963

A. INTRODUCTION

The law of limitation is that part of the law which prescribes a limit of time after which a suit or other proceeding cannot be maintained in any court of justice.

Every suit instituted after the period of limitation shall be dismissed, although limitation has not been set-up as a defence. On the other hand, the plaintiff must, when his claim is barred, show in his plaint the ground upon which he claims exemption under any of the relevant sections of the Indian Limitation Act. Otherwise, the plaint shall be rejected. The plea of limitation may be raised at any time.[1]

B. LIMITATION FOR SUIT (S. 3(2) (a))

(1) When a plaint presented in time to a proper courts said to be properly instituted.
(2) In the case of pauper, when his application for leave to sue as pauper is made in time, it is deemed to be instituted in time.
(3) In the case of claim against a company which is being wound up by the court, when the claimant first sends the claim to the official receiver in time.[2]

In all cases the presentation of the suit within time of limitation with proper authority is sufficient. It is not necessary that it must be registered within time.

In *Craft Center* v. *The Koncherry Coir Factories*,[3] the court held that the law of limitation is not meant to be an aid to unconsciousable conduct, although, if a claim is clearly barried, the court must unhesitatingly dismiss the suit. It is a law of repose, peace and justice, which bars the remedy after lapse of a particular period by way of public policy and expediency without extinguishing the right in certain cases. Therefore, the court must bar against limitation and a favour of the substance of the right to sue where two views are clearly possible.

1. See, National Council for Cooperative Training of NCUI, Legal Aspects, at 61.
2. *Ibid*.
3. AIR 1991 Ker 83. Quoted in the Limitation Act, 1963 (1998) at 3-4.

Section 4 of the Act States that the period of limitation prescribed in any suit appeal or application expires on the day when the court is closed, the suit, appeal or application may be instituted, preferred or made on the day when court reopens.

In *Amar Chand* v. *Union of India,*[4] the court held that 'court' means a proper court which has jurisdiction to entertain the suit.

A question of limitation can be raised in first appeal though the same was not raised before the trial court. The question cannot be raised at the first instance.

C. EXTENSION OF PERIOD OF LIMITATION (S. 5)

Any appeal or any application, other than an application under any of the provisions of Order XXI of the Code of Civil Procedure, 1908, may be admitted after the prescribed period, if the appellant or the applicant satisfies the court that he had sufficient cause for not preferring the appeal or making the application within such period.

Explanation: The fact that the appellant or the applicant was misled by any order, practice or Judgement of the High Court in ascertaining or computing the prescribed period may be sufficient cause within the measuring of this section.

In *M/S Rishi Prabhat* v. *Delhi Development Authority,*[5] the court held that to obtain extension of time by invoking the provisions of Section 5 of the Limitation Act, 1963 the party seeking extension has to satisfy the court that he had sufficient cause for not filling suit, appeal, revision or objections, within the prescribed time.

In *Haryana State Electricity Board* v. *Phoolchand Satyapal (Engineers and Contractors),*[6] the court held that a liberal approach is to be adopted and sufficient cause must be made out in a pragmatic manner and a pedantic approach calling upon a party to explain each day's delay is to be avoided.

D. LEGAL DISABILITY

Sections 6, 7, 8 and 9 of the Limitation Act especially deal with the matter concerning persons under legal disability.

Section 6: (1) Where a person entitled to institute a suit for make an application for the execution of a decree is, at the time from which the prescribed period is to be reckoned, a minor or insane, or an idiot, he may institute the suit or make the application within the same period after the disability has ceased, as would otherwise have been allowed from the time specified therefor in the third column of the Schedule.

4. AIR 1973 SC 313.
5. (1994) I CCC 719 (Del.).
6. (1994) 2 CCC 69 (P & H).

(2) Where such person is, at the time from which the prescribed period is to be reckoned, affected by two such disabilities, or where, before his disability has ceased, he is affected by another disability, he may institute the suit or make the application within the same period after both disabilities have ceased, as would otherwise have been allowed from the time so specified.

(3) Where the disability continues up to the death of that person, his legal representative may institute the suit or make the application within the same period after the death, as would otherwise have been allowed from the time so specified.

(4) Where the legal representative referred to in sub-section (3) is, at the date of the death of the person whom he represents, affected by any such disability, the rules contained in sub-sections (1) and (2) shall apply.

(5) Where a person under disability dies after the disability ceases but within the period allowed to him under this section, his legal representative may institute the suit or make the application within the same period after the death, as would otherwise have been available to that person had he not died.

Explanation: For the purposes of this section, 'minor' includes a child in the womb.

Section 7: Where one of the several persons jointly entitled to institute a suit or make an application for the execution of a decree is under any such disability, and a discharge can be given without the concurrence of such person, time will run against them all; but, where no such discharge can be given, time will not run as against any of them until one of them becomes capable of giving such discharge without the concurrence of the others or until the disability has ceased.

Explanation I: This section applies to a discharge from every kind of liability, including a liability in respect of any immovable property.

Explanation II: For the purposes of this section, the manager of a Hindu undivided family governed by the Mitakshara law shall be deemed to be capable of giving a discharge without the concurrence of the other members of the family only if he is in management of the joint family property.

Section 8: Nothing in section 6 or in section 7 applies to suits to enforce rights of pre-emption, or shall be deemed to extend, for more than three years from the cessation of the disability or the death of the person affected thereby, the period of limitation for any suit or application.

Section 9: Where once time has begun to run, no subsequent disability or inability to institute a suit or make an application stops it:

Provided that where letters of administration to the estate of a creditor have been granted to his debtor, the running of the period of limitation for a suit to recover the debt shall be suspended while the administration continues.

E. COMPUTATION OF PERIOD OF LIMITATION

Section 12: (1) In computing the period of limitation for any suit, appeal or application, the day from which such period is to be reckoned, shall be excluded.

(2) Computing the period of limitation for an appeal or an application for leave to appeal or for revision or for review of a judgement, the day on which the judgement complained of was pronounced and the time requisite for obtaining a copy of the decree, sentence or order appealed from or sought to be revised or reviewed shall be excluded.

(3) Where a decree or order is appealed from or sought to be revised or reviewed, or where an application is made for leave to appeal from a decree or order, the time requisite for obtaining a copy of the judgement on which the decree or order is founded shall also be excluded.

(4) In computing the period of limitation for an application to set aside an award, the time requisite for obtaining a copy of the award shall be excluded.

Explanation: In computing under this section the time requisite for obtaining a copy of a decree or an order, any time taken by the court to prepare the decree or order before an application for a copy thereof is made shall not be excluded.

In *Basavarajappa* v. *M.S. Channabasappa*,[7] the court held that the limitation for filing an appeal commences from the date of the judgement and not from the date the decree is signed.

In *State of Assam* v. *Gonda Cahndra Paul*,[8] the court held that it is now well settled that under Section 12(2) of the Limitation Act, 1963 read with the Explanation, the appellant is not entitled to exclude the time that had elapsed from the date of the judgement till signing of the decree prior to his application for a copy thereof in computing the period of limitation prescribed for filing the appeal.

Section 13: In computing the period of limitation prescribed for any suit or appeal in any case where an application for leave to sue or appeal as a pauper has been made and rejected, the time during which the applicant has been prosecuting in good faith his application for such leave shall be excluded, and the court may, or payment of the court fees prescribed for such suit or appeal, treat the suit or appeal as having the same force and effect as if the court fees had been paid in the first instance.

Section 14: (1) In computing the period of limitation for any suit the time during which the plaintiff has been prosecuting with due diligence another civil proceeding, whether in a court of first instance or of appeal or revision, against the defendant shall be excluded, where the proceeding relates to the same matter in issue and is prosecuted in good faith in a court which, from defect of jurisdiction or other cause of a like nature, is unable to entertain it.

---

7. (1991) 2 CCC 20 (Kant).
8. AIR, 1991 Gau 104.

(2) In computing the period of limitation for any application, the time during which the applicant has been prosecuting with due diligence another civil proceeding, whether in a court of first instance or of appeal or revision, against the same party for the same relief shall be excluded, where such proceeding is prosecuted in good faith in a court which, from defect of jurisdiction or other cause of a like nature, is unable to entertain it.

(3) Notwithstanding anything contained in Rule 2 of Order XXIII of the Code of Civil Procedure, 1908 (5 of 1908), the provisions of sub-section (1) shall apply in relation to a fresh suit instituted on permission granted by the court under Rule 1 of that Order, where such permission is granted on the ground that the first suit must fail by reason of a defect in the jurisdiction of the court or other cause of a like nature.

Explanation: For the purposes of this section:

(a) In excluding the time during which a former civil proceeding was pending the day on which that proceeding was instituted and the day on which it ended shall both be counted;

(b) A plaintiff or an applicant resisting an appeal shall be deemed to be prosecuting a proceeding; and

(c) Misjoinder of parties or of causes of action shall be deemed to be a cause of a like nature with defect of jurisdiction.

In *Vaditho Anantharao Naik* v. *Bhoomisetty Rajaiah,*[9] the court held that when a party has been *bonafide* pursuing a wrong remedy, it would be a fit case for applying the principle embodied in section 14 of the Limitation Act.

In *Samuel Joseph* v. *Ramachandran Chellayyan,*[10] the court held that Sections 5 and 14 of the Limitation Act, 1963, though independent, are not mutually exclusive. Even in case where section 14 applies, section 5 is not excluded.

Section 15: (1) In computing the period of limitation of any suit or application for the execution of a decree, the institution or execution of which has been stayed by injunction or order, the time of the continuance of the injunction or order, the day on which it was issued or made, and the day on which it was withdrawn, shall be excluded.

(2) In computing the period of limitation for any suit of which notice has been given, or for which the previous consent or sanction of the Government or any other authority is required, in accordance with the requirements of any law for the time being in force, the period of such notice or, as the case may be, the time required for obtaining such consent or sanction shall be excluded.

Explanation: In excluding the time required for obtaining the consent or sanction of the Government or any other authority, the date on which the application was made for obtaining the consent or sanction and the date of receipt of the order of the Government or other authority shall both be counted.

(3) In computing the period of limitation for any suit or application for execution of a decree by any receiver or interim receiver appointed in

9. 1963 (1994) 2 CCC 45 (AP).
10. (1991) 1 CCC 583 (Ker.).

proceedings for the adjudication of a person as an insolvent or by any liquidator or provisional liquidator appointed in proceedings for the winding up of a company, the period beginning with the date of institution of such proceeding and ending with the expiry of three months from the date of appointment of such receiver or liquidator, as the case may be, shall be excluded.

(4) In computing the period of limitation for any suit the time during which the defendant has been absent from India and from the territories outside India under the administration of the Central Government, shall be excluded.

In *Anandilal* v. *Ram Narain,*[11] the court held that it is a well settled principle that when the law prescribes more than one mode of execution, it is for the decree-holder to choose which of them he will pursue.

Section 16: (1) Where a person who would, if he were living, have a right to institute a suit or make an application dies before the right accrues, or where a right to institute a suit or make an application accrues only on the death of a person, the period of limitation shall be compute from the time when there is a legal representative of the deceased capable of instituting such suit or making such application.

(2) Where a person against whom, if he were living, a right to institute a suit or make an application would have accrued dies before the right accrues, or where a right to institute a suit or make an application against any person accrues on the death of such person, the period of limitation shall be computed from the time when there is a legal representative of the decreased against whom the plaintiff may institute such suit or make such application.

(3) Nothing in sub-section (1) or sub-section (2) applies to suits to enforce rights of pre-emption or to suits for the possession of immovable property or of a hereditary office.

11. AIR 1984 SC 1383.

10

The Indian Penal Code, 1860

A. INTRODUCTION

There was no criminal law in uncivilized society. Everyman was liable to be attacked in his person or property at any time by any one. The person attacked either succumbed or over-powered his opponent. "A tooth for a tooth, an eye for an eye, a life for a life" was the fore-runner of criminal justice. As time advanced, the injured person agreed to accept compensation.

The germs of criminal jurisprudence come into existence in India from the time of Manu. In the category of crimes Manu has recognized assault, theft, robbery, false evidence, slander, criminal breach of trust, cheating, adultery and rape. The king administered justice himself, and, if busy, the matter was entrusted to a Judge. If a criminal was fined, the fine went to the king's treasury, and was not given as compensation to the injured party.[1]

The Indian Penal Code was drafted by the first Indian Law Commission for which Lord McCauley was the President, and was submitted to the Governor-General of India in Council in 1837; but it was not until 1860 that it took its place on the Indian Statue Book. This central act, which was passed on October 6, 1860, is applicable to whole of Indian except Jammu and Kashmir. There are 511 sections in the Indian Penal Code.

B. OFFENCE

An act committed or omitted in violation of law is an offence. To constitute an offence two things are necessary—

(i) *Actus reus* – Act
(ii) *Mens rea* – Guilty mind

The absence of one will not constitute an offence.

Where an offence is made out within the meaning of S. 40, IPC, from the facts and circumstances of the case, it would not be an excuse to say that since the matter arose out of a contract which was not enforceable in a civil court on grounds of immortality, the accused could not be prosecuted even in regard to his criminal acts. Thus where the appellants obtained a sum of

1. Ratanlal Dhirajlal, *The Indian Penal Code* (1997) at I.

Rs. 300 on false pretence of supplying a girl for becoming the wife of his nephew and thereafter managed to slip out of his view, it was held that merely because a civil suit to recover the money or for specific performance of the contract would not lie, prosecution for cheating under Section 420 read with Section 34, IPC, could not be avoided. In *Pratibha Rani v. Suraj Kumar*, the Supreme Court also held that an act of a husband against his wife coming within the meaning of the definitions in this code, would be equally an offence.[2]

The main classification on which the offences under IPC can be divided are:

(1) Offences against state (Ss. 121-130).
(2) Offences against public including offences against public servant and offences affecting public health, safety, decency and moral; (Ss. 141-294A).
(3) Offences against human body such as murder, causing miscarriage, hurt (Ss. 299-338).
(4) Offences against corporal or incorporal properties, which include theft, misappropriation and breach of trust, fraudulent deeds and dispossession of property, forging, cheating (Ss. 378-424).
(5) Offences against reputation which classify the offences of defamation and offences of intimidation, insult (Ss. 499-511).

Keeping in view the functioning of a co-operative societies of the country, the following main provisions of Indian Penal Code relating to the misappropriation, unlawful retention of property, additions, alterations and tampering of records, wrongful furnishing of documents and criminal breach of trust are applicable to co-operative societies functioning in various activities.

C. DISHONESTY (S. 24)

Whoever does anything with the intention of causing wrongful gain to one person or wrongful loss to another person, is said to do that thing, "dishonesty."

From this definition it will appear that the term 'dishonesty' is not used in the code in its popular significance. Unless there is wrongful gain to one person, or wrongful loss to another, an act would not be 'dishonestly'. Wrongful gain includes wrongful retention and wrongful loss includes being kept out of the property as well as being wrongful deprived of property. Thus, 'dishonestly' means an intention to cause either wrongful gain or wrongful loss. In *Narendra Pratap Narain Singh v. State of U.P.*,[3] the Supreme Court held that failure of a bank in disclosing to a person the precarious economic condition of a bank customer for whom that person was called upon to give guarantee may constitute "dishonesty" and "fraud".

2. *Id.*, at 45.
3. AIR, 1991, SC 1394.

D. FRAUDULENTLY (S. 25)

A person is said to do a thing fraudulently if he does that thing with intent to defraud but not otherwise.

The Word "Fraudulently' is not confined to transactions of which deprivation of property forms a part. The intention with which an act is done is very important in determining whether that is done 'dishonestly' or 'fraudulently.' Where an offence depends upon proof of intention, the court must have proof of facts sufficient to justify it in coming to the conclusion that the intention existed. No doubt, one has usually to infer intention from conduct, and one matter that has to be taken into account is the probable effect of the conduct. But that is never conclusive.

E. 'FRAUDULENTLY'; 'DISHONESTLY'

According to the "Supreme Court" the word "defraud" includes an element of deceit. Deceit is not an ingredient of the definition of the word "Dishonestly" while it is an important ingredient of the definition of the word "fraudulently." The former involves a pecuniary or economic gain or loss while the latter by construction excludes that element.[4]

Where the accused, after the execution and registration of a document, which was not required by law to be attested, added his name to the document as an attesting witness, it was held that his act was neither fraudulent nor dishonest and the accused was, therefore, not guilty of forgery.

F. VALUABLE SECURITY (S. 30)

The word "Valuable Security" do not a document which is, or purports to be, a document whereby any legal right is created, extended, transferred, restricted, extended, transferred, restricted, extinguished or released, or where by any person acknowledges that he lies under legal liability, or has not a certain legal right.

ILLUSTRATION

A writes his name on the back of a bill of exchange. As the effect of this endorsement is to transfer the right to the bill to any person who may become the lawful holder of it, the endorsement is a "Valuable Security."

The words "Valuable Security" also occur in Ss. 329-331, 347, 348, 420, 467 and 471. Account books containing entries not signed by a party are not "Valuable Security." A copy of a valuable security is not a valuable security.[5]

4. *Id.*, at 22.
5. *Id.*, at 25.

G. DISHONEST MISAPPROPRIATION OF PROPERTY (S. 403)

Whoever dishonestly misappropriates or converts to his own use any moveable property, shall be punished with imprisonment of either description for a term which may extend to two years, or with fine, or with both.

ILLUSTRATION

A takes property belonging to Z out of Z's possession in good faith, believing, at the time when he takes it, to his own use, when he knows or has the means of discovering the owner, or before he has used reasonable means to discover and give notice to the owner and has kept the property a reasonable time to enable the owner to claim it. What are reasonable means or what is a reasonable time in such a case, is a question of fact.

It is not necessary that the finder should know who is the owner of the property, or that any particular person is the owner of it: it is sufficient if, at the time of appropriating it, he does not believe it to be his own property, or in good faith believes that the real owner cannot be found.

ILLUSTRATION

(a) A finds a cheque payable to bearer. He can form no conjecture as to the person who has lost the cheque. But the name of the person, who has drawn the cheque, appears. A knows that this person can direct him to the person in whose favour the cheque was drawn. A appropriates the cheque without attempting to discover the owner. He is guilty of an offence under this section.

(b) A finds a valuable ring, not knowing to whom it belongs. A sells it immediately without attempting to discover the owner. A is guilty of an offence under this section.

Criminal misappropriation takes place when the possession has been innocently come by, but where, by a subsequent change of intention, or from the knowledge of some new fact with which the party was not previously acquainted, the retaining becomes wrongful and fraudulent. The offence consists in that the property belongs to himself. A is not guilty of theft; but if A, after discovering his mistake, dishonestly appropriates the property to his own use, he is guilty of an offence under this section.

(c) A, being on friendly terms with Z, goes into Z's Library in Z's absence, and takes away a book without Z's express consent. Here, if A was under the impression that he had Z's implied consent to take the book for the purpose of reading it, A has not committed theft for the purpose of reading it, A has not committed theft. But, if A afterwards sells the book for his own benefit, he is guilty of an offence under this section.

(d) A and B, being joint owners of a horse, A takes the horse, out of B's possession intending to use it. Here, as A has a right to use the horse, he does not dishonestly misappropriate it. But, if A sells the horse and appropriates the whole proceeds to his own use, he is guilty of an offence under this section.

Explanation 1: A dishonest misappropriation for a time only is a misappropriation within the meaning of this section.

ILLUSTRATION

A finds a Government Promissory note belonging to Z, bearing a blank endorsement. A knowing that the note belongs to Z, pledges it with a banker as a security for a loan, intending at a future time to restore it to Z. A has committed an offence under this section.

Explanation 2: A person who finds property not in the possession of any other person, and takes such property for the purpose of protecting it for, or of restoring it to, the owner, does not take or misappropriate it dishonestly, and is not guilty of an offence; but he is guilty of the offence above defined, if he appropriates the dishonest misappropriation or conversion, either permanently or for a time, of property which is already without wrong in the possession of the offender.[6]

H. CRIMINAL BREACH OF TRUST (S. 405)

Whoever, being in any manner entrusted with property, or with any dominion over property, dishonestly misappropriates or converts his own use that property, or dishonestly uses or disposes of that property in violation of any direction of law prescribing the mode in which such trust is to be discharged, or of any legal contract, express or implied, which he has made touching the discharge of such trust, or wilfully suffer any other person so to do, commits "criminal breach of trust".

Explanation 1: A person, being an employer (of an establishment whether exempted under section 17 of the Employees' Provident Funds and Miscellaneous Provisions Act, 1952 (19 of 1952) or not, who deducts the employees' contribution from the wages payable to the employee for credit to a Provident Fund or Family Pension Fund established by any law for the time being in force, shall be deemed to have been entrusted with the amount of the contribution so deducted by him and if he makes default in the payment of such contribution to the said fund in violation of the said law, shall be deemed to have dishonestly used the amount of the said contribution in violation of a direction of law as aforesaid.

Explanation 2: A person, being an employer, who deducts the employee's contribution from the wages payable to the employee for credit to the Employee's State Insurance Fund held and administered by the Employees' State Insurance Fund held and administered by the Employees' State Insurance Corporation established under the Employees' State Insurance

6. *Id*, at 561-62.

Act, 1948, shall be deemed to have been entrusted with the amount of the contribution so deducted by him and if he makes default in the payment of such contribution to the said Fund is violation of the said Act, shall be deemed to have dishonestly used the amount of the said contribution in violation of a direction of law as aforesaid.

ILLUSTRATION

(a) A, being executor to the will of a deceased person, dishonestly disobeys the law which directs him to divide the effects according to the will, and appropriates them to his own use. A has committed criminal breach of trust.

(b) A is a warehouse keeper. Z, going on a journey, entrusts his furniture to A, under a contract that it shall be returned on payment of a stipulated sum for warehouse room. A dishonestly sells the goods. A has committed criminal breach of trust.

(c) A residing in Calcutta is agent for Z, residing at Delhi. There is an express or implied contract between A and Z, that all sums remitted by Z to A shall be invested by A, according to Z's direction. Z remits a lakh of rupees to A, with directions to A to invest the same in company's paper. A dishonestly disobeys the directions and employs the money in his own business. A has committed criminal breach of trust.

(d) But if A, in the last illustration, not dishonestly but in good faith, believing that it will be more for Z's advantage to hold shares in the Bank of Bengal, disobeys Z's directions, and lays shares in the Bank of Bengal, for Z, instead of buying Company's paper, here though Z should suffer loss, and should be entitled to bring a civil action against A, on account of that loss yet A, not having acted dishonestly, has not committed criminal breach of trust.

(e) A, a revenue-officer, is entrusted with public money and is either directed by law, or bound by a contract express or implied, with the Government, to pay into certain treasury at the public money which he holds. A dishonestly appropriates the money. A has committed criminal breach of trust.

(f) A, a carrier, is entrusted by Z with property to be carried by and or by water. A dishonestly misappropriates the property. A has committed criminal breach of trust.

I. PUNISHMENT FOR CRIMINAL BREACH OF TRUST (S. 406)

Whoever commits criminal breach of trust shall be punished with imprisonment of either description for a term which may extend to three years, or with fine or with both.

To constitute this offence there must be dishonest misappropriation by a person in whom confidence is placed as to the custody or management of the property in respect of which the breach of trust is charged. The ownership or beneficial interest in the property in respect of which criminal breach of trust is alleged to have been committed must be in some person other than the accused and the latter must hold it on account of some person or in some way for his benefit. The offence of criminal breach of trust closely resembles the offence of embezzlement under the English law. Offences committed by trustees with regard to trust property fail within the purview of this section. In *Anil Saran* v. *State of Bihar*,[7] the Supreme Court has reiterated that where a partner is entrusted with property under special contract and he holds that property in a fiduciary capacity, and misappropriation of that property would amount to criminal breach of trust.

J. CRIMINAL BREACH OF TRUST BY CARRIER ETC. (S. 407)

Whoever, being entrusted with property as a carrier, wharfinger or ware-house-keeper, commits criminal breach of trust in respect of such property, shall be punished with imprisonment of either description for a term which may extend to seven years, and shall also be liable to fine.

Those who receive property under a contract, express or implied, to carry it or to keep it in safe custody are punishable under this section for a criminal breach of trust with respect to such property.

(a) 'Carrier'

A carrier is a person who undertakes to transport the goods of other persons from one place to another for hire.

(b) 'Wharfinger'

A wharfinger is one who owns or keeps a wharf, which is a broad plain place near some creek or haven, to lay goods and wares on that are brought to or from the water.

(c) 'Warehouse-keeper'

A warehouse-keeper is one who keeps a warehouse, which is a house to deposit or keep wares in. Ware is an article or merchandise, fabric, especially in the plural, goods, commodities merchandise.

K. CRIMINAL BREACH OF TRUST BY CLERK OR SERVANT (S. 408)

Whoever, being a clerk or servant or employed as a clerk or servant, and being in any manner entrusted in such capacity with property, or with any dominion over property, commits criminal breach of trust in respect of that

7. AIR 1996 SC 204.

property, shall be punished with imprisonment of either description for a term which may extend to seven years, and shall also be liable to fine.

Section 381, punishes theft by a clerk or a servant. This section inflicts enhanced punishment on such a person for criminal breach of trust. The property must have been entrusted to the accused in his capacity as a clerk or a servant. A clerk or a servant who takes his master's property is punishable for theft.[8]

(a) 'Clerk'

A clerk is modern usage means a writer in an office, public or private, either for keeping accounts or entering minutes.[9]

(b) 'Servant'

Master and servant—a relationship where by a person calls in the assistance of others, where his own skill and labour are not sufficient to carry out his own business or purpose. A servant acts under the direct control and supervision of the master and is bound to conform to all reasonable orders given in the course of his work.

(c) 'Employed as a Clerk or Servant'

If a person acts as a clerk or servant although there is no contract binding on him to work, yet, so long as he does the duties he will come under the category of a clerk or a servant.

L. CRIMINAL BREACH OF TRUST BY PUBLIC SERVANT, OR BY BANKER, MERCHANT OR AGENT (S. 409)

Whoever, being in any manner entrusted with property, or with any dominion over property in his capacity of a public servant or in the way of his business as a banker, merchant, factor, broker, attorney or agent, commits criminal breach of trust in respect of that property, shall be punished with imprisonment for life, or with imprisonment of either description for a term which may extend to ten years, and shall also be liable to fine.

This section classes together public servants, bankers, merchants, factors, brokers, attorneys and agents. As a rule, the duties of such persons are of a highly confidential character, involving great powers of control over the property entrusted to them; and a breach of trust by such persons may often induce serious public and private calamity[10].

8. *Id.* at 577.
9. *Ibid.*
10 *Gourashankar Naik* v. *State of Orissa; ANZ Grindlays Bank* v. *Shipping and Clearing (Agents) P. Ltd.; 1992 Cr. L.J. Cal.*

M. FORGERY (S. 463)

Whoever makes any false document or part of a document, with intent to cause damage or injury to the public or to any person or to support any claim or title, or to cause any person to part with property, or to enter into any express or implied contract, or with intent to commit fraud or that fraud may be committed, commits forgery.

N. MAKING A FALSE DOCUMENT (S. 465)

A person is said to make a false document.

First: Who dishonestly or fraudulently makes, signs, seals or executes a document or part of a document, or makes any mark denoting the execution of a document, with the intention of causing it to be believed that such document or part of a document was made, signed, sealed or executed by or by the authority of a person by whom or by whose authority he knows that it was not made, signed, sealed or executed; or at a time at which he knows that it was not made, signed, sealed or executed; or

Secondly: Who, without lawful authority, dishonestly or fraudulently, by cancellation or otherwise, alters a document in any material part thereof, after it has been made or executed either by himself or by any other person, whether such person be living or dead at the time of such alteration; or

Thirdly: Who dishonestly or fraudulently causes any person to sign, seal, execute or alter a document, knowing that such person by reason of unsoundness of mind or intoxication cannot, or that by reason of deception practised upon him, he does not know the contents of the document or the nature of the alteration.

ILLUSTRATION

(a) A has a letter of credit upon B for Rs. 10,000 written by Z. A, in order to defraud B, adds a cipher to the 10,000 and makes the sum 1,00,000, intending that it may be believed by B that Z so wrote the letter. A has committed forgery.

(b) A, without Z's authority, affixes Z's seal to a document purporting to be a conveyance of an estate from Z to A, with the intention of selling the estate to B and thereby of obtaining from B the purchase money. A has committed forgery.

(c) A picks up a cheque on a banker signed by B, payable to bearer, but without any sum having been inserted in the cheque. A fraudulently fills up the cheque by inserting the sum of ten thousand rupees. A commits forgery.

(d) A leaves with B, his agent, a cheque on a banker, signed by A, without inserting the sum payable and authorizes B to fill up the cheque by inserting a sum not exceeding ten thousand rupees for the purpose of making certain payments. B fraudulently fills up the cheque by inserting the sum of twenty thousand rupees. B commits forgery.

(e) A draws a bill of exchange of himself in the make of B without B's authority, intending to discount it as a genuine bill with a banker and intending to take up the bill on its maturity. Here, as A draws the bill with intent to deceive the banker by leading him to suppose that he had the security of B, and thereby to discount the bill, A is guilty of forgery.

(f) Z's will contains these words: "I direct that all my remaining property be equally divided between A, B and C". A dishonestly scratches out B's name, intending that it may be believed that the whole was left to himself and C. A has committed forgery.

(g) A endorses a Government promissory note and makes it payable to Z or his order by writing on the bill the words "Pay to Z or his order" and singing the endorsement. B dishonestly erases the words "Pay to Z or his order" and thereby converts the special endorsement into a blank endorsement. B commits forgery.

(h) A sells and conveys an estate to Z. A afterwards, in order to defraud of his estate executes a conveyance of the same estate to B, dated six months earlier than the date of the conveyance to Z, intending it to be believed that he had conveyed the estate to B before he conveyed it to Z. A has committed forgery.

(i) Z dictates his will to A. A intentionally writes down a different legatee from the legatee named by Z, and by representing to Z that he has prepared the will according to his instructions, induces Z to sign the will. A has committed forgery.

(j) A writes a letter and signs it with B's name without B's authority, certifying that as a man of good character and in distressed circumstances from unforeseen misfortune intending by means of such letter to obtain alms from Z and other persons. Here, as A made a false document in order to induce Z to part with property, A has committed forgery.

(k) A without B's authority writes a letter and signs it in B's name certifying to A's character, intending thereby to obtain employment under Z. A has committed forgery, in as much as he intended to deceive Z by the forged certificate, and thereby to induce Z to enter into an express or implied contract for service

Explanation 1: A man's signature of his own name may amount to forgery.

ILLUSTRATION

(a) A signs his own name to a bill of exchange, intending that it may be believed that the bill was drawn by another person of the same name. A has committed forgery.

(b) A writes the word "accepted" on a piece of paper and signs it with Z's name, in order that B may afterwards write on the paper a bill of exchange drawn by B upon Z, and negotiate the bill as though it had been accepted by Z. A is guilty of forgery; and if B, knowing the fact, draws the bill upon the paper pursuant to A's intention, B is also guilty of forgery.

(c) A picks up a bill of exchange payable to the order of a different person of the same name. A endorses the bill in his own name, intending to cause it to be believed that it was endorsed by the person to whose order it was payable here. A has committed forgery.

(d) A purchases an estate sold under execution of a decree against B. B, after the seized of the estate, in collusion with Z, executes a lease of the estate to Z at a nominal rent for a long period, and dates the lease six months prior to the seizure, with intent to defraud A, and to cause it to be believed that the lease in his own name, commits forgery by antedating it.

(e) A, a trader, in anticipation of insolvency, lodges effects with B for A's benefit, and with intent to defraud his creditors; and in order to give a colour to the transaction, write a promissory note binding himself to pay to B a sum for value received, and antedates note, intending that it may be believed to have been made before A was on the pointed insolvency. A has committed forgery under the first head of the definition.

Explanation 2: The making of a false document in the name of a fictitious person, intending it to be believed that the document was made by a real person, or in the name of a deceased person, intending it to be believed that the document was made by the person in his lifetime, may amount to forgery.

ILLUSTRATION

A draws a bill of exchange upon a fictitious person, and fraudulently accepts the bill in the name of such fictitious person with intent to negotiate it. A commits forgery.

O. PUNISHMENT FOR FORGERY (S. 465)

Whoever commits forgery shall be punished with imprisonment of either description for a term which may extend to two years, or with fine, or with both.

The offence of forgery is defined in Ss. 463 and 464 of the Code Under S. 463 the making of a false document with any of the intents therein mentioned is forgery, and S. 464 sets forth when a person is said to make a false document within the meaning of the Code.

The definition of forgery in the Code is not as simple and clear as the definition of forgery in common law. Forgery in England is not defined by statute. Forgery in common law is defined as the fraudulent making or alternation of a writing to the prejudice of another man's right.

Ingredients

The elements of forgery are—

1. The making of a false document or part of it.

2. Such making should be with intent:
   (a) to cause damage or injury to (i) public, or (ii) any person; or
   (b) to support any claim or title; or
   (c) to cause any person to part with property; or
   (d) to cause any person to enter into express or implied contract; or
   (e) to commit fraud or that fraud may be committed.

P. FORGERY OF VALUABLE SECURITY, WILL ETC. (S. 467)

Whoever forges a document which purports to be a valuable security, or a will, or an authority to adopt a son, or which purports to give authority to any person to make or transfer any valuable security, or to receive the principal, interest, or dividends thereon, or to receive or deliver any money, moveable property, or valuable security, or any document purporting to be an acquaintance or receipt acknowledging the payment of money, or an acquaintance or receipt for the delivery of any moveable property or valuable security, shall be punished with imprisonment for life, or with imprisonment of either description for a term which may extend to ten years, and shall also be liable to fine.

The offence under this section is an aggravated form of the offence described in the preceding section. The forged document must be one of those mentioned in the section. A complaint by the court is necessary for cognizance of the offence.

Q. FORGED DOCUMENT (S. 470)

A false document made wholly or in part by forgery is designated "a forged document".

R. USING AS GENUINE A FORGED DOCUMENT (S. 471)

Whoever fraudulently or dishonestly uses as genuine any document which he knows or has reason to believe to be a forged document, shall be punished in the same manner as if he had forged such document.

What this section requires is the use as genuine of any document which is known or believed to be a forged document; it does not lay down that such use can only occur when the original itself is produced, for the section does not require the production of the original.

INGREDIENTS

There must be—

1. Fraudulent or dishonest use of a document as genuine.

2. The person using it must have knowledge or reason to believe that the document is a forged one.

S. FALSIFICATION OF ACCOUNTS (S. 477A)

Whoever, being a clerk, officer or servant, or employed or acting in the capacity of a clerk, officer or servant, wilfully, and with intent to defraud, destroys, alters, mutilates or falsifies any book, paper, writing, valuable security or account which belongs to or is in the possession of his employer or has been received by him for or on behalf of his employer or wilfully and with intent to defraud, makes or abets the making of any false entry in, or omits or alters or abets the omission or alteration of any material particular from or in, any such book, paper, writing, valuable security or account, shall be punished with imprisonment of either description for a term which may extend to seven years, or with fine, or with both.

Explanation: It shall be sufficient in any charge under this section to allege a general intent to defraud without naming any particular person intended to be defrauded or specifying any particular sum of money intended to be the subject of the fraud, or any particular day on which the offence was committed.

This section refers to acts relating to book-keeping or written accounts. It makes the falsification of books and accounts punishable even though there is no evidence to prove misappropriation of any specific sum on any particular occasion.

Ingredients

This section requires that—

1. The person coming within its purview must be a clerk, an officer, or a servant, or acting in the capacity of a clerk, an officer, or a servant.
2. He must wilfully and with intent to defraud—
   (i) destroy, alter, mutilate, or falsify, any book, paper, writing, valuable security, or account which—
      (a) belongs to or is in the possession of his employer; or
      (b) has been received by him for or on behalf of his employer;
   (ii) make or abet the making of any false entry in or omit or alter or abet the omission or alteration of any material particular from or in any such book, paper, writing, valuable security or account.

11

Civil Procedure Code, 1908

A. INTRODUCTION

Civil law means the law by which a person affected can get his remedy in relation to the personal right or right over the property. Civil procedure code is the most important as it contains a mass of procedural or processed rules that govern all kinds of suits or proceedings that come up before courts having civil, revenue or hindered Jurisdictions. The provisions huge in number cover a vast field and lie scattered over the body of the code a vast field and lie scattered over the body of the code containing sections expressed in more general terms and orders containing of rules giving details.

B. SUITS OF CIVIL NATURE

Section 9 of the C.P.C. says that, "The courts shall (subject to the provisions herein contained) have jurisdiction to try all suits of a civil nature excepting suits of which their cognizance is either expressly or impliedly barred.

Explanation I: A suit in which the right to property or to an office is contested is a suit of a civil nature, notwithstanding that such right may depend entirely on the decision of question as to religious rites or ceremonies.

Explanation II: For the purpose of this section, it is immaterial whether or not any fees are attached to the office referred to in Explanation I or whether or not such Office is attached to a particular place.

Section 9 confers the power upon the Civil Court Jurisdiction to try a suit of civil nature. In other words, the civil courts' power is restricted only to suits and or disputes of civil nature.

In *Shivkumar Chandha* v. *Municipal Corporation of Delhi*[1], the court held that where statutory enactments only create rights or liabilities without providing for remedies, any person having a grievance that he has been wronged or his right is being affected, can approach the ordinary civil court on the principle of law that where there is a right there is a remedy – *Ubi Jus ibi remedium*.

1. (1993) 3 SCC 161.

C. STAY OF SUIT (S. 10)

No court shall proceed with the trial of any suit in which the matter in issue is also directly and substantially in issue in a previously instituted suit between the same parties, or between parties under whom they or any of them claim litigating under the same title where such suit is pending in the same or any other court in India having Jurisdiction to grant the relief claimed, or in any court beyond the limits of India established or continued by the Central Government and having like Jurisdiction, or before the Supreme Court.

Explanation: The tendency of suit in a foreign court does not preclude the courts in India from trying a suit founded on the same cause of action.

Section 10 requires that a suit must be stayed if the matter directly and substantially in issue in it also directly and substantially in issue in a previous suit that is pending. The criterion for deciding whether the subsequent suit be stayed or not is whether there is identity of matters directly and substantially in issue in the two suits, if there is, the subsequent suit must be stayed and if there is not, it will not be stayed.[2]

The object of this section is to prevent two courts of concurrent jurisdiction from simultaneously trying two parallel suits in respect of the same matter in issue. It is to obviate conflict of decisions of two contradictory decrees being passed in respect of the same subject-matter between the same parties that the present section has been enacted. To sum up, the conditions for the application of section 10 are:

(i) the matter of issue in the second suit is directly and substantially in issue in the first suit;
(ii) the parties in the second suit are same; and
(iii) the court in which the first suit is instituted to competent to grant the relief claimed in the subsequent suit[3].

D. RES JUDICATA (S. 11)

Doctrine of *res judicata* is based upon two Roman Maxims *Nemo debt bis vexari Pro Uno eteadem cause,* i.e., no one shall be vexed twice over for the same cause of action, and interest *republicae ut sit finis litium,* i.e., it is to the interest of the state that there should be an end to litigation[4].

No court shall try any suit or issue in which the matter directly and substantially in issue has been directly and substantially in issue in a former suit between the same parties, or between parties under whom they or any of them claim, litigating under the same title, in a Court competent to try

2. Neem Kumar Agarwal *v.* Neem Kumar, 1957 ALT 734 Quoted in M.P. Tandom, *'Code of Civil Procedure'* (1997) at 10.
3. Judgemental TRG. Repulike *v.* Rungta & Son's (P) Ltd; AIR 1966 Cal. 382.
4. See *Supra* note 2 at 31-67.

such subsequent suit or the suit in which such issue has been subsequently raised, and has been heard and finally decided by such Court.

Explanation I: The expression "former suit" shall denote a suit which has been decided prior to the suit in question whether or not it was instituted prior thereto.

Explanation II: For the purposes of this section, the competence of a Court shall be determined irrespective of any provisions as to a right of appeal from the decision of such Court.

Explanation III: The matter above referred to must in the former suit have been alleged by one party and either denied or admitted, expressly or impliedly, by the other.

Explanation IV: Any matter, which might and ought to have been made ground of defence or attack in such former suit shall be deemed to have been a matter directly and substantially in issue in such suit.

Explanation V: Any relief claimed in the plaint, which is not expressly granted by the decree, shall, for the purposes of this section, be deemed to have been refused.

Explanation VI: Where persons litigate *bonafide* in respect of a public right or of a private right claimed in common for themselves and others, all persons interested in such right shall, for the purposes of this section, be deemed to claim under the persons so litigating.

Explanation VII: The provisions of this section shall apply to a proceeding for the execution of a decree and references in this section to any suit, issue or former suit shall be construed as references, respectively, to a proceeding for the execution of the decree, question arising in such proceeding and a former proceeding for the execution of that decree.

Explanation VIII: an issue heard and finally decided by a court of limited jurisdiction, competent to decide such issue, shall operate as *res judicata* in a subsequent suit, notwithstanding that such court of limited jurisdiction was not competent to try such subsequent suit in which such issue has been subsequently raised.

Doctrine of *res judicata* is based upon two Roman Maxims *Nemo debt bis vexari Pro Uno eteadem cause,* i.e., no one shall be vexed twice over for the same cause of action, and interest *republicae at sit finis litium,* i.e., it is to the interest of the state that there should be an end to litigation.

E. PLEADINGS ($O_{6\text{-}8}$, $R_{4\text{-}5}$)

The preparation of plaint by the plaintiff in the case and the written statement by the opposite parties who are called defendant are called pleadings. It includes the set-off plead by the defendant. Any defect or error in the pleadings can be amended at the instance of the parties and by the order of the Court (O_6 R_{17} and Sec. 153). The plaint must have the necessary particulars of claim, cause of action and the relief required and must be verified by the plaintiff. The plaint must be properly valued and necessary court fee stamps must be affixed. The relevant documents must be accompanied with the plaint. The written statement by the defendant must have the defence or set-off if any, and verified by the defendant[5].

F. SERVICE OF SUMMONS

If the plaint is properly presented, it is admitted as per O_4, R_2. After the plaint being admitted, summons to the defendant be sent as per O_5, $R_{7,8}$.

(a) Definition

Summon is a document issued from the office of a Court of Justice, calling upon the person to whom it is directed to attend before a judge or office of the court on the day mentioned therein.

(b) Summons to Defendants (S. 27)

Where a suit has been duly instituted, a summon may be issued to the defendant to appear and answer the claim and may be served in the manner prescribed.

Where a suit has been duly instituted by filing a plaint, the first duty of the court is to issue a summon calling on the defendant to appear and answer the claim on a day specified therein either in person or by a pleader duly instructed or accompanied by some person able to answer all material questions. A summon mentioning wrong date for appearance or appearance on a day when the court is closed, is not a summon as required under O_5, R_1. The date is essential ingredient of the summon.[6]

(c) Essentials of a Summon

Every Summons shall:

(i) Intimate to the defendant of the date of hearing and whether he is to appear in person or by a pleader;

(ii) Contain a direction whether the date is fixed for settlement of issues only or final disposal of the suit; and

(iii) Order the defendant to produce all documents in his possession or power upon which he intends to rely in support of his case.

(d) Modes of Service of Summons (O_5, R_{10})

Service of the summons shall be made by delivering or tendering a copy

5. National Council for Co-operative Training of NCUI, Legal Aspects, HDCM-2 at 71.
6. AIR 1964, M.P. 261.

thereof signed by the Judge or such officer as he appoints in this behalf, and sealed with the seal of the court.

(i) Personal or Direct Service

The summon should be handed over in person to the defendant or adult male or female member of his family. Such personal service is also called direct service because service is made by delivering a copy thereof to the defendant personally, or to an agent or other person on his behalf and the signature of the person to whom the copy is so handed over must be obtained[7].

(ii) Service by affixing a copy of summons on defendant's house with an order of the court

(a) Where the defendant or his agent or in their absence an adult member of the family refuses to sign the acknowledgment, or

(b) Where the service officer after using all due and reasonable diligence, cannot find the defendant who is absent from his residence at the time when service is sought to be effected on him at his residence and there is no likelihood of his being found at the residence, within a reasonable time and there is no other such person on whom service can be effected, the serving officer shall affix a copy of the summons on the outer door. If the court is satisfied, it declares the service to have been duly effected[8].

(iii) Service by registered post in addition to Personal Service

The summons can also be served to the defendant by registered post also. The acknowledgement of the registered post summon is essential. The court issuing the summons shall declare that the summons had been duly served on the defendant; provided that where the summons was properly addressed, prepaid and duly sent by registered post[9].

(iv) Substituted Service

Where the court is satisfied that the defendant is avoiding service, or the defendant cannot be served. In any way, the court shall order the summons to be served by affixing a copy thereof in some conspicuous part of the house. Such service is valid. Service may be ordered to be effected by publication in a local newspaper also[10].

G. FRAMING OF ISSUES

(a) Importance of Issues

The issues are the backbone of a suit. The importance of defining at the

7. See, O_5 R_{11-15}.
8. See, O_5 R_{17}.
9. See, O_5 R_{19-A}.
10. See, O_5 R_{20}.

outset the points on which a decision must turn cannot be too strongly emphasised. This, no doubt, requires thought and care, but the time is well spent, for vague and general issues for the most part mean that the case is approached without a clear idea of its essentials. By framing issues each side is fully aware of the exact questions to be tried and facilities him to produce evidence germane to the issues.

(b) Framing of Issues (O_{14})

Issues arise when one party affirms a material proposition of fact or law and denied by the other issues are of two kinds:

(i) Issues of fact, and
(ii) Issues of Law.

The third kind of issue is mixed issue of Law and fact. It is the duty of the court under Sub-rule (5) of Rule 1 of Order 14, to ascertain at the first hearing of the suit, after reading the plaint and the written statements, if any, and after such examination of the parties as may appear necessary, the material propositions of fact or law on which the parties as may appear necessary, the material propositions of fact or law on which the parties are at variance and thereafter to frame and record the issues on which the decision of the case depends[11].

The court is not required to frame and record issues if the defendant at the first hearing of the suit makes no defence.

In *Alleemuddin* v. *Haji Bashir*[12] the court held that while it is true the parties are expected to be vigilant and must see that proper issues are framed in the case, but primarily it is the duty of the court and the court cannot be absolved of its responsibility merely because a party has been negligent. Even in an undefended case it is the duty of the court to frame proper issues with a view to inform the plaintiff what points he has to establish before a decree could be claimed.[13]

H. HEARING OF THE SUIT—EXAMINATION OF WITNESS (O_{18}, R_l)

As a rule the plaintiff has to prove his case and therefore he must begin. But if the defendant admits the facts alleged by the plaintiff and contends that either in point of law or on some additional facts alleged by the defendant the plaintiff is not entitled to any part of the relief, which he seeks, the defendant has the right to begin. Similarly, if on the issue or issues of fact the burden of proof is on the defendant who has the right to begin. In a suit for restitution of conjugal rights, where the marriage is admitted but coercion

11. *Supra* Note 2 at 155.
12. (1977) AWC 682.
13. *Ibid.* for further details pl. See O_{11} & O_{15}.

and non-consent is pleased or in a suit where the defendant pleads minority, it is the defendant who has to begin first.

The party having the right to begin states his case on the date fixed for the hearing of the suit and produces his evidence in support of the issues, which he is bound to prove.[14] The right to begin is mostly determined by the rule of evidence, relating to the burden of proof,[15] right to begin means the privilege to opening the case.[16]

The evidence of witnesses shall be taken orally in open court in the presence and under the personal direction and superintendence of the Judge.[17]

When the party first examines witness, this is called examination in chief or direct examination. Next the adverse party examines him, this is called cross-examination. Lastly, the party who called him for clearing up some ambiguity may reexamine him. Under Section 118 of Evidence Act, all persons are competent to testify unless the court considers that by reason of tender years, extreme old age or infirmity and incapacity of understanding the questions put and of giving rational answers. Deaf and dumb persons may be witnesses if they are able to communicate their ideas by writing signs.[18]

I. MODE OF RECORDING EVIDENCE

The mode of recording evidence is contained in Order 18 of Rules 5 to 14. In summary cases the evidence of witnesses can be taken as a memorandum of evidence.[19]

In the case of the suit, the evidence shall be taken down in writing by the judge or may be dictated by the Judge directly to the typewriter or recorded mechanically.[20] Where the English is not the court language and parties or their pleaders do not object, the evidence given in English, it may be recorded in English if the parties do have no objection to this.[21] The court may of its own motion or on application of the parties take down any particular question and answer or any objection to any question, if there appears to be any special reason.[22]

The court may at any stage recall a witness already examined and put such questions to him as it thinks fit.[23] Court may of its own accord summon any person including a party to the suit as a witness.[24]

14. See, O_{18}, $R_{2,3\ \&\ 3A}$.
15. Sec, 101-114, Evidence Act.
16. See, O_{18} R_{1-2}.
17. See, O_{18}, R_4.
18. Sec, Sec. 119 of Evidence Act.
19. See, O_{18}, R_{13}.
20. See, O_{18}., R_5.
21. See, O_{18}., R_9.
22. See, O_{18}., R_{10}.
23. See, O_{18}., R_{17}.
24. See, O_{16}., R_{14}.

J. JUDGEMENT (S_{33}, O_{20})

The court, after the case has been heard, shall pronounce Judgement, and on such Judgement a decree shall follow.

Once a judgement is signed, it shall not be altered or added to, save as provided by section 152 or a review[25] under Section 152 only clerical or arithmetical mistake or any accidental slip or omission may at any time be corrected by the court.

In the decree for payment of money, the court may order interest at such rate as it deem reasonable. When the decree is silent about further interest, it shall be deemed to have been refused.[26]

K. APPEALS (S_{96-122}, $O_{41, 43, 44, 45}$)

An appeal shall be from every decree passed by any court exercising original jurisdiction to the court authorised to hear appeals from the decision of such courts.[27]

L. EXECUTION OF DECREES

All proceedings in execution are commenced by an application for execution. The application for execution must be in writing and should contain the particulars set forth in Rules 11-24. The only exception is where the decree is for the payment of money and the Judgment debtor is in the precincts of the court when the decree is passed, in which case the court may order immediate execution on the oral application of the decree-holder at the time of passing the decree.[28]

M. MODE OF EXECUTION

Execution may be effected by delivery of property, by attachment and sale, by arrest, by appointing a Receiver or in such other manner as the nature of relief granted may require.[29] Execution by arrest is not now available as a matter of right or course and arrest or detention cannot be ordered unless it is proved to the satisfaction of the court that the debtor is unwilling to pay in spite of present means to pay and the burden of proving is on the decree holder.[30] According to Section 136 of the Limitation Act, 1963, the period of limitation for executing any decree is 12 years other than the decree of mandatory injunction.

---

25. See, O_{20}. , R_3.
26. See, *Supra* Note 5 at 72-73.
27. See, *Supra* Note 2 at 354-79.
28. See, S.P. Padhi, *Allied Laws for Co-operatives* (1968) at 82.
29. Sec, 51, O_{21}, $R_{30, 36}$.
30. Sec, 51, O_{21}, R_{37-40}.

The Co-operative Societies Act provides for execution of any award or a decision or an order passed under this Act either by Departmental Officer or by Revenue Court meant for recovery of arrears of land-revenue or by a civil court. If any award passed under the Co-operative Societies Act is transferred to a civil court for execution, the Civil Court executes the award in the same manner in which it executes its own decree.[31]

N. REFERENCE, REVISION AND REVIEW ($SS_{113\text{-}115}$, $O_{46,47}$)

Order 46, Rule 1, C.P.C., prescribes the conditions to be satisfied to enable a subordinate court to make a reference, either of its own motion or on the application of any of the parties.[32]

The person aggrieved by an order of the court, can file petition to review the same under certain circumstances. The review power must be given under the statute,

(1) Discovery of new and important matter or evidence which were not on record at the time of passing the order.
(2) Mistake or error apparent on the face of the record.
(3) For other sufficient reason.[33]

The High Court may call for the records of any case which has been decided by any court subordinate to High Court and in which no appeal lies thereto and if such subordinate courts appears:

(1) to have exercised a jurisdiction not vested in it by law; or
(2) to have failed to exercise a jurisdiction so vested; or
(3) to have acted in the exercise of its jurisdiction illegally.

The time limitation for filing revision is 90 days from the date of any order in question.

31. See, *Supra* Note 27 at 101.
32. Sec. 113.
33. Sec. 114.

12

The Industrial Dispute Act, 1947

A. INTRODUCTION

The object of the Act, as the preamble indicates is to make provision for the investigation and settlement of industrial disputes, which means adjudication of such disputes also. The act envisages collective bargaining, contracts between union representing the workmen and the management, a matter of which is outside the realm of the common law or the Indian Law of Contracts. The Civil Court will have no jurisdiction to try and adjudicate upon an industrial dispute, if it is concerned with the enforcement of certain rights or liability created under the Industrial Dispute Act.[1]

The scheme of the act is to codify the law bearing an industrial dispute, strikes and lockouts, stem from such disputes, the machinery for settlement of such disputes at various stages is provided for by the Act. Special forums of remedy have been created under the act and all Industrial disputes are to be referred to a Board, Labour Court or Tribunal constituted thereon. The intention of the Act is to vest exclusive Jurisdiction. In the Board, Labour Court or Tribunal, as the case may be, in respect of all industrial disputes between the workmen and management.[2] The Statutory Imprimatur is given to settlements and awards, and norms of discipline during the pendency of the proceedings are set down in the Act. This Central Act came into force from 1.4.1947 and extends to the whole of India.

B. DEFINITION

(a) Closure (S. 2 (CC))

"Closure" means the permanent closing down of a place of employment or part thereof.

(b) Industry (S. 2(j))

"Industry" means any business, trade, undertaking, manufacture of calling

1. See, National Council for Co-operative Training of NCUI, Legal Aspects (1994) at 30.
2. *Ibid.*

employers and includes any calling, service, employment, handicraft, or industrial occupation or a vocation of workmen.

"Industry" means any systematic activity carried on by co-operation between an employer and his workmen (whether such workmen are employed by such employer directly or by or through any agency, including a contractor) for the production, supply or distribution of goods or services with a view to satisfy human wants or wishes (not being wants or wishes which are merely spiritual or religious in nature). Co-operative societies, clubs are included in the definition of industries.

In *S.K. Verma v. Masheshchandra,*[3] the Supreme Court of India has held that it is necessary to interpret the definition of 'industry', 'workman', 'industrial dispute', etc. so as not to whittle down, but to advance the object of the Act. A pragmatic approach must be adopted.

In *Niemla Taxtile Finishing Mills* v. *Second Punjab Tribunal,*[4] the Supreme Court of India has held that the definition of 'industry' in Section 2(i) is within the legislative competence of the Central Legislature.

In *Akil Raj, Rajya Hand Pump Mistries Sangathan* v. *State of Rajasthan,*[5] it has been held that a Panchayat Samiti providing drinkable water and installing hand pumps and getting them maintained and repaired, is an 'industry'.

(c) Industrial Dispute (S. 2(k))

"Industrial dispute" means any dispute or difference between employers and employees, or between employers and workmen, or between workmen and workmen, which is connected with the employment or non-employment or the terms of employment or with the conditions of labour, of any person.

In *Village Papers (P) Ltd.* v. *State of H.P.,*[6] it has been held that on industrial dispute can arise only when a demand is made by the workmen and denied by the employer.

In *Workmen* v. *Hindustan Lever (P) Ltd.,*[7] it has been held that the expression "term of employment" would ordinarily include not only the contractual terms and conditions but those terms which are understood and applied by the parties in practice or habitually or by common consent whatever being incorporated in the contract.

In *Jagdish Narain Sharma* v. *Rajasthan Patrika Ltd.,*[8] it has been held that dispute relating to transfer of a workman can be adjudicated by Labour Court/ Industrial Tribunal only when it becomes industrial dispute otherwise only the civil court conducive the validity of transfer.

3. (1983) 4 SCC 214 Quoted in P.L. Malik, *Handbook of Labour and Industrial Law,* 1996 at 394.
4. *Ibid.* (1957) S.C. 329
5. (1995) 86 FJR 167.
6. *Id.* at 395, 1993 ILLJ 99.
7. (1984) ISCC 392.
8. (1994) 2 LJJ 600.

(d) Retrenchment (S. 2(00))

Retrenchment means the termination by the employer of the service of a workman for any reason whatsoever, otherwise than as a punishment inflicted by way of disciplinary action, but does not include:

(a) voluntary retirement of the workman; or
(b) retirement of the workman on reaching the age of superannuation if the contract of employment between the employer and the workman concerned contains a stipulation in that behalf; or
(bb) termination of the service of the workman as a result of the non-renewal of the contract of employment between the employer and the workman concerned on its expiry or of such contract being terminated under a stipulation in that behalf contained therein; or
(c) termination of the service of a workman on the ground of continued ill-health.

In *Santosh Gupta* v. *Bank of Patiala,*[9] it has been held that Retrenchment includes all kinds of termination of service by employer for any reason whatsoever except those not expressly included in Section 25-F or not expressly provided for in section 25-FF and 25-FFF. Discharge of a workman on ground of his failure to pass confirmation test would amount to retrenchment.

In *Koodaranji Service Co-Op. Bank* v. *M.M. Lissy,*[10] it has been held that the termination of service of a person appointed *de hors* the rules cannot be considered as retrenchment.

(e) Workman (S. 2(S))

'Workman' means any person (including an apprentice) employed in any industry to do any manual, unskilled, skilled, technical, operational, clerical or supervisory work for hire or reward, whether the terms of employment be express or implied, and for the purposes of any proceeding under this Act in relation to an industrial dispute, includes any such person who has been dismissed, discharged or retrenched in connection with, or as a consequence of, that dispute, or whose dismissal, discharge or retrenchment has led to that dispute, but does not include any such person—

(i) Who is subject to the Air Force Act, 1950, or the Army Act, 1950, the Navy Act 1957; or
(ii) Who is employed in the police service or as an officer or other employee of a prison; or
(iii) Who is employed mainly in a managerial or administrative capacity; or
(iv) Who, being employed in a supervisory capacity, draws wages exceeding one thousand six hundred rupees per menses or exercises, either by

9. (1980) 3 SCC 340.
10. (1994) 2 LLJ 97.

the nature of the duties attached to the office or by reason of the powers vested in him, functions mainly of a managerial nature.

Casual worker or temporary workman comes under this definition.

An appraiser was engaged by a bank purely on commission basis for weighing and testing gold ornaments offered to be pledged to the bank to secure loans, with a fair element of freedom in the manner of doing his work and without obligation on the part of the bank to allot him work. Such an appraiser, although undertaking to indemnify the bank in case of any loss, was held to be not a workman.[11]

In *Caronasahu Co. Ltd.* v. *Labour Court,*[12] it has been held that a salesman, whose duties included manual as well as clerical work such as to attend to the customer, prepare cash memos, to assist the manager in daily routine etc., is a workman.

In *S.K. Maini* v. *Carona Sahu Co. Lt.,*[13] it has been held that a shop manager, although incidentally doing some clerical work, is not a workman.

(f) Dismissal (S. 2-A)

Where any employer discharges, dismisses, retrenches or otherwise terminates the services of an individual workman, any dispute or difference between that workman and his employer connected with, or arising out of, such discharge, dismissal, retrenchment or termination shall be deemed to be an industrial dispute notwithstanding that no other workman nor any union of workmen is a party to the dispute.

Where the High Court, after analysing the powers and responsibilities of the employee and the evidence on record reversed the decision of the labour court and declared that the employee was not a workman, held, the High Court rightly interfered with the labour court's finding as the same was the very foundation of the Labour Court's Jurisdiction.

C. AUTHORITIES UNDER THE ACT

The Industrial Dispute Act has provided a set of machinery for the maintenance of industrial peace and good relation between employees and workmen. Section 3 recommends for the establishment of works committee, where the industrial establishment has 100 or more workmen. The appropriate Government by general or special order require the employer to constitute the works committee.

(a) Conciliation Officers (S. 4)

(1) The appropriate Government may, by notification in the Official Gazette, appoint such number of persons as it thinks fit, to be

11. Puri Urban Co-operative Bank *v.* Madhusudhan Sahu (1992) 3 SCC 323.
12.. (1993) 1 LLJ 997.
13. (1994) 3 SCC 510.

conciliation officers, charged with the duty of mediating in and promoting the settlement of industrial disputes.

(2) A conciliation officer may be appointed for a special area or for specified industries in a specified area or for one or more specified industries and either permanently or for a limited period.

(b) Boards of Conciliation

(1) The appropriate Government may as occasion arises by notification in the Official Gazette constitute a Board of Conciliation for promoting the settlement of an industrial dispute.

(2) A Board shall consist of a chairman and two or four other members, as the appropriate Government thinks fit.

(3) The chairman shall be an independent person and the other members shall be persons appointed in equal numbers to represent the parties to the dispute and any person appointed to represent a party shall be appointed on the recommendation of that party:

Provided that, if any party fails to make a recommendation as aforesaid within the prescribed time, the appropriate Government shall appoint such persons as it thinks fit to represent that party.

(4) A Board, having the prescribed quorum, may act notwithstanding the absence of the chairman or any of its members or any vacancy in its number:

Provided that if the appropriate Government notifies the Board that the services of the chairman or of any other member have ceased to be available, the Board shall not act until a new chairman or member, as the case may be, has been appointed.

(c) Courts of Inquiry (S. 6)

(1) The appropriate Government may as occasion arises by notification in the Official Gazette, constitute a Court of Inquiry for inquiring into any matter appearing to be and connected with or relevant to an industrial dispute.

(2) A court may consist of one independent person or of such number of independent persons as the appropriate Government may think fit and where a Court consists of two or more members, one of them shall be appointed as the chairman.

(3) A court, having the prescribed quorum, may act notwithstanding the absence of the chairman or any of its members or any vacancy in its number:

Provided that, if the appropriate Government notifies the court that the services of the chairman have ceased to be available, the court shall not act until a new chairman has been appointed.

(d) Labour Courts (S. 7)

(1) The appropriate Government may, by notification in the Official Gazette, constitute one or more Labour Courts for the adjudication of industrial disputes relating to any matter specified in the Second Schedule and for performing such other functions as may be assigned to them under this Act.

(2) A labour court shall consist of one person only to be appointed by the appropriate Government.

(3) A person shall not be qualified for appointment as the presiding officer or a Labour Court, unless—

(a) he is, or has been, a Judge of a High Court; or
(b) he has, for a period of not less than three years, been a District Judge or an Additional District Judge; or
(c) he has held any judicial office in India for not less than seven years; or
(d) he has been the presiding officer of a Labour Court constituted under any Provincial Act or State Act for not less than five years.

(e) Tribunals (S. 7-A)

(1) The appropriate Government may, by notification in the Official Gazette, constitute one or more Industrial Tribunals for the adjudication of industrial disputes relating to any matter, whether specified in the Second Schedule or the Third Schedule [and for performing such other functions as may be assigned to them under this Act].

(2) A Tribunal shall consist of one person only to be appointed by the appropriate Government.

(3) A person shall not be qualified for appointment as the presiding officer of a Tribunal, unless—

(a) he is, or has been, a Judge of a High Court; or
(aa) he has, for a period of not less than three years, been a District Judge or an Additional District Judge;

(4) The appropriate Government may, if it so thinks fit, appoint two persons as assessors to advise the Tribunal in the proceeding before it.

(f) National Tribunals (S. 7-B)

(1) The Central Government may, by notification in the Official Gazette, constitute one or more National Industrial Tribunals for the adjudication of industrial disputes which, in the opinion of the Central Government involve questions of national importance or are of such a nature that industrial establishments situated in more than one State are likely to be interested in, or affected by, such disputes.

(2) A National Tribunal shall consist of one person only to be appointed by Central Government.

(3) A person shall not be qualified for appointment as the Presiding Officer of a National Tribunal [unless he is, or has been, a judge of a High Court].

(4) The Central Government may, if it so thinks fit, appoint two persons as assessors to advise the National Tribunal in the proceeding before it.

(g) Disqualification for the Presiding Officers of Labour Courts, Tribunals and National Tribunals (S. 7-C)

No person shall be appointed to, or continue in, the office of the presiding officer of a Labour Court, Tribunal or National Tribunal, if—

(a) he is not an independent person; or
(b) he has attained the age of sixty-five years.

(h) Filing of Vacancies (S. 8)

If, for any person a vacancy (other than a temporary absence) occurs in the office of the presiding officer of a Labour Court, Tribunal or National Tribunal or in the office of the Chairman or any other member of a Board or Court, then, in the case of a National Tribunal, the Central Government and in any other case, the appropriate Government, shall appoint another person in accordance with the provisions of this Act to fill the vacancy, and the preceding may be continued before the Labour Court, Tribunal, National Tribunal, Board or Court, as the case may be, from the state at which the vacancy is filled.

(i) Finality of Orders Constituting Boards, etc. (S. 9)

(1) No order of the appropriate Government or of the Central Government appointing any person as the chairman or any other member of a Board or Court or as the presiding officer of a Labour Court, Tribunal or National Tribunal shall be called in question in any manner; and no act or proceeding before any Board or Court shall be called in question in any manner on the ground merely of the existence of any vacancy in, or defect in the constitution of, such Board or Court.

(2) No settlement arrived at in the course of a conciliation proceeding shall be invalid by reason only of the fact that such settlement was arrived at after the expiry of the period referred to in sub-section (6) of Section 12 or sub-section (5) of Section 13, as the case may be.

(3) Where the report of any settlement arrived at in the course of conciliation proceeding before a Board is signed by the Chairman and all the other members of the Board, no such settlement shall be invalid by reason only of the casual or unforeseen absence of any of the members (including the Chairman) of the Board during any stage of the proceeding.]

In *State of Haryana* v. *Haryana Co-op. Transport Ltd.,* the court held that Section 9(1) cannot Whittle down the rights conferred by Articles 226 and 227 of the Constitution.

(j) Notice of Change (S. 9-A)

No employer, who proposes to effect any change in the conditions of service applicable to any workman in respect of any matter specified in the Fourth Schedule, shall effect such change,—

(a) without giving to the workman likely to be affected by such change a notice in the prescribed manner of the nature of the change proposed to be effected; or

(b) within twenty-one days of giving such notice:

Provided that no notice shall be required for effecting any such change—

(a) where the change is effected in pursuance of any [settlement or award]; or

(b) where the workmen likely to be affected by the change are persons to whom the Fundamental and Supplementary Rules, Civil Services (Classification, Control and Appeal) Rules, Civil Services (Temporary Service) Rules, Revised Leave Rules, Civil Service Regulations, Civilians in Defence Services (Classification, Control and Appeal) Rules or the Indian Railway Establishment Code or any other rules or regulations that may be notified in this behalf by the appropriate Government in the Official Gazette, apply.

(k) Power of Government to Exempt (S. 9-B)

Where the appropriate Government is of opinion that the application of the provisions of Section 9-A to any class of industrial establishments or to any class of workmen employed in any industrial establishment affect the employers in relation thereto so prejudicially that such application may cause serious repercussion on the industry concerned and that public interest so requires, the appropriate Government may, by notification in the Official Gazette, direct that the provisions of the said section shall not apply, or shall apply, subject to such conditions as may be specified in the notification, to that class of industrial establishments or to that class of workmen employed in any industrial establishment.]

(l) Setting up of Grievance Settlement Authorities and Reference of Certain Individual Disputes to Such Authorities (S. 9-C)

(1) The employer in relation to every industrial establishment in which fifty or more workmen are employed or have been employed on any day in the preceding twelve months, shall provide for, in accordance with the rules made in that behalf under this Act, a Grievance Settlement Authority for the settlement of industrial disputes connected with an individual workmen employed in the establishment.

(2) Where an industrial dispute connected with an individual workman arises in an establishment referred to in sub-section (l), a workman or any trade union of workmen of which such workman is a member, refer, in such manner as may be prescribed such dispute to the Grievance Settlement Authority provided for by the employer under that sub-section for settlement.

(3) The Grievance Settlement Authority referred to in sub-section (l) shall follow such procedure and complete its proceedings within such period as may be prescribed.

(4) No reference shall be made under Chapter III with respect to any dispute referred to in this section unless such dispute has been referred to the Grievance Settlement Authority concerned and the decision of the Grievance Settlement Authority is not acceptable to any of the parties to the dispute.

(m) Reference of Disputes to Boards, Courts or Tribunals (S. 10)

(1) [Where the appropriate Government is of opinion that any industrial dispute exists or is apprehended, it may at any time], by order in writing,—

(a) refer the dispute to a Board for promoting a settlement thereof; or

(b) refer any matter appearing to be connected with or relevant to the dispute to a Court for inquiry; or

[(c) refer the dispute or any matter appearing to be connected with, or relevant to, the dispute, if it relates to any matter specified in the Second Schedule, to a Labour Court for adjudication; or

(d) refer the dispute or any matter appearing to be connected with, or relevant to the dispute, whether, it relates to any matter specified in the Second Schedule or the Third Schedule, to a Tribunal for adjudication:

Provided that where the dispute relates to any matter specified in the Third Schedule and is not likely to affect more than one hundred workmen, the appropriate Government may, if it so thinks fit, make the reference to a Labour Court under clause (*c*):]

[Provided further that] where the dispute relates to a public utility service and a notice under Section 22 has been given, the appropriate Government shall, unless it considers that the notice has been frivolously or vexatiously given or that it would be inexpedient so to do, make a reference under this sub-section notwithstanding that any other proceedings under this Act in respect of the dispute may have commenced:

Provided also that where the dispute in relation to which the Central Government is the appropriate Government, it shall be competent for that Government to refer the dispute to a Labour Court or an Industrial Tribunal, as the case may be, constituted by the state Government.

(1-A) Where the Central Government is of opinion that any Industrial dispute exists or is apprehended and the dispute involves any question of national importance or is of such a nature that industrial establishments situated in more than one State are likely to be interested in, or affected by, such dispute and that the dispute should be adjudicated by a National Tribunal, then, the Central Government may, whether or not it is the appropriate Government in relation to that dispute, at any time, by order in writing, refer the dispute or any matter appearing to be connected with, or relevant to, the dispute, whether it relates to any matter specified in the Second Schedule or the Third Schedule, to a National Tribunal for adjudication.]

(2) Where the parties to an industrial dispute apply in the prescribed manner, whether jointly or separately, for a reference of the dispute to a Board, Court, [Labour Court, Tribunal or National Tribunal], the appropriate Government, if satisfied that the persons applying represent the majority of each party, shall make the reference accordingly.

[(2-A) An order referring an industrial dispute to a Labour Court, Tribunal or National Tribunal under this section shall specify the period within which such Labour Court, Tribunal or National Tribunal shall submit its award on such dispute to the appropriate Government:

Provided that where such industrial dispute is connected with an individual workman, no such period shall exceed three months:

Provided further that where the parties to an industrial dispute apply in the prescribed manner, whether jointly or separately, to the Labour Court, Tribunal or National Tribunal for extension of such period or for any other reason, and the presiding officer of such Labour Court, Tribunal or National Tribunal considers it necessary or expedient to extend such period, he may for reasons to be recorded in writing, extend such period by such further period as he may think fit:

Provided also that in computing any period specified in this sub-section, the period, if any, for which the proceedings before the Labour Court, Tribunal or National Tribunal had been stayed by any injunction or order of a Civil Court shall be excluded:

Provided also that no proceedings before a Labour Court, Tribunal or National Tribunal shall lapse merely on the ground that any period specified under this sub-section had expired without such proceedings being completed.]

(3) Where an industrial dispute has been referred to a Board, [Labour Court, Tribunal or National Tribunal] under this section, the appropriate Government may by order prohibit the continuance of any strike or lock-out in connection with such dispute which may be in existence on the date of the reference.

(4) Where in an order referring an industrial dispute to [a Labour Court, Tribunal or National Tribunal] under this section or in a subsequent order, the appropriate Government has specified the points of dispute for adjudication, [the Labour Court or the Tribunal or the National Tribunal, as the case may be,] shall confine its adjudication to those points and matters incidental thereto.

(5) Where a dispute concerning any establishment or establishments has been, or is to be, referred to a [Labour Court, Tribunal or National Tribunal]

under this section and the appropriate Government is of opinion, whether on an application made to it in this behalf or otherwise, that the dispute is of such a nature that any other establishment, group or class of establishments of a similar nature is likely to be interested in or affected by, such dispute, the appropriate Government may, at the time of making the reference or at any time thereafter but before the submission of the award, include in that reference such establishment, group, or class of establishments, whether or not at the time of such inclusion any dispute exists or is apprehended in that establishment, group or class of establishments.

(6) Where any reference has been made under sub-section (1-A) to a National Tribunal, then notwithstanding anything contained in this Act, no Labour Court or Tribunal shall have jurisdiction to adjudicate upon any matter which is under adjudication before the National Tribunal, and accordingly,—

(a) if the matter under adjudication before the National Tribunal is pending in a proceeding before a Labour Court or Tribunal, the proçeeding before the Labour Court or the Tribunal, as the case may be, in so far as it relates to such matter, shall be deemed to have been quashed on such reference to the National Tribunal; and

(b) it shall not be lawful for the appropriate Government to refer the matter under adjudication before the National Tribunal to any Labour Court or Tribunal for adjudication during the pendency of the proceeding in relation to such matter before the National Tribunal.

[*Explanation.*—In this sub-section "Labour Court" or "Tribunal" includes any Court or Tribunal or other authority constituted under any law relating to investigation and settlement of industrial disputes in force in any State.]

(7) Where any industrial dispute, in relation to which the Central Government is not the appropriate Government, is referred to a National Tribunal, then, notwithstanding anything contained in this Act, any reference in Section 15, Section 17, Section 19, Section 33-A, Section 33-B and Section 36-A to the appropriate Government in relation to such dispute shall be construed as a reference to the Central Government but, save as aforesaid and as otherwise expressly provided in this Act, any reference in any other provision of this Act to the appropriate Government in relation to that dispute shall mean a reference to the State Government.]

[(8) [No proceedings pending before a Labour Court, Tribunal or National Tribunal in relation to an industrial dispute shall lapse merely by reason of the death of any of the parties to the dispute being a workman, and such Labour Court, Tribunal or National Tribunal shall complete such proceedings and submit its award to the appropriate Government.]

(n) Voluntary Reference of Disputes to Arbitration (S.10-A)

(1) Where any industrial dispute exists or is apprehended and the employer and the workmen agree to refer the dispute to arbitration, they may, at any time before the dispute has been referred under Section 10 to a

Labour Court or Tribunal or National Tribunal, by a written agreement, refer the dispute to arbitration and the reference shall be to such person or persons (including the presiding officer of a Labour Court or Tribunal or National Tribunal) as an arbitrator or arbitrators as may be specified in the arbitration agreement.

[(1-A) Where an arbitration agreement provides for a reference of the dispute to an even number of arbitrators, the agreement shall provide for the appointment of another person as umpire who shall enter upon the reference, if the arbitrators are equally divided in their opinion, and the award of the umpire shall prevail and shall be deemed to be the arbitration award for the purposes of this Act.]

(2) An arbitration agreement referred to in sub-section (1) shall be in such form and shall be signed by the parties thereto in such manner as may be prescribed.

(3) A copy of the arbitration agreement shall be forwarded to the appropriate Government and the conciliation officer and the appropriate Government shall, within [one month] from the date of the receipt of such copy, publish the same in the Official Gazette.

[(3-A) Where an industrial dispute has been referred to arbitration and the appropriate Government is satisfied that the persons making the reference represent the majority of each party, the appropriate Government may, within the time referred to in sub-section (3), issue a notification in such manner as may be prescribed; and when any such notification is issued, the employers and workmen who are not parties to the arbitration agreement but are concerned in the dispute, shall be given an opportunity of presenting their case before the arbitrator or arbitrators.]

(4) The arbitrator or arbitrators shall investigate the dispute and submit to the appropriate Government the arbitration award signed by the arbitrator or all the arbitrators, as the case may be.

(4-A) Where an industrial dispute has been referred to arbitration and a notification has been issued under sub-section (3-A), the appropriate Government may, by order, prohibit the continuance of any strike or lock-out in connection with such dispute which may be in existence on the date of the reference.]

(5) Nothing in the Arbitration Act, 1940 (10 of 1940), shall apply to arbitrations under this section.

(o) Procedure and Powers of Conciliation Officers, Boards, Courts and Tribunals (S.11)

(1) Subject to any rules that may be made in this behalf, an arbitrator, a Board, Court, Labour Court, Tribunal or National Tribunal shall follow such procedure as the arbitrator or other authority concerned may think fit.]

(2) A conciliation officer or a member of a Board, [or Court or the presiding officer of a Labour Court, Tribunal or National Tribunal] may for the purpose of inquiry into any existing or apprehended industrial dispute, after giving

reasonable notice, enter the premises occupied by any establishment to which the dispute relates.

(3) Every Board, Court, [Labour Court, Tribunal and National Tribunal] shall have the same powers as are vested in a Civil Court under the Code of Civil Procedure, 1908 (5 of 1908), when trying a suit, in respect of the following matters, namely—

(a) enforcing the attendance of any person and examining him on oath;
(b) compelling the production of documents and material objects;
(c) issuing commissions for the examination of witnesses;
(d) in respect of such other matters as may be prescribed;

and every inquiry or investigation by a Board, Court, [Labour Court, Tribunal or National Tribunal], shall be deemed to be a judicial proceeding within the meaning of Sections 193 and 228 of the Indian Penal Code (45 of 1860).

(4) A conciliation officer [may enforce the attendance of any person for the purpose of examination of such person or call for] and inspect any document which he has ground for considering to be relevant to the industrial dispute [or to be necessary for the purpose of verifying the implementation of any award or carrying out any other duty imposed on him under this Act, and for the aforesaid purposes, the conciliation officer shall have the same powers as are vested in a Civil Court under the Code of Civil Procedure, 1908 (5 of 1908), [in respect of enforcing the attendance of any person and examining him or of compelling the production of documents].

(5) A Court, Labour Court, Tribunal or National Tribunal may, if it so thinks fit, appoint one or more persons having special knowledge of the matter under consideration as assessor or assessors to advise it in the proceeding before it.

(6) All conciliation officers, members of a Board or Court and the presiding officers of a Labour Court, Tribunal or National Tribunal shall be deemed to be public servants within the meaning of Section 21 of the Indian Penal Code (45 of 1860).

(7) Subject to any rules made under this Act, the costs of, and incidental to, any proceeding before a Labour Court, Tribunal or National Tribunal shall be in the discretion of that Labour Court, Tribunal or National Tribunal and the Labour Court, Tribunal or National Tribunal, as the case may be, shall have full power to determine by and to whom and to what extent and subject to what conditions, if any, such costs are to be paid, and to give all necessary directions for the purposes aforesaid and such costs may, on application made to the appropriate Government by the person entitled, be recovered by that Government in the same manner as an arrear of land revenue.]

(8) Every Labour Court, Tribunal or National Tribunal shall be deemed to be a civil court for the purposes of Sections 345, 346 and 348 of the code of Criminal Procedure, 1973 (2 of 1974).

Violation of requirement under Section 11(2) of reasonable notice to enter premises does not affect conciliation proceedings.[14] Sub-section (7) of Section 11 gives a discretion to the Tribunal and it has full power to determine by and to whom and to what extent and subject to that conditions, if any, the costs are to be paid. However, the discretion is a judicial discretion and must be exercised according to the rules of reasons and justice—not by chance or caprice or private opinion or some fanciful idea of benevolence or sympathy. The general rule is that costs follow the event unless the Court, for good reason, otherwise orders. The power to order the payment of costs granted under it to industrial tribunals is made comprehensive and is not even fettered by a provision like Section 35(2), CPC. 'Costs of and incidental to' has no reference to costs payable in advance or to be incurred in future by a party, for less do they refer to halting and travelling allowances to be incurred by a party while attending the court on his own behalf. As the Code of Civil Procedure applies to the proceedings before Labour Appellate Tribunal, it has jurisdiction to review its own order under Order XLVII of the CPC. Where the Tribunal has passed orders for inspection of documents in contravention of Order XI, Rules 15 and 18, CPC the order must be set aside.[15]

Quasi-judicial Tribunals like the Industrial Tribunal, not hampered by the rules of evidence applicable to proceedings in a court of law, would be entitled to rely on data available to it, otherwise than from evidence adduced on behalf of the parties and it is not open to the court in an application for an issue of a writ of *certiorari* to go into the matters of the conclusion of the Tribunal.

The Industrial Tribunal and the Labour Court are not bound by technical rules of procedure.[16] Strict rules of pleading governing the proceedings before a civil court do not govern the pleadings before the Labour and Industrial Courts.

The power conferred on the industrial forum for getting the documents produced, is not intended to enable any litigant to embark upon a fishing enquiry, with a hope to search for some material on which reliance could be placed.

(p) Powers of Labour Courts, Tribunals and National Tribunals to give appropriate relief in case of discharge or dismissal of workmen (S. 11-A)

Where an industrial dispute relating to the discharge or dismissal of a workman has been referred to a Labour Court, Tribunal or National Tribunal for adjudication and, in the course of the adjudication proceedings, the Labour Court, Tribunal or National Tribunal, as the case may be, is satisfied

14. State of Bihar *v.* Kripa Shankar Jaiswal, AIR 1961 SC 304; (1961) 1 LLJ 334.
15. Shambhu Nath and Sons Ltd. *v.* Additional Industrial Tribunal, Delhi, 12 FJR 203.
16. Sarva Shramik Sangh *v.* Indian Hume Pipe Co. Ltd., (1993) 2 SCC 386: 1993 SCC (L & S) 627.

that the order of discharge or dismissal was not justified, it may, by its award, set aside the order of discharge or dismissal and direct reinstatement of the workman on such terms and conditions, if any, as it thinks fit, or give such other relief to the workman including the award of any lesser punishment in lieu of discharge or dismissal as the circumstances of the case may require:

> Provided that in any proceeding under this section the Labour Court, Tribunal or National Tribunal, as the case may be, shall rely only on the materials on record and shall not take any fresh evidence in relation to the matter.

In *Hospital Employers* v. *Christian Medical College,*[17] the court held that the powers of Tribunals or Courts under Section 11-A are not arbitrary, unguided and uncanalised.

In *Karnataka SRTC* v. *N. Nagendrappa,*[18] the court held that the power of the Labour Court is not without limitation. It can interfere only when punishment is disproportionate to the proved guilt and it should give reasons in support of its decision. Section 11-A is equally applicable to minority educational institutions, protected under Article 30(1) of the Constitution of India.[19]

Section 11-A applies only to disputes which are referred for adjudication after the section has come into force. It has no retrospective operation.[20]

In *Rama Kant Misra* v. *State of U.P.,* [21] the court held that the Tribunal or the Court has to be satisfied that even though misconduct is proved and a penalty has to be imposed, the extreme penalty of dismissal or discharge was not justified in the facts and circumstances of the case, meaning thereby that the punishment was either disproportionately heavy or excessive. In order to avoid the charge of vindictiveness, justice, equity and fair play demand that punishment must always be commensurate with the gravity of the offence charged.

In *Gujarat SRTC* v. *Danaji Sukaji Kodiyar,*[22] the court held that the Labour Court has jurisdiction to give direction for reinstatement even without back wages.

In *Rajasthan State Road Transport Corporation* v. *Kailash Chand Sharma*[23] the court held that the Labour Court has got no jurisdiction under Section 11-A to interfere with the punishment of removal or substitute it with a lesser punishment in cases of embezzlement or misappropriation of public money.

In *Mohini* v. *General Manager, Syndicate Bank*[24] the court held that the power of the Court or Tribunal under Section 11-A may not be exercisable by the High Court under Article 226 of the Constitution.

17. (1987) 4 SCC 691: 1988 SCC (L & S) 53.
18. (1992) LLJ 168 (Kant.)
19. Hospital Employees' Union *v.* Christian Medical College (1987) 4SCC 691.
20. Workmen *v.* Firestone Tyre & Rubber Co. (1973) SCC (L & S) 341.
21. (1982) 3 SCC 346.
22. (1994) 2 LLJ 1113.
23. (1995) 1 LLJ 268 (Raj.).
24. (1995) 1 LLJ, 351.

In *Rameshwar Manihi* v. *Sangramgarh Colliery*[25], the court held that even in case of an individual dispute under Section 2-A the Tribunal does not become *functus officio* nor does the reference abate merely on account of death of the workman during the pendency of adjudication.

D. ILLEGAL DISMISSAL: REINSTATEMENT WHEN CAN BE REFUSED

In *Workmen* v. *Hindustan Steel Ltd.*[26], the court held that where the findings of misconduct are based on no legal evidence and the conclusion is one to which no reasonable man would come, the arbitrator appointed under Section 10-A or the Supreme Court in appeal under Article 136 can reject the findings as perverse. Holding that the findings are perverse does not constitute reappraisal of evidence, though in exercise of the jurisdiction conferred by Section 11-A both the arbitrator and the Supreme Court can re-appraise the evidence led in the domestic enquiry and satisfy itself whether the evidence led by the employer established misconduct against the workman.[27]

In *Ved Prakash Gupta* v. *Delton Cable India (P) Ltd.*[28], the court held that where the charge against the workman was of abusing a co-worker in filthy language and no previous adverse remarks against the delinquent workman was shown, the extreme penalty of dismissal was disproportionately excessive.

E. DUTIES OF CONCILIATION OFFICERS (S. 12)

(1) Where an industrial dispute exists or is apprehended, the conciliation officer may, or where the dispute relates to a public utility service and a notice under Section 22 has been given, shall, hold conciliation proceedings in the prescribed manner.

(2) The conciliation officer shall, for the purpose of bringing about a settlement of the dispute, without delay, investigate the dispute and all matters affecting the merits and the right settlement thereof and may do all such things as he thinks fit for the purpose of inducing the parties to come to a fair and amicable settlement for the dispute.

(3) If a settlement of the dispute or of any of the matters in a dispute is arrived at in the course of the conciliation proceedings the conciliation officer shall send a report thereof to the appropriate Government or an officer authorized in this behalf by the appropriate Government together with a memorandum of the settlement signed by the parties to the dispute.

(4) If no such settlement is arrived at, the conciliation officer shall, as soon as practicable after the close of the investigation, send to the appropriate Government a full report setting forth the steps taken by him for ascertaining

25. (1994) 1 SCC 292
26. (1984) SUPP SCC (L & S).
27. Rajender Kumar Kindru *v.* Delhi Administration, (1984) 4 SCC 635.
28. (1984) 2 SCC 569

the facts and circumstances relating to the dispute and for bringing about a settlement thereof, together with a full statement of such facts and circumstances, and the reasons on account of which, in his opinion, a settlement could not be arrived at.

(5) If, on a consideration of the report referred to in sub-section (4), the appropriate Government is satisfied that there is a case for reference to a Board, Labour Court, Tribunal or National Tribunal, it may make such reference. Where the appropriate Government does not make such a reference it shall record and communicate to the parties concerned its reasons therefor.

(6) A report under this section shall be submitted within fourteen days of the commencement of the conciliation proceedings or within such shorter period as may be fixed by the appropriate Government.

Provided that, subject to the approval of the conciliation officer, the time for the submission of the report may be extended by such period as may be agreed upon in writing by all the parties to the dispute.

Section 10 is independent of Section 12. It is not necessary that the procedure laid down in Section 12 regarding conciliation proceedings should be complied with before reference is made by the Government under Section 10(1) makes reference. The obligation to refer dispute relating to a public utility service under the proviso to Section 10(1) is independent of duty to refer a dispute under Section 12 (1) because (i) under the proviso a reference may be made, notwithstanding that any other proceedings under the Act have commenced, and (ii) under Section 10(1) the Government need not communicate the reasons while under Section 12(5) it must do so.[29]

F. CONCILIATION PROCEEDINGS AND PROCEDURE

When conciliation proceedings have commenced under Section 12(1) the further procedure enjoined by the Act has to be followed. When no settlement is arrived at, during conciliation proceedings, it is the duty of the appropriate Government to proceed under sub-section (5) of the section either to make a reference or to record and communicate to the parties concerned its reasons for not making reference. Where Government refuses to make reference on irrelevant grounds, Supreme Court in appeal can direct it to perform its statutory duty of making reference.[30]

Where as many as twenty meetings held by the conciliation officer yielded no result, a writ of *mandamus* could be issued to him to forward a failure report to the Government.[31]

A writ of *mandamus* can be issued directing the appropriate Government to discharge the duty cast on them under Section 12(5).

29. Ramchandra Abaji Pawar *v.* State pf Bombay, 4 FJR 93 (Bom HC).
30. Sankari Cement Alai Thozhitalar Munnetra Sangam *v.* Govt. of T. N. (2983) 1 SCC 304: 1983 SCC (L & S) 139.
31. All India Bombay Tyres International Employees' Federation *v.* C.B. Dinagre, 1993 Lab IC 817: (1992) 2 LLN 887: (1992) 2 Cur LR 225 (Bomb).

The Government is entitled to go into *prima facie* merits of dispute for declining whether to refer the same or not. The High Court under Article 226 cannot sit in appeal over Government's order refusing to make a referene.[32] If however a party can show that the refusal to refer a dispute is not *bonafide* or is based on a consideration of wholly irrelevant facts and circumstances a writ of *mandamus* would lie.

G. COMMENCEMENT AND CONCLUSION OF PROCEEDINGS (S. 20)

(1) Conciliation proceedings shall be deemed to have commenced on the date on which a notice of strike or lock-out under Section 22 is received by the conciliation officer or on the date of the order referring the dispute to a Board, as the case may be:

(2) A conciliation proceeding shall be deemed to have concluded—

(a) where a settlement is arrived at, when a memorandum of the settlement is signed by the parties to the dispute;

(b) where no settlement is arrived at, when the report of the conciliation officer is received by the appropriate government or when the report of the Board is published under section 17; as the case may be; or

(c) when a reference is made to a court, Labour Court, Tribunal or National Tribunal under section 10 during the tendency of conciliation proceedings.

(3) Proceedings before an arbitrator under Section 10-A or before a Labour Tribunal or National Tribunal shall be deemed to have commenced on the date of the reference of the dispute for arbitration or adjudication, as the case may be, and such proceedings shall be deemed to have concluded [on the date on which the award becomes enforceable under Section 17-A].

H. CERTAIN MATTERS TO BE KEPT CONFIDENTIAL (S. 21)

There shall not be included in any report or award under this Act any information obtained by a conciliation officer, Board, Court, [Labour Court, Tribunal, National Tribunal or an arbitrator] in the course of any investigation or inquiry as to a trade union or as to any individual business (whether carried on by a person, firm or company) which is not available otherwise than through the evidence given before such officer, Board, Court, [Labour Court, Tribunal, National Tribunal or arbitrator], as the case may be, that such information shall be treated as confidential; nor shall such conciliation officer or any individual member of the Board, [or Court or the presiding officer of the Labour Court, Tribunal or National Tribunal or the arbitrator] or any person present at or concerned in the proceedings disclose any such information without the consent in writing of the secretary of the trade union or the person, firm or company in question, as the case may be:

32. Bombay Union of Journalists *v.* State of Bombay, (1964) 1 LLJ 351.

Provided that nothing contained in this section shall apply to a disclosure of any such information for the purposes of a prosecution under Section 193 of the Indian Penal Code (45 of 1860).

Section 21 does not prevent the inspection of documents by the adversary of the party, who claims them to be confidential but produces them and intends to use them in evidence. The section only prevents a conciliation officer, Board, Court or Tribunal to include in its report or award the contents of any document claimed to be confidential. The Tribunal may, however, without violating the provision of Section 21 take notice of the fact that the profit and loss account in the document discloses loss for the year.[33]

I. STRIKES AND LOCK-OUTS

(a) Prohibition of Strikes and Lock-outs (S. 22)

(1) No person employed in a public utility service shall go on strike in breach of contract:

(a) without giving to the employer notice of strike, as herein after provided, within six weeks before striking; or
(b) within fourteen days of giving such notice; or
(c) before the expiry of the date of strike specified in any such notice as aforesaid; or
(d) during the pendency of any conciliation proceedings before a conciliation officer and seven days after the conclusion of such proceedings.

(2) No employer carrying on any public utility service shall lock-out any of his workmen:

(a) without giving them notice of lock-out as hereinafter provided—within six weeks before locking out; or
(b) within fourteen days of giving such notice; or
(c) before the expiry of the date of lock-out specified in any such notice as aforesaid; or
(d) during the pendency of any conciliation proceedings before a conciliation officer and seven days after the conclusion of such proceedings.

(3) The notice of lock-out or strike under this section shall not be necessary where there is already in existence a strike or, as the case may be, lock-out in the public utility service, but the employer shall send intimation of such lock-out or strike on the day on which it is declared, to such authority as may be specified by the appropriate Government either generally or for a particular area or for a particular class of public utility services.

33. Kanpur Hosiery Workers' Union, Kanpur *v.* The Pakka Hosiery Mills, Kanpur, 1952 LAC 19 (LAT).

(4) The notice of strike referred to in sub-section (1) shall be given by such number of persons or persons and in such manner as may be prescribed.

(5) The notice of lock-out referred to in sub-section (2) shall be given in such manner as may be prescribed.

(6) If on any day an employer receives from any person employed by him any such notices as are referred to in sub-section (1) or gives to any persons employed by him any such notices as are referred to in sub-section (2), he shall within five days thereof report to the appropriate Government or to such authority as that Government may prescribe, the number of such notices received or given on that day.

The legality of the strike depends on the provisions of Section 22 in the case of a public utility service and the question whether it was provoked or not in immaterial.

In *Ramnagar Cane & Sugar Co.* v. *Jain Chakravarty*,[34] the court held that during pendency of conciliation proceedings between public utility concern and one of its unions, strike by another union of the same concern, held, illegal.

(b) General Prohibition of Strikes and Lock-outs (S. 23)

No workman who is employed in any industrial establishment shall go on strike in breach of contract and no employer of any such workman shall declare a lock-out;

(a) during the pendency of conciliation proceedings before a Board and seven days after the conclusion of such proceedings;

(b) during the pendency of proceedings before [a Labour Court, Tribunal or National Tribunal] and two months after the conclusion of such proceedings;

(bb) during the pendency of arbitration proceedings before an arbitration and two months after the conclusion of such proceedings, where a notification has been issued under sub-section (3-A) of Section 10-A; or]

(c) during any period in which a settlement or award is in operation in respect of any of the matters covered by the settlement or award

(c) Illegal Strikes and Lock-out (S. 24)

(1) A strike or a lock-out shall be illegal if—

(i) it is commenced or declared in contravention of Section 22 or Section 23; or

(ii) it is continued in contravention of an order made under sub-section (3) of Section 10 [or sub-Section (4A) of Section 10-A].

(2) Where a strike or lock-out in pursuance of an industrial dispute has already commenced and is in existence at the time of the reference of the

34. AIR 1960 SC 1012: (1961) 1 LLJ 244.

dispute to a Board, [an arbitrator, a] [Labour Court, Tribunal or National Tribunal], the continuance of such strike or lock-out shall not be deemed to be illegal, provided that such strike or lock-out was not at its commencement in contravention of the provisions of this Act or the continuance thereof was not prohibited under sub-section (3) of Section 10 [or sub-section (4-a) of Section 10-A].

(3) A lock-out declared in consequence of an illegal strike or a strike declared in consequence of an illegal lock-out shall not be deemed to be illegal.

Legal lock-out does not give a licence to the management to act unreasonably. Where a strike is unjustified and it is followed by a lock-out which becomes unjustified a case of apportionment of blame arises. Illegal strike cannot be half legitimate. Mere breach of standing order cannot render strike illegal.[35]

In *Nellimarla Jute Mills Karmika Sangham* v. *State of Andhra Pradesh,*[36] the court held that the lock-out is declared to be illegal, the principle of 'no work no pay' does not apply.

J. LAY-OFF AND RETRENCHMENT

(a) Definition of Continuous Service (S. 25-B)

For the purpose of this chapter:

(1) a workman shall be said to be in continuous service for a period if he is, for that period, uninterrupted service, including service which may be interrupted on account of sickness or authorized leave or an accident or a strike which is not illegal, or a lock-out or a cession of work which is not due to any fault on the part of the workman;

(2) where a workman is not in continuous service within the meaning of clause (1) for a period of one year or six months, he shall be deemed to be in continuous service under an employer—

(a) for a period of one year, if the workman, during a period of twelve calendar months preceding the date with reference to which calculation is to be made, has actually worked under the employer for not less than—
   (i) one hundred and ninety days in the case of a workman employed below ground in a mine; and
   (ii) two hundred and forty days, in any other case;

(b) for a period of six months, if the workman, during a period of six calendar months preceding the date with reference to which calculation is to be made, has actually worked under the employer for not less than—

35. India Marine Service (P) Ltd. *v.* Workmen, (1963) 1 LLJ 122, Chandramalai Estate *v.* Workmen, (Workmen), (1960) 3 SCR 451: (1960) 2 LLJ 243.
36. 1995 Lab IC 1041 (AP).

(i) ninety-five days, in the case of a workman employed below ground in a mine; and in the

(ii) one hundred and twenty days, in any other case.

Explanation: For the purpose of clause (2), the number of days on which a workman has actually worked under an employer shall include the days on which—

(i) he has been laid-off under an agreement or as permitted by standing orders made under the Industrial Employment (Standing Orders) Act, 1946 (20 of 1946), or under this Act or under any other law applicable to the industrial establishment;

(ii) he has been on leave with full wages, earned in the previous year;

(iii) he has been absent due to temporary disablement cause by accident arising out of and in the course of his employment; and

(iv) in the case of a female, she has been on maternity leave; so however, that the total period of such maternity leave does not exceed twelve weeks].

In *Sur Enamel & Stamping Works Ltd.* v. *Workmen,*[37] the court held that when a temporary employee is re-appointed on a fresh basis then his previous service cannot be taken into consideration. Service for 240 days in a period of 12 calendar months is equal not only to service for a year but is to be deemed continuous service even if interrupted.[38] The period of 240 days need not be in the same service in the same capacity.[39]

In computing 240 days' service notional breaks of service cannot be ignored.[40]

In *Ramakrishna Ram Nath* v. *Presiding Officer, Labour Court,*[41] the court held that a workman after satisfying the test under Section 25-B need not further show that he has worked during all the period he has been in the service of the employer for 240 days in a year.

(b) Right of Workmen Laid-Off for Compensation (S. 25-C)

Whenever a workman (other than a *badli* workman or a casual workman) whose name is borne on the muster-rolls of an industrial establishment and who has completed not less than one year of continuous service under an employer is laid-off, whether continuously or intermittently, he shall be paid by the employer for all days during which he is so laid-off, except for such weekly holidays as may intervene, compensation which shall be equal to fifty per cent of the total of the basic wages and dearness allowance that would have been payable to him had he not been so laid-off:

37. (1964) 3 SCR 616: (1963) 2 LLJ 367.
38. Digwadih Colliery *v.* Workmen, AIR 1956 SC 75: (1965) 2 (LLJ 118).
39. Prabhu Dayal Jat *v.* Alwar Sahakari Bhumi Vikas Bank Ltd., 1991 Lab IC 944: (1991) 2 LLJ 130: (1991) 2 Cr LR 526 (Raj) (DB).
40. Eicher Goodearth *v.* Industrial Tribunal, (1986) 1 LLN 219 (P & H).
41. (1985) 3 SCC 67.

Provided that if during any period of twelve months, a workman is so laid-off for more than forty-five days, no such compensation shall be payable in respect of any period of the lay-off after the expiry of the first forty-five days, if there is an agreement to that effect between the workman and the employer:

Provided further that it shall be lawful for the employer in any case falling within the foregoing proviso to retrench the workman in accordance with the provisions contained in Section 25-F at any time after the expiry of the first forty-five days of the lay-off and when he does so, any compensation paid to the workman for having been laid-off during the preceding twelve months may be set-off against the compensation payable for retrenchment.

Explanation: "Badi workman means a workman who is employed in an industrial establishment in the place of another workman whose name is borne on the muster-rolls of the establishment, but shall cease to be regarded as such for the purposes of this section, if he has completed one year of continuous service in the establishment.

(c) Duty of an Employer to Maintain Muster-Rolls of Workmen (S. 25-D)

Notwithstanding that workmen in any industrial establishment have been laid-off, it shall be the duty of every employer to maintain for the purposes of this Chapter a muster-roll, and to provide for the making of entries therein by workmen who may present themselves for work at the establishment at the appointed time during normal working hours.

Workmen Not Entitled to Compensation in Certain Cases (S. 25-E)

No compensation shall be paid to a workman who has been laid off—

(i) If he refuses to accept any alternative employment in the same establishment from which he had been laid-off, or in any other establishment belonging to the same employer situate in the same town or village or situate within a radius of five miles from the establishment to which he belongs, if, in the opinion of the employer, such alternative employment does not call for any special skill or previous experience and can be done by the workman, provided that the wages which would normally have been paid to the workman are offered for the alternative employment also;

(ii) If he does not present himself for work at the establishment at the appointed time during normal working hours at least once a day.

(iii) If such laying-off is due to the strike or slowing-down of production on the part of the workmen in another part of the establishment.

(d) Conditions Precedent to Retrenchment of Workmen (S. 25-F)

No workman employed in any industry who has been in continuous service for not less than one year under an employer shall be retrenched by that employer until—

(a) the workman has been given one month's notice in writing indicating the reasons for retrenchment and the period of notice has expired, or the workman has been paid in lieu of such notice, wages for the period of the notice;

(b) the workman has been paid, at the time of retrenchment, compensation which shall be equivalent to fifteen days' average pay [or every completed year of continuous service] or any part thereof in excess of six months; and

(c) notice in the prescribed manner is served on the appropriate Government [or such authority as may be specified by the appropriate Government by notification in the Official Gazette].

In *Automobiles Coop. Workshop Ltd.* v. *Jethmal Aggarwal,*[42] the court held that the payment of retrenchment compensation by cheque along with the order of termination, even though the cheque could not be encased on the same day, satisfied the requirement of simultaneous payment. Section 25-F is applicable to *ad hoc* temporary employees also, if they have worked for more than 240 days in a year continuously immediately preceding the order of termination of service.

(e) Procedure for Retrenchment (S. 25-G)

Where any workman in an industrial establishment, who is a citizen of India, is to be retrenched and he belongs to a particular category of workmen in that establishment, in the absence of any agreement between the employer and the workman in this behalf, the employer shall ordinarily retrench the workman who was the last person to be employed in that category, unless for reasons to be recorded the employer retrenches any other workman.

Departure forms the 'last come first go' rule is permissible on valid and justifiable grounds. Burden is on the management to prove existence of such ground. Grade-wise classification of women will not create different categories so as to exclude operation of Section 25-G in case of retrenchment of some of the workmen falling under a different grade.[43] The provisions of Section 25-G are directory but a departure from the principle of last come first go can be made only for sufficient grounds.

K. CONDITIONS OF SERVICE, ETC. TO REMAIN UNCHANGED UNDER CERTAIN CIRCUMSTANCES DURING PENDENCY OF PROCEEDINGS (S. 33)

(1) During the pendency of any conciliation proceedings before a conciliation officer or a Board or of any proceeding before [an arbitrator or] a Labour Court or Tribunal or National Tribunal in respect of an industrial dispute, no employer shall,—

42. (1993) 2 LLJ 62 (1993) 66 FLR 711: (1993) 1 Cur LR 264.

43. Workmen *v.* Jorhaut Tea Co. Ltd., (1980) 3 SCC 406: 1980 SCC (L & S) 427.

(a) In regard to any matter connected with the dispute, alter, to the prejudice of the workmen concerned in such dispute, the conditions of service applicable to them immediately before the commencement of such proceedings; or
(b) For any misconduct connected with the dispute, discharge or punish, whether by dismissal or otherwise, any workmen concerned in such dispute, save with the express permission in writing of the authority before with the proceeding is pending.

(2) During the pendency of any such proceeding in respect of an industrial dispute, the employer may, in accordance with the standing orders applicable to a workman concerned in such dispute [for, where there are no such standing orders, in accordance with the terms of the contract, whether express or implied, between him and the workman],—

(a) alter, in regard to any matter not connected with the dispute, the conditions of service applicable to that workman immediately before the commencement of such proceeding; or
(b) for any misconduct not connected with the dispute, discharge or punish, whether by dismissal or otherwise, that workman:
Provided that no such workman shall be discharged or dismissed, unless he has been paid wages for one month and an application has been made by the employer to the authority before which the proceeding is pending for approval of the action taken by the employer.

(1) Notwithstanding anything contained in sub-section (2), no employer shall during the pendency of any such proceeding in respect of an industrial dispute, take any action against any protected workman concerned in such dispute—

(a) by altering, to the prejudice of such protected workman, the conditions of service applicable to him immediately before the commencement of such proceedings; and
(b) by discharging or punishing whether by dismissal or otherwise, such protected workman save with the express permission in writing of the authority before which the proceeding is pending.

Explanation: For the purposes of this sub-section, a "protected workman", in relation to an establishment, means a workman who, being [a member of the executive or other officer-bearer) of a registered trade union connected with the establishment, in recognized as such in accordance with rules made in this behalf.

(4) In every establishment, the number of workmen to be recognized as protected workmen for the purposes of sub-section (3) shall be one per cent of the total number of workmen employed therein subject to a minimum number of five protected workmen and a maximum number of one hundred protected workmen and for aforesaid purpose, the appropriate Government may make rules providing for the distribution of such protected workmen among various trade unions, if any, connected with the establishment and

the manner in which the workmen may be chosen and recognized as protected workmen.

(5) Where an employer makes an application to a conciliation officer, Board, an arbitrator, a Labour Court, Tribunal or National Tribunal under the proviso to sub-section (2) for approval of the action taken by him, the authority concerned shall, without delay, hear such application and pass, [within a period of three months from the date of receipt of such application, such order in relation thereto at it deems fit.]

> Provided that where any such authority considers it necessary or expedient so to do, it may, for reasons to be recorded in writing, extend such period by such further period as it may think fit:
> Provided further that no proceedings before any such authority shall lapse merely on the ground that any period specified in this sub-section had expired without such proceedings being completed.]

(a) Special provision for adjudication as to whether conditions of service, etc., changed during pendency of proceedings (S. 33-A)

Where an employer contravenes, the provisions of Section 33 during the pendency of proceedings [before a conciliation officer, Board, an arbitrator, a Labour Court, Tribunal or National Tribunal}. Any employee aggrieved by such contravention, may make a complaint in writing, [in the prescribed manner.

(a) to such conciliation officer or Board, and the conciliation officer or Board shall take such complaint into account in mediating in, and promoting the settlement of, such industrial dispute; and

(b) to such arbitrator, Labour Court, Tribunal or National Tribunal and on receipt of such complaint, the arbitrator, Labour Court, Tribunal or National Tribunal, as the case may be, shall adjudicate upon the complaint as if it were a dispute referred to or pending before it, in accordance with the provisions of this Act and shall submit his or its award to the appropriate Government and the provisions of this Act shall apply accordingly.]

L. RECOVERY OF MONEY DUE FROM AN EMPLOYER (S. 33-C)

(1) Where any money due to a workman from an employer under a settlement or an award or under the provisions of [Chapter V-A or Chapter V-B], the workman himself or any other person authorized by him in writing in this behalf, or, in the case of the death of the workman, his assignee or heirs may, without prejudice to any other mode of recovery, make an application to the appropriate Government is satisfied that any money is so due, it shall issue a certificate for that amount to the collector who shall proceed to recover the same in the same manner as an arrear of land revenue:

Provided that every such application shall be made within one year from the date on which the money became due to the workman from the employer:
Provided further that any such application may be entertained after the expiry of the said period of one year, if the appropriate Government is satisfied that the applicant had sufficient cause for not making the application within the said period.

(2) Where any workman is entitled to receive from the employer any money and if any question arises as to amount of money due or as to the amount at which such benefit should be computed, then the question may, subject to any rules that may be made under this Act, be decided by such Labour Court as may be specified in this behalf by the appropriate Government within a period not exceeding three months.

[Provided that where the presiding officer of a Labour Court considers it necessary or expedient so to do, he may, for reasons to be recorded in writing, extend such period by such further period as he may think fit.]

(3) For the purposes of computing the money value of a benefit, the Labour Court may, if it so thinks fit, appoint a Commissioner who shall, after taking such evidence as may be necessary, submit a report to the Labour Court and the Labour Court shall determine the amount after considering the report of the Commissioner and other circumstances of the case.

(4) The decision of the Labour Court shall be forwarded by it to the appropriate Government and any amount found due by the Labour Court may be recovered in the manner provided for a sub-section (1).

(5) Where workmen employed under the same employer are entitled to receive from him any money or any benefit capable of being computed in terms of money, then, subject to such rules as may be made in this behalf, a single application for the recovery of the amount due may be made on behalf of or in respect of any number of such workmen.

Explanation: In this section "Labour Court" includes any court constituted under any law relating to investigation and settlement of industrial disputes in force in any State.

In *Reserve Bank of India* v. *Bhopal Singh Panchal,*[44] the court held that a disputed question about entitlement to full pay and allowances for the period of deemed suspension due to involvement in criminal case till reinstatement on acquittal, is beyond the scope of Section 33-C(2). A dispute question about entitlement to full pay and allowances for the period in respect of which he claims relief, even though he is no longer employed at the time of the application.[45]

44. (1994) 1 SCC 54: 1994 (L & S) 594: (1994) 26 ATC 619.
45. National Building Construction Corpn. *v.* Pritam Singh Gill, (1972) 2 SSC 1

13

The Payment of Wages Act, 1936

A. INTRODUCTION

The Payment of Wages Act is designed to secure payment of wages to the employees on due dates and expeditions disposal of claims relating to wages or any portion thereof wrongly withheld. It provides for payment of wages to employees at regular intervals without any unauthorised deductions.

The Act extends to the whole of India and applies to "factories" covered by the Factories Act, 1948 and to the following industrial establishments[1]:

(a) Tramway service or motor transport service engages in carrying passengers or goods or both, by road for hire or reward.
(b) Air transport service other than such service belonging to or exclusively employed in the military, naval or air forces of the Government of India or the Civil Aviation Department of the Central Government.
(c) Dock, Wharf, or Jetty.
(d) Inland Vessel, Mechanically propelled.
(e) Mines or quarries covered by the Mines Act, 1952 and oil field.
(f) Plantations covered by the Plantation Labour Act, 1951.
(g) Workshop or other establishment, in which articles are produced, adopted or manufactured, with a view to their use, transport or sale.
(h) Establishments in which any work relating to the construction development or maintenance of buildings, roads, bridges or canals, or relating to operations corrected with navigation, irrigation or supply of water or relating to the generation, transmission and distribution of electricity or any other form of power is being carried on.
(i) Railway administration covered by the Indian Railways Act, 1890 and contractors fulfilling a contract with the Railway Administration.

Section 1(5) of the Act empowers the state Governments power to extend the provisions of the Act to any class of persons employed in any industrial establishments, or class or group of industrial establishments, after giving three months notice of their intention to do so, in the official Gazette. Where,

1. See, National Council for Co-operative Training of NCUI, Legal Aspects, (1994) at 39.

however, the extension covers any industrial undertaking owned by the Central Government with objects not confined to one state, any such notification can be issued only in consultation with the Central Government[2].

The Act now covers all persons in covered establishments drawing "wages" upto Rs. 1000 per month[3].

B. DEFINITION OF WAGES (SEC. 2 (VI))

"Wages" means all remuneration (whether by way of salary, allowances or otherwise) expressed in terms of money or capable of being so expressed which would, if the terms of employment, express or implied, were fulfilled, be payable to a person employed in respect of his employment or of work done in such employment and includes:

(a) any remuneration payable under any award or settlement between the parties or order of a court;

(b) any remuneration to which the person employed is entitled in respect of overtime work or holidays or any leave period;

(c) any additional remuneration payable under the terms of employment (whether called a bonus or by any other name);

(d) any sum which by reason of termination of employment of the person employed is payable under any law, contract or instrument which provides for the payment of such sum, whether with or without deductions, but does not provide for the time within which the payment is to be made;

(e) any sum to which the person employed is entitled under any scheme framed under any law for the time being in force; but does not include:

  (i) any bonus (whether under a scheme of profit-sharing or otherwise) which does not form part of remuneration payable under the terms of employment or which is not payable under any award or settlement between the parties or order of a court;

  (ii) the value of any house-accommodation, or of the supply of light, water, medical attendance or other amenity or of any service excluded from the computation of wages by a general or special order of the State Government;

  (iii) any contribution paid by the employer to any pension or provident fund, and the interest which may have accrued thereon;

  (iv) any travelling allowance or the value of any travelling concession;

  (v) any sum paid to the employed person to defray special expenses entitled on him by the nature of his employment; or

  (vi) any gratuity payable on the termination of employment in cases other than those specified in sub-clause (d).

---

2. *Ibid.*
3. The Original Coverage of up to Rs. 200 p.m. was extended to Rs. 400 p.m. by Amendment Act, 68 of 1957 and further extended to Rs. 1000 by ordinance dated 12.11.75 ratified by Amendment Act, 1976.

Wages are the remunerations payable according to the terms of contract and rules framed by the Government for payment of allowances to its employees which must be included in the term of contract. Whether house rent in wages, depends upon the terms of the contract. It is so, if its payment is compulsory otherwise not[4].

The subsistence allowance is an allowance payable under section 10-A of the Industrial Employment (Standing Orders) Act, 1946, which is a term of employment. Hence, subsistence allowance falls within the definition of wages[5].

The remuneration payable to a workman which is 'wages' as defined by Section 2(vi) of the Payment of Wages Act, does not cease to be 'wages' so defined merely because the wage-period, on the basis of which remuneration is calculated, is a month.[6]

The amount of bonus payable under the Bonus Act, 1965 would be covered within the definition of 'wages' as defined in the Payment of Wages Act[7].

C. PAYMENT OF WAGES (Ss. 3-6)

It is the responsibility of the manager of a factory or in the case of an industrial establishment of the person in control of that establishment, to pay wages on the due date. The wage period shall be fixed and notified in the establishment daily, weekly, fortnightly or monthly, as the case may be. A Register of wages must be maintained giving particulars of the gross wages for the wage period the total of all deductions made therefrom, and the actual wages paid to each person, the date of payment, and bear the signature or thumb impression of the wage respective employees. The wages in respect of any month must be paid on or before the 7th of the subsequent month in the case of establishments where in less than 1000 workers are employed; where, however, the services of an employed person are terminate, the wages due to him/her shall be paid before the expiry of two working days from the date of termination. Wages have to be paid in current coins or currency notes or both. By the 1976 Amendment Act, which came into force on 12-11-1975, in accordance with the proviso to Section 6, the employer may, after obtaining the authorisation of the employed person, pay the wages either by a cheque or by crediting the wages in his bank account.[8]

D. DEDUCTION FROM WAGES (S. 7)

Deduction could be made from wages in respect of fines, for absence from duty, for damages or loss of goods expressly entrusted to the employed

4. See, P.L. Malik, *'Hand Book of Labour and Industrial Law'* (1996) at 765.
5. India Leaf Spring Manufacturing Company (P) Ltd. *v.* Appellate, authority under Payment of Wages Act, (1993) ILLN 105 (A.P.)
6. Modern Printing Press *v.* Brijnandan Baj Pal, (1960) ILLJ 182.
7. Junior Labour Inspector *v.* Appellate Authority, (1976) ILLJ.
8. See, *Supra* Note 1 at 41.

person or loss of money or which he is required to account, where such loss or damage is directly attributable to his neglect or default; for house accommodation or other amenities supplied by the employer, recovery of advance or loans, Income Tax, Profession Tax, deduction made in accordance with a court order, contributions to provident fund or E.S.I.S., payment cooperatives stores credit society, Insurance premium in the case of Salary Savings policies or premium on fidelity Guarantee Bonds and deductions made with the written authorisation towards purchase of state or central government Securities or for being deposited in the post office in furtherance of any savings scheme of Government etc[9]. The total deductions shall not exceed 75% of an employed normal gross wages earned[10]. By the Amendment Act of 1976, deduction, with the written authorisation of an employee, could also be made for contribution to the Prime Minister's National Relief Fund or to such other fund as the Central Government, by notification, specify[11].

If 10 or more persons acting in concert absent themselves without due notice and without reasonable cause, or being present in the work spot refuse to carry out their normal work insurance of a "Stay-in-Strike", or for any other cause, which is not reasonable in the circumstances, the employees will render themselves liable to a deduction from their earned wages of an amount not exceeding eight days wages. In all other cases, deduction for absence shall be made on proportionate basis.

In respect of fines, after obtaining the approval of the state government, the employer should publish as notice specifying acts or omissions in respect of which fines shall be imposed. No fine shall be imposed without a proper enquiry and giving an opportunity to the employee for showing cause way the fine should not be imposed. The maximum fine that can be imposed is limited to 3% of wages and cannot be recovered after the expiry of 60 days from the date on which it is imposed.

Deduction for damages or loss shall be maintained in a Register in Form II Prescribed under the Tamil Nadu Payment of Wages Rules[12].

Any agreement or contract by which an employee agrees to any deduction other than those authorized under the Act would be null and void[13] by virtue of Section 13. Deductions can be made for voluntary absence from duty of the employee and absence from duty between the period of his dismissal and his reinstatement is not a voluntary act on his part and no deduction can therefore be made. The Indian Railway Establishment Code is a body of statutory rules under Article 309, read with Article 372 of the constitution.

'Deduction from Wages' has not been defined in the Act. Some illustrations of such deduction are, however, to be found in Sections 7 to 13. One of them

9. For Notices, Registers and Returns, Pl. See, Rules of *Ibid.* Act.
10. Withholding of increment at the efficiency bar, reduction to a lower rank or time scale, or suspension for a good and sufficient cause, shall not be deemed to be deduction from wages.
11. *Id.*, at 42
12. *Ibid.*
13. Armugham *v.* Jawahar Mills, AIR 1956. Mad. 79.

in section 7(2) (b) is 'deductions for absence from duty', which indicates that such a deduction can be total deduction also. That is to say, 'deduction from wages' may be the same thing as 'deduction from wages[14].' Section 7(2) enumerates the permissible deductions and not any obligatory deductions[15].

In *Chandra Sekhar Banerjee*[16] case the court held that even where the terms of contract stipulated that in case of non-utilisation of the building loans the entire amount would become repayable immediately together with interest, paying the debtor-employee a salary of Rs. 5 only and deducting the remaining part has been held to be arbitrary[17].

E. CLAIMS ARISING OUT OF DEDUCTION FROM WAGES OR DELAY IN PAYMENT OF WAGES (Ss. 15-16)

The State Government has been authorized to appoint Presiding Officers of Labour Courts or Industrial Tribunals constituted under the Industrial Disputes Act, 1947, or any commissioner appointed under the Workmen's Compensation Act, to bear and decide claims arising out of deducting from wages or delay in payment of wages. Any such applications must be submitted within 12 months of the cause of the action, provided however, where the authority is satisfied on an application made by the petitioner giving reasons for the delay, the application may be admitted by such Authority, condoning the delay. Any enquiry by the authority shall be deemed judicial proceedings. The amount awarded by the authority can be recovered from the employer in the same manner as a fine imposed by a magistrate[18]. The affected workers can make the application to the authority under section 16.

An application beyond time should be admitted only after hearing the opposite party. Admission should be conscious[19]. In *Sita Ram Charan*[20] case the court held that the point of sufficiency of cause is to be directed by proper legal principles. There is a clear distinction between ignorance of laws and mistake of law... Where there is a mistake of law the delay should be excused, but ignorance of law does not constitute sufficient cause and it cannot be interfered with under Articles 226 and 227 of the constitution[21]. The Madras High Court in *Armugam* v. *Javahar Mills*[22] held that the expression "delayed wages" can only means wages admitted due but the payment of which has been postponed on some excuse or other.

14. Dilbagh Rai Jarry *v.* Union of India, (1974) 3 SCC, 554.
15. Hill Plantation Workers, Union *v.* Anamalai Plantars' Association, (1987) ILLN 249 (Mad.)
16. Chander Sekhar Banerjee *v.* Union of India, (1995) Lab. IC 1305 (Cal.)
17. See *Supra* Note 4 at 765.
18. See *Supra* Note 1 at 43.
19. See *Supra* Note 4 at 774.
20. Seetaram Ramcharan *v.* M.N. Nagrashna, AIR 1954, Bom. 537.
21. Ramla Sahkari Chini Mills Ltd. Payment of Wages Act, 1995 ILLJ 90.
22. 1956 ILLJ, 519.

F. JURISDICTION OF THE AUTHORITY

Under this Section the authority is a tribunal of limited Jurisdiction and it cannot determine any controversy, which is not in its ambit within the provisions[23]. The authority under the Act can only decide claims regarding deductions alleged to have been made contrary to the provisions of the Act and cannot adjudicate upon any dispute regarding wages[24].

In *Payment of Wages Inspector* v. *Surajmal Mehta*[25], it has been held that the authority has the Jurisdiction to determine the actual wages but not the potential wages. The Jurisdiction of the authority really is to determine the terms of contract in so far as they relate to the payment of wages and in so far as he has to declare the liability of the employer to pay wages under the terms of the contract. But that Jurisdiction does not extend to determining the question as to whether that contract has terminated as alleged by the employer or the contract still subsists as alleged by the servant.

In *H. Watts Case*[26] the court has held that the Additional Magistrate has Jurisdiction to entertain and decide cases of delay and deduction of wages under this act.

G. RETRENCHMENT COMPENSATION

The Supreme Court of India has held any claim under Section 25F, 25FF, 25FFF of the Industrial Disputes Act should be taken up under section 33-C of the Industrial Dispute Act and not under the Payment of Wages Act[27].

H. APPEALS (S. 17)

The Payment of Wages Authority is not an authority within the meaning of section 19(1) (a) of the Administrative Tribunals Act, 1985 nor is an order passed by it Under Section 15(3) of the Payment of Wages Act, a service matter within Section 3(q) of the Tribunal Act. Hence, such an order of that Authority can be challenged by an appeal Under the Payment of Wages Act and not by an application Under Section 19 of the Tribunal Act[28].

By virtue of section 28 of the Administrative Tribunal Act, the Jurisdiction of the appellate authority Under Section 17 of the Payment of Wages Act remains undistributed by the establishment of Administrative Tribunals. Consequently, an appeal contemplated Under Section 17 would neither stand transferred to, nor can be filed before, the Administrative Tribunal[29].

23. A.V.D. Costa *v.* B.C. Patel, IR (1955) SC 412.
24. Raj Kumar Mills *v.* Inspector, P.W.N.B., AIR 1955 MB, 60.
25. (1969) ISCC 52.
26. H. Watts *v.* B.N. Rai, AIR 1960 All. 200.
27. Payment of Wages Inspector, Ujjain *v.* Surajmal Mehta and others, 1959 ILLJ, 762.
28. General Manager, Western Railway *v.* Authority under Payment of Wages Act, (1994) ILLJ 1066 Raj. Quoted in *Supra* Note 4 at 780.
29. Krisan Prasad Gupta *v.* Controller, Printing and Stationary, (1996) 1 SCC.

For the purpose of fixing the pecuniary limit for the right of appeal under Section 17(1) (a) the total amount awarded in a single application is the guiding factor[30].

In orde that an employee may have a right to appeal in two conditions are necessary, firstly, the petition must be entertained by the authority and, secondly, a refusal to give direction on merits. If after entertainment the application the authority holds that it has no jurisdiction it is not refusal to give direction and the applicant has no right to appeal. The only remedy is to approach the High Court to compel the authority to assume Jurisdiction[31].

An appeal Under Section 17 must be preferred within limit from the date of the direction sought to be appealed against. This period cannot be extended for any sufficient cause under the provisions of Section 5, Limitation Act, the act not having been made applicable to such an appeal. The provisions of sections 6-8, 19-81. Limitation Act, will also not apply, while the provisions contained in Sections 4, 9 to 12 and 22 will apply to such appeals. Thus, the time spent in obtaining a copy of the directions sought to be appealed against shall be excluded[32]. An appeal under section 17 cannot be dismissed for non-prosecution[33].

Unless the amount involved exceeds Rs. 300 an employer cannot prefer an appeal against the decision of the payment of wages authority; in the case of a workman, the amount involved should be not less than Rs. 25 or in the case of a body of workmen or group Rs. 50.

30. See *Supra* Note 26 at 20.
31. C.S. Lal *v.* Sheikh, Badshah, AIR 1955 Bom. 75.
32. Section 12, Limitation Act, 1879, 4 AC 504.
33. Jai Prakash *v.* Seventh Addl. District Judge (1985) 2 LLN 93 (All.)

14

Workmen's Compensation Act, 1923

A. INTRODUCTION

The growing complexity of industry in this country, with the increasing use of machinery and consequent danger to workmen, along with the comparative poverty of the workmen themselves renders it advisable that they should be protected as far as possible, from hardship arising from accidents. A legislation of this kind helps to reduce the number of accidents. In a manner that cannot be achieved by official inspection and to mitigate the effect of accidents by provision for suitable medical treatment, thereby making industry more attractive to labour and increasing its efficiency. The act provides for cheaper and quicker disposal of disputes relating to compensation through special tribunals then possible under the civil law.[1]

An act to provide for the payment by certain classes of employers to their workmen of compensation for injury by accident. The act extends to the whole of India.

B. WORKMEN'S COMPENSATION

(a) Employer's Liability for Compensation

(1) If personal injury is caused to a workman by accident arising out of and in the course of his employment, his employer shall be liable to pay compensation in accordance with the provision of this chapter.

Provided that the employer shall not be so liable—

(a) In respect of any injury which does not result in the total or partial disablement of the workman for a period exceeding three days.

(b) In respect of any injury, not resulting in death or permanent total disablement caused by an accident which is directly attributed to—

   (i) The workman having been at the time therefore under the influence of drink of drugs, or

   (ii) The wilful disobedience of the workman to an order expressly given, or to a rule expressly framed, for the purpose of securing the safety of workman, or

1. P.L. Malik, *"Handbook of Labour and Industrial Law,"* (1976) at 862.

(iii) The wilful removal or disregard by the workman of any safety guard or other device which he knew to have been provided for the purpose of securing the safety of workmen.

(2) If a workman employed in any employment specified in Part A of Schedule III contracts any disease specified therein as an occupational disease peculiar to that employment, or if a workman, whilst in the service of an employer in whose service he has been employed for a continuous period of not less than six months which period shall not include a period of service under any other employer in the same kind of employment in any employment specified in Part B of Schedule III, contracts any disease specified therein as an occupational disease peculiar to that employment, or if a workman whilst in the service of one or more employers in any employment specified in Part C of Schedule III for such continuous period as the Central Government may specify in respect of each such employment, contracts any disease specified therein as an occupational disease peculiar to that employment, the contracting of the disease shall be deemed to be an injury by accident within the meaning of this section and, unless the contrary is proved, the accident shall be deemed to have arisen out of, and in the course of, the employment.

Provided that if it is proved—

that a workman whilst in the service of one or more employers in any employment specified in Part C of Schedule III has contracted a disease specified therein as an occupational disease peculiar to that employment during a continuous period which is less than the period specified under this sub-section for that employment, and

that the disease has arisen out of and in the course of the employment; the contracting of such disease shall be deemed to be an injury by accident within the meaning of this section:

Provided further that if it is proved that a workman who having served under any employer in any employment specified in Part B of Schedule III or who having served under one or more employers in any employment specified in Part C of that Schedule, for a continuous period specified under this sub-section for that employment and he has after the cessation of such service contracted any disease specified, in the said Part B or the said Part C, as the case may be, as an occupational disease contracting of the disease shall be deemed to be an injury by accident within the meaning of this section.

(2-A) If a workman employed in any employment specified in Part C of Schedule III contracts any occupational disease peculiar to that employment, the contracting whereof is deemed to be an injury by accident within the meaning of this section, and such employment was under more than one employer, all such employers shall be liable for the payment of the compensation in such proportion as the Commissioner may, in circumstances, deem just.

(3) The Central Government or the State Government, after giving, by notification in the official Gazette, not less than three months notice of its intention so to do, may, by like notification, add by description of employment to the employment specified in Schedule III, and shall specify in the case of employments so added the diseases which shall be deemed for the purposes of this section to be occupational diseases peculiar to those employments respectively and thereupon the provisions of sub-section (2) shall apply, in the case of a notification by the Central Government, within the territories to which this Act extends or, in case of a notification by the State Government, within the State as if such diseases had been declared by this Act to be occupational diseases peculiar to those employments.

(4) Save as provided by [sub-sections (2), (2-A)] and (3), no compensation shall be payable to a workman in respect of any disease unless the disease is directly attributable to a specific injury by accident arising out of and in the course of his employment.

(5) Nothing herein contained shall be deemed to confer any right to compensation on a workman in respect of any injury if he has instituted in a Civil Court a suit for damages in respect of the injury against the employer or any other person; and no suit for damages shall be maintainable by a workman in any court of law in respect of any injury—

(a) if he has instituted a claim to compensation in respect of the injury before a Commissioner; or
(b) if an agreement has been come to between the workman and his employer providing for the payment of compensation in respect of the injury in accordance with the provisions of this act.

The burden of proving that the accident arose out of employment is upon the workman. Where a worker was stabbed on his way to work and there was no motive behind the murder, held that the accident arose out of employment. Where a workman leaves an employer and he alleges that he contracted disease under employment of previous master, the burden of proof is upon him. Although the onus of proving that the injury by accident arose both out of and in the course of employment rests upon the applicant, these essentials may be inferred when the facts proved justify the inference.[2]

In *Leela Devi* v. *Ram Lal Rahu,*[3] the court held that the employee's unexplained or apparently natural death has occurred during the course of employment, the adjudicator is not relieved of the responsibility of finding out whether there were any factors rendering the employer liable for compensation.

"Accident" in course of employment—A boy, remaining to the factory canteen after having served tea in his usual round to certain persons in the factory premises was struck by a bullet and he died the following day. It was held that death of the boy was due as an accident arising out of and in the course of his employment.[4] Normally when a person is proceeding from

2. Bhayadhai *v.* Central Railway, Bombay, AIR 1955 Bom. 105.
3. 1989 Lab IC 758: (1990) LLJ 364 (HP).
4. AIR 1952 Bom. 382.

his home to the place of work, he cannot be in the course of his employment. It is especially so if he proceeds by a public transport which is available for every citizen. But there may be circumstances which would indicate that even before he reaches the work spot and is on his journey from his home to the place of work or from the place of work back to his home, it would still be in the course of employment. It is not necessary that the workman should either travel in a conveyance provided by the employee or that it would be obligatory on their part to do so in order to conclude that they were in the course of employment while travelling in that conveyance. The question has to be considered with reference to the fact and circumstances of each case.[5]

The broad points in deciding as to whether in case of an accident suffered by an employee on a public street while proceeding to or returning from his place of duty, he is entitled to compensation are whether as that moment he was obliged to be on that site by the express or implied terms of contract or his service, whether he was there in his capacity as an employee or merely as a member of public, whether he was at that time under the control or direction of the employer or was acting as a completely free person whether his presence on the sport was incidental to his employment, and whether there was a proximate connection between the employment and the accident.[6]

In *Steel Authority of India Ltd.* v. *Kanchanbala Mohanty*,[7] the court held that the travelling a far distance in the opposite direction and taking a circuitous route cannot be said to be a normal route and as such the doctrine of national extension is not applicable.

Death Independent of an accident Compensation for – Where incapacity or death results from a disease independent of accident, the workman or his dependants as the case may be will not be allowed compensation under the Act.

Where a workman while going to his work spot jumped from a running train to catch another train held, the injury sustained by him could not be attributed to any accident which arose out of and in the course of his employment.[8]

Where the workman despite written instructions on the notice board did not inform the manager or the mechanic of the absence of safeguards to the machine and while working on the same got his fingers crushed, held, mere such negligent conduct on the part of the workman did not amount to wilful disobedience to an order expressly given so as to exonerate under sub-section (1)(b)(ii) the employer from liability to pay compensation.[9]

5. Patel Engg. Co. *v.* Commt. of Workmen's Compensation, 1978 Lab 1279 (AP).
6. Union of India *v.* Noor Jahan, 1979, Lab IC 652 (All).
7. (1994) 2 LLJ 1167: 1967: 1994 Lab IC 1528: (1994) 2 LLN 1133 (Ori).
8. Combat Vehicles and Research Establishments *v.* Deputy Commissioner of Labour, (1995) LLN 675:
9. Ramrao Zingraji Shende *v.* Indian Yarn Manufacturing Company; (1993) 1 LLJ 442: (1993) 1 LLN 487: (1994) 2 ACJ 916 (Bom).

(b) Amount of Compensation (S. 4)

(1) Subject to the provisions of this Act, the amount of compensation shall be as follows, namely—

(a) Where death results from the injury.	An amount equally to fifty per cent of the monthly wages of the deceased workman multiplied by the relevant factor; or an amount to fifty thousand rupees, whichever is more.
(b) Where permanent total disablement results from the injury.	An amount equally to sixty percent of the monthly wages of the injured workman multiplied by the relevant factor; an amount of sixty thousand and rupees whichever is more; by the relevant factor.

Explanation I: For the purposes of clause (a) and clause (b) "relevant factor", in relation to a workman means the factor specified in the second column of Schedule IV against the entry in the first column of that Schedule specifying the number of years which are the same as the completed years of the age of the workman on his last birthday immediately preceding the date on which the compensation fell due.

Explanation II: Where the monthly wages of a workman exceed two thousand rupees, his monthly wages for the purposes of clause (a) and clause (b) shall be deemed to be two thousand rupees only;

(iii) Where permanent partial disablement results from the injury.	(i) In the case of an injury specified in Part II of Schedule I, such percentage of the compensation which would have been payable in the case of permanent total disablement as is specified therein as being the percentage of the loss of earning capacity caused by that injury; and (ii) In the case of an injury not specified in Schedule I. Such percentage of the compensation payable in the case of permanent total disablement as is proportionate to the loss of earning capacity as assessed by the qualified medical practitioner permanently caused by the injury.

Explanation I: Where more injuries than one are caused by the same accident, the amount of compensation payable under this head shall be aggregated but not so in any case as to exceed the amount which would have been payable if permanent total disablement had resulted from the injuries.

Explanation II: In assessing the loss of earning capacity for the purposes of sub-clause (ii) the qualified medical practitioner shall have due regard to the percentages of loss of earning capacity in relation to different injuries specified in Schedule I:

(iv) Where temporary disablement, whether total or partial results from the injury.	A half-monthly payment of the sum equivalent to twenty-five percent of monthly wages of the workman, to be paid in accordance with the provisions of sub-section (2).

[(1-A) Notwithstanding anything contained in sub-section (1), while fixing the amount of compensation payable to a workman in respect of an accident occurred outside India, the Commissioner shall take into account the amount of compensation, if any, awarded to such workman in accordance with the law of the country in which the accident occurred and shall reduced the amount fixed by him by the amount of compensation awarded to the workman in accordance with the law of that country.

(2) The half-monthly payment referred to in clause (d) of sub-section (1) shall be payable on the sixteenth day—

(i) from the date of disablement where such disablement lasts for a period of twenty-eight days or more, or

(ii) after the expiry of a waiting period of three days from the date of disablement where such disablement lasts for a period of less than twenty-eight days; and thereafter half monthly during the disablement or during a period of five years, whichever period is shorter:

Provided that—

(a) there shall be deducted from any lump sum or half-monthly payments to which the workman is entitled the amount of any payment or allowance which the workman has received from the employer by way of compensation during the period of disablement prior to the receipt of such lump sum or of the first half-monthly payment as the case may be, and

(b) no half-monthly payment shall in any case exceed the amount, if any, by which half the amount of the monthly wages of the workman before the accident exceeds half the amount of such wages which he is earning after the accident.

Explanation: Any payment or allowance which the workman has received from the employer towards his medical treatment shall not be deemed to be a payment or allowance received by him by way of compensation within the meaning of clause (a) of the proviso.

(3) On the ceasing of the disablement before the date on which any half-monthly payment falls due there shall be payable in respect of that half-month a sum proportionate to the duration of the disablement in that half-month.

(4) If the injury of the workman results in his death, the employer shall, in addition to the compensation under sub-section (1), deposit with the Commissioner a sum of one thousand rupees for payment of the same to the eldest surviving dependant of the workman towards the expenditure of the funeral of such workman or where the workman did not have a

dependant or was not living with his dependant at the time of his death to the person who actually incurred such expenditure.

In view of Supreme Court's decision in *Pratap Narain Singh Deo* v. *Srinivas Sabata,*[10] compensation is to be awarded not with reference to the loss of physical capacity but with reference to the loss of earning capacity, which is to be examined with reference to the nature of the job the workman was doing.

The employer becomes liable to pay the compensation as soon as the personal injury is caused to the workman by the accident arising out of and in the course of employment. There is no suspension of compensation pending settlement. In computing compensation for partial disablement the Commissioner has to accept the certificate of the Medical Officer. In the absence of other data the assessment by the qualified medical practitioner as to the loss of earning capacity should be the basis for assessing the quantum of compensation.[11]

Compensation is to be awarded under the Workmen's Compensation Act on the basis of 'wages' of the injured employee. When the question is what compensation is to be awarded to an employee who has been injured, the term 'wages' is to be interpreted in the light of the definition given in Section 2(n) of the Workmen's Compensation Act, and not in the light of the definition given in the Payment of Wages Act. The words "Privilege or Benefit" in the definition of "Wages" in the Workmen's Compensation Act includes the benefit of free accommodation. It is, therefore, clear that the monetary value of such accommodation, since free accommodation is capable of being estimated in money, when provided free to an applicant falls within the term 'wages' for the purpose of assessing the amount of compensation.

(C) COMPENSATION TO BE PAID WHEN DUE AND PENALTY FOR DEFAULT (S. 4-A)

(1) Compensation under Section 4 shall be paid as soon as it falls due.

(2) In cases where the employer does not accept the liability for compensation to the extent claimed, he shall be bound to make provisional payment based on the extent of liability which he accepts, and, such payment shall be deposited with the Commissioner or made to workman, as the case may be, without prejudice to the right of the workman to make any further claim.

(3) Where an employer is in default in paying the compensation due under this Act within one month from the date it fell due, the Commissioner shall—

(a) direct that the employer shall, in addition to the amount of the arrears, pay simple interest thereon at the rate of twelve percent per annum or

10. (1976) 1 SCC 289: 1976 SCC (L & S) 52.

11. New India Assurance Co. Ltd. *v.* K. Abdullakuty, (1993) I LLJ 1122: 1993 Lab IC 761: (1993) 2 Cur LR 1061 (Ker.) (DB).

at such higher rate not exceeding the minimum of the lending rates of any schedule bank as may be specified by the Central Government, by notification in the Official Gazette, on the amount due; and

(b) if, in his opinion there is no justification for the delay, direct that the employer shall, in addition to the amount of the arrears and interest thereon, pay a further sum not exceeding fifty percent of such amount by way of penalty:

Provided that an order for the payment of penalty shall not be passed under caluse (b) without giving a reasonable opportunity to the employer to show cause why it should not be passed.

Explanation I: For the purposes of this sub-section, "Schedule bank" means a bank for the time being included in the Second Schedule to the Reserve Bank of India Act, 1934 (2 of 1934).

(3-A) The interest payable under sub-section (3) shall be paid to the workman or his dependant, as the case may be, and the penalty shall be credited to the State Government.

An employer making a default in timely payment of compensation and contesting the claim of the dependants of the deceased workman is not entitled to any relief in penalty merely on the ground that he had made some *ex gratia* payment to the dependants.[12]

D. POWERS AND PROCEDURE OF COMMISSIONERS (S. 23)

The Commissioner shall have all the powers of a Civil Court under the Code of Civil Procedure, 1908 (5 of 1908), for the purpose of taking evidence on oath (which such Commissioner is hereby empowered to impose) and of enforcing the attendance of witnesses and compelling the production of documents and material objects (and the Commissioner shall be deemed to be Civil Court for all the purposes of [Section 195 and of Chapter XXVI of the Code of Criminal Procedure, 1973 (2 of 1974)].

A proceeding arising out of a claim application for workmen's compensation before the Commissioner has no difference from a suit in legal phraseology. The institution of the case will be on the date when the claim application is filled before the Commissioner. The word 'suit', since the Limitation Act, applies to all claims and application to court under any act, must be given a wider meaning, so as to include a claim, in what ever form it is presented to court either by plaint or otherwise, whereon a proceeding before the court commences. Accordingly, on the application in the statutory form being filed, the suit under the Limitation Act, 1963 on the claim is to be deemed to be instituted by the aggrieved party.[13]

The Commissioner has no inherent power to review his earlier judgement on the ground of illegility. In the absence of the workman's counsel, the Commissioner should, ordinarily, adjourn the case unless the adjournment

12. Ram Dulari Kalia *v.* H.P. State Electricity Board, (1987) 1 LLN 825: 1987 Lab IC 748 (H.P.).
13. Indian Iron & Steel Co. Ltd. *v.* Shish Ram, (1979) 2 LLJ 94 Cal: 1979 Lab IC 707.

is likely to result in grave miscarriage of justice or is occasioned on account of utter lack of *bonafides* or diligence on the part of the workman.[14]

E. METHOD OF RECORDING EVIDENCE

The Commissioner shall make a brief memorandum of the substance of the evidence of every witness as the examination of the witness proceeds, and such memorandum shall be written and signed by the Commissioner with his own hand and shall form a part of the record:

> Provided that, if the Commissioner is prevented from making such memorandum, he shall record the reason of his inability to do so and shall cause such memorandum to be made in writing from his dictation and shall sign the same, and such memorandum shall form a part of the record:
>
> Provided further that the evidence of any medical witness shall be taken down as nearly as may be word for word.[15]

F. APPEALS (S. 30)

(1) An appeal shall lie to the High Court from the following orders of a Commissioner, namely—

(a) an order awarding as compensation a lump sum whether by way of redemption of a half-monthly payment or otherwise or disallowing a claim in full or in part for a lump sum;

(aa) an order awarding interest on penalty under Section 4-A.

(b) an order refusing to allow redemption of a half-monthly payment;

(c) an order providing for the distribution of compensation among the dependants of a deceased workman, or disallowing any claim of a person alleging himself to be such dependent;

(d) an order allowing or disallowing any claim for the amount of an indemnity under the provisions of sub-section (2) of Section 12; or

(e) an order refusing to register a memorandum of agreement or registering the same or providing for the registration of the same subject to conditions:

Provided that no appeal shall lie against any order unless a substantial question of law is involved in the appeal and, in the case of an order other than an order such as is referred to in clause (b), unless the amount in dispute in the appeal is not less than three hundred rupees:

Provided further that no appeal shall lie in any case in which the parties have agreed to abide by the decision of the Commissioner, or

14. Gain Chand *v.* Mani Karan, (1990) 1 LLJ 565.

15. Without examining the medical officer, the medical certificate ought not be made on the basis of award. M.S.N. Co. Ltd. *v.* Moht. Kunjee, AIR 1956 Tra. Co. 935.

in which the order of the Commissioner gives effect to an agreement come to by the parties:

Provided further that no appeal by an employer under clause (a) shall lie unless the memorandum of appeal is accompained by a certificate by the Commissioner to the effect that the appellant has deposited with him the amount payable under the order appealed against.

(2) The period of limitation for an appeal under this section shall be sixty days.

(3) The provisions of Section 5 of the Limitation Act, 1963 (36 of 1963), shall be applicable to appeals under this section.

The phrase 'substantial question of law' must be given a wider construction than Section 110 of the Civil Procedure Code. It should cover even cases in which the Commissioner has clearly misdirected himself on a question of law such as awarding compensation without giving notice to employer. This section does not exclude application of Section 12 of the Indian Limitation Act. Where the order is not pronounced in the presence of the parties and the information is given only on a subsequent date then limitation will start from such a date.

A substantial question of law exists where there is some doubt or difference of opinion. An appeal lies against the order directing payment of lump sum compensation. A memorandum of appeal without a certificate from the Commissioner cannot amount in law to a formal presentation of an appeal. An appeal without a certificate of deposit within time is barred by limitation. Mere admission of a belated appeal does not mean implied condonation of delay. A substantial question of law is involved in the finding of a Commissioner not based on evidence and as such an appeal lies under Section 30. Proviso I, Workmen's Compensation Act if a finding is recorded without any evidence whatsoever, the question is one of law and therefore an appeal under Section 30(1) of the Act is maintainable. [16]

In *Kap. Steel* v. *R. Sasikala,*[17] the court held that the period of limitation for an appeal u/s 30 is to be computed from the date of pronouncement of the impugned order and not from the date of communication thereof.

An application under Order 9 of the CPC, 1908, for setting aside an *ex-parte* order can be filed before the Workmen's Compensation Authority by virtue of Rule 41. But, his order dismissing such application is not appealable under Rule I of Order 43 of the Code or even u/s 30 of the Act.[18]

16. For detailed case laws pl. See, *Supra* Note 1 at 898-99.
17. (1990) 2 LLN 738.
18. Praveen Industries *v.* Banawar Singh (1990) I LLN 915: (1990) 2 LLJ 412 (Kant) (DB).

15

Factories Act, 1948

A. INTRODUCTION

The Factories Act, 1948 provides for the health, safety, welfare and other aspects of workers in factories. The Act is enforced by the State Governments through their Factory inspectorates. The Act also empowers the State Governments to frame rules, so that the local conditions prevailing in the state are appropriately reflected in the enforcement.[1]

B. DEFINITION OF FACTORY [S. 2(m)]

"Factory" means any premises including the precincts thereof—

(i) Where on ten or more workers are working, or were working on any day of the preceding twelve months, and in any part of which a manufacturing process is being carried on with the aid of power, or is ordinarily so carried on, or

(ii) Where on twenty or more workers are working, or were working on any day of the preceding twelve months, and in any part of which a manufacturing process is being carried on without the aid or power, or is ordinarily so carried on, —

but does not in a mine or mobile unit belonging to armed forces of the union, a railway running shed or a hostel, restaurant or eating place.

C. IMPORTANT PROVISION OF THE ACT

(A) HEALTH

Cleanliness (S. 11)

(1) Every factory shall be kept clean and free from effuvia arising room any drain, privy or other nuisance, and in particular—
   (a) accumulations of dirt and refuse shall be removed daily by sweeping or by any other effective method from the floors and

1. See, P.L. Malik, *"Handbook of Labour and Industrial Law"* (1996) at 298.

benches of workrooms and from staircases and passages, and disposed of in a suitable manner;

(b) the floor of every workroom shall be cleaned at least once in every week by washing, using disinfectant, where necessary, or by some other effective method;

(c) where a floor is liable to become wet in the course of any manufacturing process to such extent as is capable of being drained, effective means of drainage shall be provided as maintained;

(d) all inside walls and partitions, all ceilings or tops of rooms and all walls, sides and tops of passages and staircases shall—

(i) where they are [painted otherwise than with washable water paint] at least once in every year period of five years;

(ia) where they are painted with washable water paint at least once in every period of three years and washed at least once in every period of six months;

(ii) where they are painted or varnished or where they have smooth impervious surfaces, be cleaned at least once in every period of fourteen months by such method as may be prescribed;

(iii) in any other case, be kept whitewashed, or colour washed, and the whitewashing or colour washing shall be carried out at least once in every period of fourteen months;

(dd) all doors and window frames and other wooden or metallic framework and shutters shall be kept painted or varnished and the painting or varnishing shall be carried out at least once in every period of five years;]

(a) the dates on which the processes required by clause (d) are carried out shall be entered in the prescribed register.

(2) If, in view of the nature of the operations carried on [in a factory or class or description of factories or any part of a factory or class or description of factories}, it is not possible for the occupier to comply with all or any of the provisions of sub-section (1), the State Government may by order exempt such factory or class or description of factories [or part] from any of the provisions of that sub-section and specify alternative methods for keeping the factory in a clean state.

Disposal of Wastes and Effluents (S. 12)

(1) Effective arrangements shall be made in every factory for the treatment of wastes and effluents due to the manufacturing process carried on therein, so as to render them innocuous, and for their disposal.

(2) The State Government may make rules prescribing the arrangements to be made under sub-section (1) or requiring that the arrangements made in accordance with sub-section (1) shall be approved by such authority as may be prescribed.

The norms or guidelines passed by the Effluent Board must satisfy the test of reasonableness.[2] A factory can be prosecuted even if plans for arrangement of wastes and effluents have neither been approved nor disapproved.[3]

In the absence of any rule under the U.P. Factories Rules, 1950 that the existing factory must stop functioning till fresh plans are approved by the Board, even if the existing factory continues working after the original plans for the disposal of wastes and effluents have been disapproved by the Board, it cannot be held that it has violated Section 12(1).[4]

Ventilation and Temperature (S. 13)

(1) Effective and suitable provision shall be made in every factory for securing and maintaining in every workroom—
   (a) adequate ventilation by the circulation of fresh air, and
   (b) such a temperature as will secure to workers therein reasonable conditions of comfort and prevent injury to health; and in particular,
      (i) walls and roofs shall be of such material and so designed that such temperature shall not be exceeded but kept as low as practicable;
      (ii) where the nature of the work carried on in the factory involves, or is likely to involve, the production of excessively high temperatures such adequate measures as are practicable shall be taken to protect the workers therefrom, by separating the process which produces such temperatures from the workroom, by insulating the hot parts or by other effective means.

(2) The State Government may prescribe a standard of adequate ventilation and reasonable temperature for any factory or class or description of factories or parts thereof and direct that (proper measuring instruments, at such places and in such position as may be specified, shall be provided and such records, as may be prescribed shall be maintained).

(3) If it appears to the Chief Inspector that excessively high temperatures in any factory can be reduced by the adoption of suitable measures, he may, without prejudice to the rules made under sub-section (2), serve on the occupier, an order in writing specifying the measures which, in his opinion, should be adopted, and requiring them to be carried out before a specified date.]

Dust and Fume (S. 14)

(1) In every factory in which, by reason of the manufacturing process carried on, there is given-off any dust or fume or other impurity of

2. Article 19 (6), *id.* 315.
3. 43 FLR 233.
4. K.L. Vij *v.* State of U.P., 1978 Lab IC 446 (All): 53 FJR 244.

such a nature and to such an extent as is likely to be injurious or offensive to the workers employed therein, or any dust in substantial quantities, effective measures shall be taken to prevent its inhalation and accumulation in any workroom, and if any exhaust appliance is necessary for this purpose, it shall be applied as near as possible to the point of origin of the dust, fume or other impurity, and such point shall be enclosed so far as possible.

(2) In any factory no stationary internal combustion engine shall be operated unless the exhaust is conducted into the open air, and no other internal combustion engine shall be operated in any room unless effective measures have been taken to prevent such accumulation of fumes therefrom as are likely to be injurious to workers employed in the room.

Artificial Humidification (S. 15)

(1) In respect of all factories in which the humidity of the air is artificially increased, the State Government may make rules,—
   (a) prescribing standard of humidification;
   (b) regulating the methods used for artificially increasing the humidity of the air;
   (c) directing prescribed tests for determining the humidity of the air to be correctly carried out and recorded; and
   (d) prescribing methods to be adopted for securing adequate ventilation and cooling of the air and the workrooms.

(2) In any factory in which the humidity of the air is artificially increased, the water used for the purpose shall be taken from a public supply, or other source of drinking water, or shall be effectively purified before it is so used.

(3) If it appears to an Inspector that the water used in a factory for increasing humidity which is required to be effectively purified under sub-section (2) is not effectively purified he may serve on the manager of the factory an order in writing, specifying the measures which in his opinion should be adopted, and requiring them to be carried out before specified date.

Overcrowding (S. 16)

(1) No room in any factory shall be overcrowded to an extent injurious to the health of the worker employed therein.

(2) Without prejudice to the generality of sub-section (1), there shall be in every workroom of a factory in existence on the date of the commencement of this Act at least (9.9 cubic meters) and of a factory built after the commencement of this Act at least (4.2 cubic meters) of space for every worker employed therein, and for the purposes of this sub-section no account shall be taken of any space which is more than (4.2 cubic meters) above the level of the floor of the room.

(3) If the Chief Inspector by order in writing so requires, there shall be posted in each workroom of a factory a notice specifying the maximum number of workers who may, in compliance with the provisions of this section, be employed in the room.

(4) The Chief Inspector may, by order in writing exempt, subject to such conditions, if any, as he may think fit to impose, any workroom from the provisions of this section if he is satisfied that compliance therewith in respect of the room is unnecessary in the interest of the health of the workers employed therein.

Lighting (S. 17)

(1) In every part of a factory where workers are working or passing there shall be provided and maintained sufficient and suitable lighting, natural or artificial or both.

(2) In every factory all glazed windows and skylights used for the lighting of the workroom shall be kept clean on both the inner and outer surfaces and, so far as compliance with the provisions of any rules made under sub-section (3) of Section 13 will allow, free from obstruction.

(3) In every factory effective provision shall, so far as is practicable, be made for the prevention of—
   (a) glare, either directly from a source of light or by reflection from a smooth or polished surface; and
   (b) the formation of shadows to such an extent as to cause eye-strain or the risk of accident to any worker.

(4) The State Government may prescribe standards of sufficient and suitable lighting for factories or for any class or description of factories or for any manufacturing process.

Drinking Water (S. 18)

(1) In every factory effective arrangements shall be made to provide and maintain at suitable points conveniently situated for all workers employed therein a sufficient supply of wholesome drinking water.

(2) All such points shall be legibly marked "drinking water" in a language understood by majority of the workers employed in the factory, and no such point shall be situated within (six meters of any washing place, urinal, latrine, spittoon, open drain carrying, sullage or effluent or any other source of contamination) unless a shorter distance is approved in writing by the Chief Inspector.

(3) In every factory wherein more than two hundred and fifty workers are ordinarily employed, provisions shall be made for cooling drinking water during hot weather by effective means and for distribution thereof.

(4) In respect of all factories or any class or description of factories the State Government may make rules for securing compliance with the

provisions of sub-sections (1), (2) and (3) and for the examination by prescribed authorities of the supply and distribution of drinking water in factories.

Latrines and Urinals (S. 19)

(1) In every factory—
  (a) sufficient latrine and urinal accommodation of prescribed types shall be provided conveniently situated and accessible to workers at all times while they are at the factory;
  (b) separate enclosed accommodation shall be provided for male and female workers;
  (c) such accommodation shall be adequately lighted and ventilated, and no latrine or urinal shall, unless specially exempted in writing by the Chief Inspector, communicate with any workroom except through an intervening open space or ventilated passage;
  (d) all such accommodations shall be maintained in a clean and sanitary condition at all times; and
  (e) sweepers shall be employed whose primary duty would be to keep clean latrines, urinals and washing places.

(2) In every factory wherein more than two hundred and fifty works are ordinarily employed—
  (a) all latrine and urinal accommodation shall be of prescribed sanitary types;
  (b) the floors and internal walls, up to a height of (ninety centimeters), of the latrines and urinals and the sanitary blocks shall be laid in glazed tiles or otherwise finished to provide a smooth polished impervious surface; and
  (c) without prejudice to the provisions of clauses (d) and (e) of sub-section (1), the floors, portions of the walls and blocks so laid or finished and the sanitary pans of latrines and urinals shall be thoroughly washed and cleaned at least once in every seven days with suitable detergents or disinfectants or with both.

(3) The State Government may prescribe the number of latrines and urinals to be provided in any factory in proportion to the number of male and female workers ordinarily employed there, and provide for such further matters in respect of sanitation in factories, including the obligation of workers in this regard, as it considers necessary in the interest of the health of the workers employed therein.

Spittoons (S. 20)

(1) In every factory there shall be provided a sufficient number of spittoons in convenient places and they shall be maintained in a clean and hygienic condition.

(2) The State Government may make rules prescribing the type and the number of spittoons to be provided and their location in any factory and provide for such further matters relating to their maintenance in a clean and hygienic condition.

(3) No person shall spit within the premises of a factory except in the spittoons provided for the purpose and a notice containing this provision and the penalty for its violation shall be prominently displayed at suitable places in the premises.

(4) Whoever spits in contravention of sub-section (3) shall be punishable with fine not exceeding five rupees.

This Section enacts an important discipline for the employees and every one spitting in contravention of sub-section (3) of this section will do so at the pain of punishment with fine nor exceeding five rupees. Sufficient number of spittoons must be provided in every factory and the same must be at convenient places spitting must be done in spittoons only and the penalty for the violation of this direction shall be predominantly displayed at suitable places in the premises of the factory.

The Courts of Justice have no jurisdiction to inquire into the suitability or sufficiency of the sanitary accommodation excising at the factory or required by the notice of the Inspect.[5]

(B) SAFETY

Fencing of Machinery (S. 21)

(1) In every factory the following, namely—

(i) every moving part of a prime mover and every flywheel connected to a prime mover, whether the prime mover or flywheel is in the engine house or not;

(ii) the headrace and tailrace of every water-wheel and water turbine;

(iii) any part of a stock-bar which projects beyond the head stock of a lathe; and

(iv) unless they are in such position or of such construction as to be safe to every person employed in the factory as they would be if they were securely fenced, the following, namely—

(a) every part of an electric generator, motor or rotary converter;

(b) every part of transmission machinery; and

(c) every dangerous part of any other machinery,

shall be securely fenced by safeguards of substantial construction which (shall be constantly maintained and kept in position while the parts of machinery they are fencing are in motion or in use:

Provided that for the purpose of determining whether any part of machinery is in such position or is of such construction as to be safe as aforesaid, account shall not be taken of any occasion when—

5. Tracey *v.* Pretly & Sons, (1901) 1 QB 444; R *v.* Stepney Corporation, (1902) 1 KB 317.

(i) it is necessary to make an examination of any part of the machinery aforesaid while it is in motion or, as a result of such examination, to carry out lubrication or other adjusting operation while the machinery is in motion, being an examination or operation which it is necessary to be carried out while that part of the machinery is in motion, or

(ii) in the case of any part of a transmission machinery used in such process as may be prescribed (being a process of a continuous nature the carrying on of which shall be, or is likely to be, substantially interfered with by the stoppage of that part of the machinery, it is necessary to make an examination of such part of the machinery while it is in motion or, as a result of such examination, to carry out any mounting or shipping of belts or lubrication or other adjusting operation while the machinery is in motion.

And such examination or operation is made or carried out in accordance with the provisions of sub-section (1) of Section 22.

(2) The State Government may by rules prescribe such further precautions as it may consider necessary in respect of any particular machinery or part thereof, or exempt, subject to such condition as may be prescribed, for securing the safety of the workers, any particular machinery or part thereof from the provisions of this section.

Dangerous part of the machinery fencing of—The duty to fence such machinery as contemplated by this section is absolute.[6] In *Hindle v. Birtwistle*,[7] the expressions "dangerous part" was held to mean any machinery from which in the ordinary course of working it, danger may reasonably be anticipated, even if such danger would arise from negligence or some outside source.

"In motion" — The duty cast by this section applies to machinery in use or in motion. The obligation, however, does not extend to cases of parts flying out of a broken machinery.[8] Secure fencing includes proper maintenance and repair.

Practicability: It is the absolute liability of the employer to securely fence by safety guards every dangerous part of any machinery and the practicability of providing a safety guard should not be taken into consideration.[9]

Safety: Section 21 does not contemplate a provision being made for the safety of an employee who is assigned the work of repairing machinery or of shifting machinery or installing new machinery.

Observance of the safety measures under Section 21 cannot depend on the occurring of any particular accident but it depends on whether such safety measures are dispensable regard being had to the nature of machine

6. Davies *v.* Thomas Owen & Co. Ltd. (1919) 3 KB 39; Pursel *v.* Clement Talbot Ltd. (1914) 111 LJ 827: Warkins *v.* Naval Collery Co. 1921 An. 693.
7. (1897) 1 QB 192
8. Carrols *v.* Andrew Bareley & Sons Ltd. (1908) 2 All. ER 386.
9. (1966) 2 LLJ 867: AIR 1966 MP 324].

as also the foreseeable possibility of the workmen in the factory coming into contract therewith in the course of their duties deliberately or accidentally.[10]

Work on or near Machinery in Motion (S. 22)

(1) Where in any factory it becomes necessary to examine any part of machinery referred to in Section 21, while the machinery is in motion, or, as a result of such examination, to carry out—

(a) in a case referred to in clause (i) of the proviso to sub-section (1) of Section 21, lubrication or other adjusting operation; or

(b) in case referred to in clause (ii) of the aforesaid, any mounting or shipping of belts or lubrication of other adjusting operation.

While the machinery is in motion such examination or operation shall be made or carried only by a specially trained adult male worker wearing tight fitting clothing (which shall be supplied by the occupier) whose name has been recorded in the register prescribed in this behalf and who has been furnished with a certificate of his appointment, and while he is so engaged—

(a) such worker shall not handle a belt at a moving pulley unless—

(i) the belt is not more than fifteen centimeters in width;

(ii) the pulley is normally for the purpose of drive and not merely a flywheel or balance wheel (in which case a belt is not permissible);

(iii) the belt joint is either laced or flush with the belt;

(iv) the belt, including the joint and the pulley rim, are in good repair;

(v) there is reasonable clearance between the pulley and any fixed plant or structure;

(vi) secure foothold and, where necessary, secure hand-hold, are provided for the operator; and

(vii) any ladder in use for carrying out any examination or operation aforesaid is securely fixed or lashed or is firmly held by a second person;

(b) without prejudice to any other provision of this Act relating to the fencing of machinery, every set screw, bolt and key on any revolving shaft, spindle, wheel or pinion, and all spur, worm and other toothed or friction gearing in motion with which such worker would otherwise be liable to come into contact, shall be securely fenced to prevent such contact.

(2) No woman or young person shall be allowed to clean, lubricate or adjust any part of a prime mover or of any transmission machinery while the prime mover or transmission machinery is in motion, or to clean, lubricate or adjust any part of any machine if the cleaning, lubrication or adjustment thereof would expose the woman or young

10. E.S.I. Corpn. *v.* Shree Sitaram Mills Ltd., 1978 Lab IC 1220 (Bomb).

person to risk of injury from any moving part either of that machine or of any adjacent machinery.

(3) The State Government may, by notification in the Official Gazette, prohibit in any specified factory or class or description of factories the cleaning, lubricating or adjusting by any person of specified parts of machinery when those parts are in motion.

While this section prohibits women and children from working on moving part, the English law goes a step further to the effect that they are prohibited from working on stationary parts, while any other part is in motion.[11]

Employment of Young Persons on Dangerous Machines (S. 23)

(1) No young person (shall be required or allowed to work at any machine to which this section applied, unless he has been fully instructed as to the dangers arising in connection with the machine and the precautions to observed and—

(a) has received sufficient training in work at the machine, or

(b) is under adequate supervision by a person who has a thorough knowledge and experience of the machine.

(2) Sub-section (1) shall apply to such machines as may be prescribed by the State Government (being machines which in its opinion are of such a dangerous character that young persons ought not to work at them unless the foregoing requirements are complied with).

Striking Gear and Devices for Cutting-off Power (S. 24)

(1) In every factory—

(a) suitable striking gear or other efficient mechanical appliance shall be provided and maintained and used to move driving belts to and from fast and loose pulleys which form part of the transmission machinery, and such gear or appliances shall be so constructed, placed and maintained as to prevent the belt from creeping back on to the fast pulley;

(b) driving belts when not in use shall not be allowed to rest or ride upon shafting in motion.

(2) In every factory suitable devices for cutting off power in emergencies from running machinery shall be provided and maintained in every workroom:

Provided that in respect of factories in operation before the commencement of this Act, the provisions of this sub-section shall apply only to workrooms in which electricity is used as power.

(3) When a device, which can inadvertently shift from 'off' to 'on' position, is provided in a factory to cut-off power, arrangements shall be provided for locking the device in safed position to prevent accidental

11. Pearson *v.* Belgiam Mills Co. (1886) 1 QB 244; Crabtree *v.* Commercial Mills Ltd. (1910) 103 LT 8791.

starting of the transmission machinery or other machines to which the device is fitted.]

Self-acting Machines (S. 25)

No traversing part of a self-acting machine in any factory and no material carried thereon shall, if the space over which it runs is a space over which any person is liable to pass, whether in the course of his employment or otherwise, be allowed to run on its outward or inward traverse within a distance of (forty-five centimeters) from any fixed structure which is not part of the machine:

Provided that the Chief Inspector may permit the continued use of a machine installed before the commencement of this Act, which does not comply, with the requirements of this section on such conditions for ensuring safety as he may think fit to impose.

Casing of New Machinery (S. 26)

(1) In all machinery driven by power and installed in any factory after the commencement of this Act,—

(a) every set screw, bolt or key on any revolving shaft, spindle, wheel or pinion shall be so sunk, encased or otherwise effectively guarded as to prevent danger; and

(b) all spur, worm and other toothed or friction gearing which does not require frequent adjustment while in motion, shall be completely encased, unless it is so situated as to be as safe as it would be if it were completely encased.

(2) Whoever sells or lets on hire or, as agent of a seller or hirer, causes or procures to be sold or let on hire, for use in a factory any machinery driven by power which does not comply with the provisions of [sub-section (1) or any rules made under sub-section (3), shall be punishable with imprisonment for a term which may extend to three months or with fine which may extend to five hundred rupees or with both.

(3) The State Government may make rules specifying further safeguards to be provided in respect of any other dangerous part of any particular machine or class or description of machines.]

This section empowers State Government to make rules specifying further safeguards to be provided in respect of any other dangerous part of any particular machine or class or description of machines. It is noteworthy that the section places an obligation on the agent, sellers, and hires also and provides for a fine in case of breach. The obligation is caste upon middlemen also.[12]

12. *Id.* at 322.

Prohibition of Employment of Women and Children Near Cotton Openers (S. 27)

No woman or child shall be employed in any part of a factory for pressing cotton in which a cotton opener is at work:

> Provided that if the feed-end of a cotton-opener is in a room separated from the delivery end by a partition extending to the roof or to such height as the Inspector may in any particular case specify in writing, women and children may be employed on the side of the partition where the feed-end is situated.

A woman or child may be employed in any part of a factory for pressing cotton in which a cotton-opener is at work only if feed-end of a cotton-opener is in a room separated from the delivery end by a partition extending to the roof or to such height as the Inspector may specify in any particular case in writing. It is to be noted however that in such a case women and children may be employed on the side of the partition where the feed-end is situated.

The requirement is not met if there is a door made in a partition between the portions of the room and that the door is shown to be open at a particular time, or even although it is shut, yet it is not locked or other effective means taken to prevent it being operated by a woman or child wishing to get into the press room.[13]

Hoists and Lifts (S. 28)

(1) In every factory—

- (a) every hoist and lift shall be—
  - (i) of good mechanical construction, sound material and adequate strength;
  - (ii) properly maintained, and shall be thoroughly examined by a competent person at least once in every period of six months, and a register shall be kept containing the prescribed particulars of every such examination.
- (b) every hoist way and lift way shall be sufficiently protected by an enclosure fitted with gates, and the hoist or life and every such enclosure shall be so constructed as to prevent any person or thing from being trapped between any part of the hoist or lift and any fixed structure or moving part;
- (c) the maximum safe working load shall be plainly marked on every hoist or lift, and no load greater than such load shall be carried thereon;
- (d) the case of every hoist or lift used for carrying persons shall fitted with a gate on each side from which access is afforded to a landing;
- (e) every gate referred to in clause (b) or clause (d) shall be fitted with interlocking or other efficient device to secure that the gate cannot

13. B.N. Gamadia *v.* Emperor, 50 Bom 34: AIR 1926 Bom 57.

be opened except when the cage is at the landing and that the cage cannot be moved unless the gate is close.

(2) The following additional requirements shall apply to hoists and lifts used for carrying persons and installed or reconstructed in a factory after the commencement of this Act, namely—

(a) Where the cage is supported by rope or chain, there shall be at least two ropes or chains separately connected with the cage and balance weight, and each rope or chain with its attachment shall be capable of carrying the whole weight of the cage together with its maximum load;

(b) efficient devices shall be provided and maintained capable of supporting the cage together with its maximum load in the event of breakage of ropes, chains or attachments; and

(c) an efficient automatic device shall be provided and maintained to prevent the cage from over-running.

(3) The Chief Inspector may permit the continued use of a hoist or lift installed in a factory before the commencement of this Act, which does not fully comply with the provisions of sub-section (1) upon such conditions for ensuring safety as he may think fit to impose.

(4) The State Government may, if in respect of any class or description of hoist or lift, it is of opinion that it would be unreasonable to enforce any requirement of sub-sections (1) and (2), by order direct that such requirement shall not apply to such class or description of hoist or lift.

Explanation—For the purposes of this section, no lifting machine or appliance shall be deemed to be a hoist or lift unless it has a platform or cage, the direction or movement of which is restricted by a guide or guides.

Properly maintained—"Properly maintained" imposes an absolute and regular obligation. The injured party is not required to furnish any proof of any breach in case of a failure of the mechanism and consequent injury.[14]

Lifting Machines, Chains, Ropes and Lifting Tackles (S. 29)

(1) In any factory the following provisions shall be complied with in respect of every lifting machine (other than a hoist and lift) and every chain, rope and lifting tackle for the purpose of raising or lowering persons, goods or materials—

(a) all parts, including the working gear, whether fixed or moveable, or every lifting machine and every chain, rope or lifting tackle shall be—

(i) of good construction, sound material and adequate strength and free from defects;

(ii) properly maintained; and

(iii) thoroughly examined by a competent person at least, once in every period of twelve months, or at such intervals as the

14. Galashiels Gas Co. Ltd. *v.* O'Donnel, (1949) 1 All ER 319.

Chief Inspector may specify in writing; and a register shall be kept containing the prescribed particulars of every such examination;

(b) no lifting machine and no chain, rope or lifting tackle shall, except for the purpose of test, be loaded beyond the safe working load which shall be plainly marked thereon together with an identification mark and duly entered in the prescribed register; and where this is not practicable, a table showing the safe working loads of every kind and size of lifting machine or chain, rope or lifting tackle in use shall be displayed in prominent positions on the premises; and

(c) while any person is employed or working on or near the wheel track of a travelling crane in any place where be would be liable to be struck by the crane, effective measures shall be taken to ensure that the crane does not approach within (six meters) of that place.

(2) The State Government may make rules in respect of any lifting machine or any chain, rope or lifting tackle used in factories—

(a) prescribing further requirements to be complied with in addition to those set out in this section; and

(b) providing for exemption from compliance with all or any of the requirements of this section, where in its opinion, such compliance is unnecessary or impracticable.

(3) For the purpose of this section a lifting machine or a chain, rope or lifting tackle shall be deemed to have been thoroughly examined if a visual examination supplemented, if necessary, by other means and by the dismantling of parts of the gear, has been carried out as carefully as the conditions permit in order to arrive at a reliable conclusion as to the safety of the parts examined.

Explanation—In this section—

(a) "lifting machine" means a crane, crab, winch, teagle, pulley block, gin wheel, transporter or runway;

(b) "lifting tackle" means any chain sling, rope sling, hook, shackle, swivel, coupling, socket, clamp, tray or similar appliance, whether fixed or movable, used in connection with the raising or lowering of persons, or loads by use of lifting machines.

Revolving Machinery (S. 30)

(1) In every factory in which the process of grinding is carried on there shall be permanently affixed to or placed near each machine in use a notice indicating the maximum safe working peripheral speed of every grindstone or abrasive wheel, the speed of the shaft or spindle upon which the wheel is mounted, and the diameter of the pulley upon such shaft or spindle necessary to secure such safe working peripheral speed.

(i) The speeds indicated in notices under sub-section (1) shall not be exceeded.

(ii) Effective measures shall be taken in every factory to ensure that the safe working peripheral speed of every revolving vessel; cage, basket, flywheel, pulley, disc or similar appliance driven by power is not exceeded.

Sub-section (3) speaks of "Effective measures" which shall be taken in every factory to ensure that the safe working peripheral speed of every revolving vessel, cage, basket, fly wheel, pulley, disc or similar appliance driven by power is not exceeded. Each particular case has to be decided with reference to its circumstances to decide what "Effective measures" have been taken.[15]

Pressure Plant (S. 31)

(1) If in any factory, any plant or machinery or any part thereof is operated at a pressure above atmospheric pressure, effective measures shall be taken to ensure that the safe working pressure of such plant or machinery or part is not exceeded.

(2) The State Government may make rules providing for the examination and testing of any plant or machinery such as is referred to in sub-section (1) and prescribing such other safety measures in relation thereto as may in its opinion be necessary in any factory or class or description of factories.

(3) The State Government may, by rules, exempt, subject to such conditions as may be specified therein, any part of any plant or machinery referred to in sub-section (1) from the provisions of this section.

This section specifies what precaution has to be taken when working any part of plant or machinery in a factory in a manufacturing process operated at a pressure above atmospheric pressure.[16]

Floor, Stairs and Means of Access—in every Factory (S. 32)

(a) all floors, steps, stairs, passages and gangways shall be of sound conditions and properly maintained (and shall be kept free from obstructions and substances likely to cause persons to slip), and where it is provided with substantial handrails;

(b) there shall, so far as is reasonably practicable, be provided and maintained safe means of access to every place at which any person is at any time required to work; and

(c) when any person has to work at a height from where he is like to fall, provision shall be made, so far as is reasonably practicable, by fencing or otherwise, to ensure the safety of the person so working.

15. *Id.* at 325.
16. *Ibid.*

Pits, Sumps, Openings in Floors, etc. (S. 33)

(1) In every factory every fixed vessel, sump, tank, pit or opening in the ground or in a floor which, by reasons of its depth, situation, construction, or contents, is or may be a source of danger, shall be either securely covered or securely fenced.

(2) The State Government may, by order in writing, exempt, subject to such conditions as may be prescribed, any factory or class or description of factories in respect of any vessel, sump, tank, pit or opening from compliance with the provisions of this section.

Failure in securely fence—The failure to securely fence fermenting vats is a contravention of Section 33 and is an offence under Section 92 thereof. It is a continuing offence and every day the contravention is continued while the factory is worked a fresh offence is committed for which the owner and occupier would be liable.[17] Securely fencing a pit means covering or fencing it in such a way what it ceases to be a source of danger.

Excessive Weights (S. 34)

(1) No person shall be employed in any factory to lift, carry or move any load so heavy as to be likely to cause him injury.

(2) The State Government may make rule prescribing the maximum weights which may be lifted, carried or moved by adult men, adult women, adolescents and children employed in factories or in any class or description of factories or in carrying on any specified process.

Protection of Eyes (S. 35)

(1) In respect of any such manufacturing process carried on in any factory as may be prescribed, being a process, which involves—
    (a) risk of injury to the eyes from particles or fragments thrown-off in the course of the process, or
    (b) risk to the eyes by reason of exposure to excessive light, the State Government may by rules require that effective screens or suitable goggles shall be provided for the protection of persons employed on, or in the immediate vicinity of, the process.

'Suitable' is not equivalent to perfect; it means well adapted for the process under consideration and that it must fit him. The words 'to protect the eyes' were describing the end, which is sought to be achieved by the provision of goggles.[18]

It is not enough if the goggles were hung in the office room, the workers must be informed of their whereabouts. In such a case only it can be said that the requirements of this section are complied with.[19]

17. State *v.* Umashanker, (1962) 23 FJR 162.
18. AIR 1955 NUC 1933.
19. Finch *v.* Telegraph Construction & Maintenance Co. Ltd., (1949) All ER 4520.

Precautions Against Dangerous Fumes, Gases, etc. (S. 36)

(1) No person shall be required or allowed to enter any chamber, tank, vat, pit, piple, flue or other confined space in any factor in which any gas, fume, vapour or dust is likely to be present to such an extent as to involve risk to persons being overcome thereby, unless it is provided with a manhole of adequate size or other effective means of egress.

(2) No person shall be required or allowed to enter any confined space as it referred to in sub-section (1), until all practicable measures have been taken to remove any gas, fume, vapour or dust, which may be present so as to bring its level within the permissible limits and to prevent any ingress of such gas, fume, vapour or dust and unless—
   (a) a certificate in writing has been given by a competent person, based on a test carried out by himself that the space is reasonably free from dangerous gas, fume, vapour or dust; or
   (b) such person is wearing suitable, breathing apparatus and a belt securely attached a rope the free end of which is held by a person outside the confined space.]

Precautions Regarding the Use of Portable Electric Light (S. 36-A)

In any factory—

(a) no portable electric light or any other electric appliance of voltage exceeding twenty-four volts shall be permitted for use inside any chamber, tank, vat, pit, pipe, flue or other confined space (unless adequate safety devices are provided, and

(b) if any inflammable gas, fume or dust is likely to be present in such chamber, tank, vat, pit, pipe, flue or other confined space, no lamp or light other than that of flame-proof construction shall be permitted to be used therein.

Explosive or Inflammable Dust, Gas, etc. (S. 37)

(1) Where in any factory a manufacturing process produces dust, gas, fume or vapour of such character and to such extent as to be likely to explode to ignition, all practicable measures shall be taken, to prevent any such explosion by—
   (a) effective enclosure of the plant or machinery used in the process;
   (b) removal or prevention of the accumulation of such dust, gas, fume or vapour; and
   (c) exclusion or effective enclosure of all possible sources of ignition.

(2) where in any factory the plant or machinery used in a process such as is referred to in sub-section (1) is not so constructed as to withstand the probable pressure which such an explosion as aforesaid would produce, all practicable measures shall be taken to restrict the spread and effects of the explosion by the provision in the plant or machinery of chokes, baffles, vents or other effective appliances.

(3) Where any part of the plant or machinery is a factory contains any explosive or inflammable gas or vapour under pressure greater than atmospheric pressure, that part shall not be opened except in accordance with the following provisions, namely—

(a) before the fastening of any joint of any pipe connected with the part or the fastening of the cover or any opening into the part is loosened, any flow of the gas or vapour into the part or any such pipe shall be effectively stopped by a stop valve or other means;

(b) before any such fastening as aforesaid is removed, all practicable measures shall be taken to reduce the pressure of the gas or vapour in the part or pipe to atmospheric pressure; and

(c) where any such fastening as aforesaid has been loosened or removed, effective measures shall be taken to prevent any explosive or inflammable gas or vapour from entering the part of the pipe until the fastening has been secured, or, as the case may be, securely replaced:

Provided that the provisions of this sub-section shall not apply in the case of plant or machinery installed in the open air.

(4) No plant, tank or vessel which contains or has contained any explosive or inflammable substance shall be subjected in any factory to any welding, brazing, soldering or cutting operation which involves the application of heat unless adequate measures have first been taken to remove such substance and any fumes arising therefrom or to render such substance and fumes non-explosive or non-inflammable, and no such substance shall be allowed to enter such plant, tank or vessel after any such operation until the metal has cooled sufficiently to prevent any risk of igniting the substance.

(5) The State Government may by rules exempt, subject to such conditions as may be prescribed, any factory or class or description of factories from compliance with all or any of the provisions of this section.

"Amongst the most important new provisions are those directed against the dangers which arise from inflammable dust, gases and vapours produced or used in industry. Most people know that coal dust is explosive and this leads to many disasters in coalmines, but it may be a surprise to come to learn that other familiar domestic articles such as flour, sugar and starch are also explosive if they are ignited when in the form of a dust cloud. Hence, where inflammable dust are produced by grinding or other process, the new Act requires special precautions to be taken, such as enclosing the plant, keeping rooms free from dust and keeping away naked lights."[20]

Precautions in Case of Fire (S. 38)

(1) In every factory, all practicable measures shall be taken to prevent outbreak of fire and its spread, both internally and externally, and to provide and maintain—

(a) safe means of escape for all persons in the event of a fire, and

(b) the necessary equipment and facilities for extinguishing fire.

20. *Id.* at 328.

(2) Effective measures shall be taken to ensure that in every factory all the workers are familiar with the means of escape in case of fire and have been adequately trained in the routine to be followed in such cases.

(3) The State Government may make rules, in respect of any factory or class or description of factories, requiring the measures to be adopted to give effect to the provisions of sub-sections (1) and (2).

(4) Notwithstanding anything contained in clause (a) of sub-section (1) or sub-section (2), if the Chief Inspector, having regard to the nature of the work carried on in any factory, the construction of such factory, special risk to life or safety, or any other circumstances, is of the opinion that the measures provided in the factory, whether as prescribed or not, for the purposes of clause (a) of sub-section (1) or sub-section (2), are inadequate, he may, by order in writing, require that such additional measures as he may consider reasonable and necessary, be provided in the factory before such date as is specified in the order.

Factories and workshops are to be furnished with a certificate that they are provided with such means of escape in case of fire as can reasonably be required. It is the duty of the District Council to ascertain whether factories and workshops are provided with such means of escape from fire where necessary to require its provision. The country court has jurisdiction, on necessary application to apportion the cost of complying with the requirement between the owner and the occupier of the factory or workshop in a just and equitable manner.[21]

Power to Require Specifications of Defective Parts or Tests of Stability (S. 39)

If it appears to the Inspector that any building or part of building or any part of the ways, machinery or plant in a factory is in such a condition that it may be dangerous to human life or safety, he may serve on (the occupier or manager or both) of the factory an order in writing requiring him before a specified date—

(a) to furnish such drawings, specifications and other particulars as may be necessary to determine whether such building, ways, machinery or plant can be used with safety, or

(b) to carry out such tests in such manner as may be specified in the order, and to inform the Inspector of the results thereof.

Safety of Buildings and Machinery (S. 40)

(1) If it appears to the Inspector that any building or part of a building or any part of the ways, machinery or plant in a factory is in such a condition that it is dangerous to human life or safety, he may serve or (the occupier or manager or both) of the factory an order in writing

21. Monk *v.* Arnold (1902) 1 KB 761; Homer *v.* Franklin, (1904) 2 KB 877.

specifying the measures which in his opinion should be adopted, and requiring them to be carried out before a specified date.

(2) It appears to the Inspector that the use of any building or part of a building or any part of the ways, machinery or plant is a factory involves imminent danger to human life or safety, he may serve on [the occupier or manager or both] of a factory an order in writing prohibiting its use until it has been properly repaired or altered.

Maintenance of Building (S. 40-A)

If it appears to the Inspector that any building or part of a building in a factory is in such a state of disrepair as is likely to lead to conditions detrimental to the health and welfare of the workers, he may serve on the occupier or manager or both of the factory on order in writing specifying the measures which in his opinion should be taken and require the same to be carried out before such date as in specified in the order.

Safety Officers (S. 40-B)

(1) In every factory,—

  (i) wherein one thousand or more workers are ordinarily employed, or

  (ii) wherein, in the opinion of the State Government, any manufacturing process or operation is carried on, which process or operation involves any risk of bodily injury, poisoning or disease, or any other hazard to health, to the persons employed in the factory, the occupier shall, if so required by the State Government by notification in the Official Gazette, employ such number of Safety Officers as may be specified in that notification.

(2) The duties, qualifications and conditions of service of Safety Officers shall be such as may be prescribed by the State Government.

Power to Make Rules to Supplement this Chapter (S. 41)

The State Government may make rules requiring the provisions in any factory or in any class or description of factories of such further [devices and measures] for securing the safety of persons employed therein as it may deem necessary.

(C) Provisions Relating To Hazardous Processes

Constituting of Site Appraisal Committees (S. 41)

(1) The State Government may, for purposes of advising it to consider applications for grant of permission for the initial location of a factory involving a hazardous process or for the expansion of any such factory, appoint a Site Appraisal Committee consisting of—

(a) the Chief Inspector of the State who shall be its Chairman;

(b) a representative of the Central Board for the Prevention and Control of Water Pollution appointed by the Central Government under Section 3 of the Water (Prevention and Control of Pollution) Act, 1974;

(c) a representative of the State Board appointed under Section 4 of the Water (Prevention and Control of Pollution) Act, 1981;

(d) a representative of the State Board appointed under Section 4 of the Water (Prevention and Control of Pollution) Act, 1974;

(e) a representative of the State Board for the Prevention and Control of Air Pollution referred to in Section 5 of the Air (Prevention and Control of Pollution) Act, 1981;

(f) a representative of the Department of Environment in the State;

(g) a representative of the Meteorological Department of the Government of India;

(h) an expert in the field of occupational health; and

(i) a representative of the Town Planning Department of the State Government, and not more than five other members who may be co-opted by the State Government who shall be—

 (i) a scientist having specialized knowledge of the hazardous process which will be involved in the factory,

 (ii) a representative of the local authority within whose jurisdiction the factory is to be established, and

 (iii) not more than three other persons as deemed fit by the State Government.

(2) The Site Appraisal Committee shall examine an application for the establishment of a factory involving hazardous process and make its recommendation to the State Government within a period of ninety days of the receipt of such applications in the prescribed form.

(3) Where any process relates to a factory owned or controlled by the Central Government or to a corporation or a company owned or controlled by the Central Government, the State Government shall co-opt in the Site Appraisal Committee, representative nominated by the Central Government as a member of that Committee.

(4) The Site Appraisal Committee shall have power to call for any information from the person making any application for the establishment or expansion of a factory involving a hazardous process.

(5) Where the State Government has granted approval to an application for the establishment or expansion of a factory involving a hazardous process, it shall not be necessary for an applicant to obtain a further approval from the Central Board or the State Board established under the Water (Prevention and Control of Pollution) Act, 1981 (14 of 1981).

Compulsory Disclosure of Information by the Occupier (S. 41-B)

(1) The occupier of every factory involving a hazardous process shall disclose in the manner prescribed all information regarding dangers,

including health hazards and the measures to overcome such hazards arising from the exposure to or handling of the materials or substances in the manufacture, transportation, storage and other processes, to the workers employed in the factory. The Chief Inspector, the local authority within whose jurisdiction the factory is situate and the general public in the vicinity.

(2) The occupier shall, all the time or registering the factory involving a hazardous process lay down a detailed policy with respect to the health and safety of the workers employed therein and intimate such policy to the Chief Inspector and the local authority and, thereafter, at such intervals as may be prescribed, inform the Inspector and the local authority of any change made in the said policy.

(3) The information furnished under sub-section (1) shall include accurate information as to the quality, specifications and other characteristics of wastes and the manner of their disposal.

(4) Every occupier shall, with the approval of the Chief Inspector, draw up an on-site emergency plan and detailed disaster control measures for his factor.

(D) WELFARE

Washing Facilities (S. 42)

(1) In every factory—
   (a) adequate and suitable facilities for washing shall be provided and maintained for the use of the workers therein;
   (b) separate and adequately screened facilities shall be provided for the use of male and female workers; and
   (c) such facilities shall be conveniently accessible and shall be kept clean.

(2) The State Government may, in respect of any factory or class or description of factories or of any manufacturing process, prescribe standards or adequate and suitable facilities for washing.

The report of Royal Commission says that "The provisions of suitable washing facilities for all employees is even desirable, and here many factories are deficient. The workers who live in crowded areas have inadequate facilities for washing at their homes and bathing facilities would add to their comfort, health and efficiency. We recommend that for workers engaged in dirty processes, the provision for washing place and water should be made obligatory".

The section enjoins *inter alia* that separate and adequately screened facilities shall be provided for the use of male and female workers.[22]

22. Section 42(1)(b).

Facilities for Storing and Drying Clothing (S. 43)

The State Government may, in respect of any factory or class or description of factories, make rules requiring the provision therein of suitable places for keeping clothing not worn during working hours and for the drying of wet clothing.

"Suitable places for keeping clothing not worn during working hours and for the drying of wet clothing"—What is a suitable place is a disputable question, and it depends on the circumstances of each case. The court held that the risk of theft was an element which mush be taken into consideration in deciding whether the accommodation was suitable.[23]

Facilities for Sitting (S. 44)

(1) In every factory suitable arrangements for sitting shall be provided and maintained for all workers obliged to work in a standing position, in order that they may take advantage of any opportunities for rest which may occur in the course of their work.
(2) If, in the opinion of the Chief Inspector, the workers in any factory engaged in a particular manufacturing process or working in a particular room are able to do their work efficiently in a sitting position, he may, by order in writing, require the occupier of the factory to provide before a specified date such seating arrangements as may be practicable for all the workers so engaged or working.
(3) The State Government may, by notification, in the Official Gazette, declare that the provisions of sub-section (1) shall not apply to and specified factory or class or description of factories or to any specified manufacturing process.

First Aid Appliances (S. 45)

(1) There shall in every factory be provided and maintained, so as to be readily accessible during all working hours first aid boxes or cupboards equipped with the prescribed contents, and the number of such boxes or cupboards to be provided and maintained shall not be less than on for every one hundred and fifty workers ordinarily employed (at any one time) in the factory.
(2) Nothing except the prescribed contents shall be kept in a first aid box or cupboard.
(3) Each first-aid box or cupboard shall be kept in the charge of a separate responsible person who holds a certificate in first-aid treatment recognized by the State Government and who shall always be readily available during the working hours of the factory.

23. McCarthy *v.* Daily Mirror Ltd., (1949) 1 All ER 801 CA.

(4) In every factory wherein more than five hundred workers are ordinarily employed there shall be provided and maintained an ambulance room of the prescribed size, containing the prescribed equipment and in the charge of such medical and nursing staff as may be prescribed and those facilities shall always be made readily available during the working hours of the factory.

Report of Royal Commission on Labour said that "We recommend that, in the case of all factories where mechanical power is used a first-aid box of prescribed standard, which need not involve any great outlay, should be provided and maintained in the different departments according to the number of workers employed, on the basis to be laid down by local Governments. Steps should be taken to ensure that there are persons on the staffs of the different departments in every large factory capable of utilizing the appliances in the proper manner in case of need."

Canteens (S. 46)

(1) The State Government may make rules requiring that in any specified factory wherein more than two hundred and fifty workers are ordinarily employed, a canteen or canteens shall be provided and maintained by the occupier for the use of the workers.

(2) Without prejudice to the generality of the foregoing power, such rules may provided for—

- (a) the date by which such canteen shall be provided;
- (b) the standards in respect of construction, accommodation, furniture and other equipment of the canteen;
- (c) the foodstuffs to be served therein and the charges which may be made therefor;
- (d) the constitution of the managing committee for the canteen and representation of the workers in the management of the canteen;
  - (dd) the items of expenditure in the running of the canteen which are not be taken into account in fixing the cost of foodstuffs and which shall be borne by the employer; and
- (e) the delegation to the Chief Inspector, subject to such conditions as may be prescribed, of the power to make rules under clause (C).

"This section enables State Governments to make rules requiring specified factories employing more than 250 persons, to set-up canteens in conformity with prescribed standards and conditions as regards construction, accommodation, equipment, foodstuffs to be served and the prices to be charged, representation of workmen in the management of the canteen."[24]

The liability of the company under Section 46 is only to set-up and maintain a canteen, so that the workers may have benefit of its existence. The terms and conditions of the service of the staff of the canteen do not come under that liability. Section 46 does not cast an obligation on the

24. S.R.O., Gazette of India, 1946, Part V, p. 348.

proprietor of the factory to run the canteen itself by employing its own workmen.[25] Where the canteen ceased to function as a result of heavy losses, the factory was not bound to provide re-employment to the erstwhile employees of the canteen.[26]

Shelters, Rest Rooms and Lunch Rooms (S. 47)

(1) In every factory wherein more than one hundred and fifty workers are ordinarily employed, adequate and suitable shelters or rest rooms and a suitable lunch room, with provision for drinking water, where can eat meals brought by them, shall be provided and maintained for the use of the workers:

Provided that any canteen maintained in accordance with the provisions of Section 46 shall be regarded as part of the requirements of this sub-section:

Provided further that where a lunchroom exists no worker shall eat any food in the workroom.

(i) The shelters or rest rooms or lunch rooms to be provided under sub-section (1) shall be sufficiently lighted and ventilated and shall be maintained in cool and clean conditions.

(ii) The State Government may—

(a) prescribe the standards in respect of construction, accommodation, furniture and other equipment of shelters, rest rooms and lunch rooms to be provided under this section; and

(b) by notification in the Official Gazette, exempt any factory or class or description of factories from the requirements of this section.

Crèches (S. 48)

(1) In every factory wherein more than (thirty women workers) are ordinarily employed there shall be provided and maintained a suitable room or rooms for the use of children under the age of six years of such women.

(2) Such rooms shall provide adequate accommodation, shall be adequately lighted and ventilated, shall be maintained in a clean and sanitary condition and shall be under the charge of women trained in the care of children and infants.

(3) The State Government may make rules—

(a) prescribing the location and the standards in respect of construction, accommodation, furniture and other equipment of rooms to be provided under this section;

---

25. Workmen Employed in Canteen run by SRF Ltd. *v.* Government of T.N. (1995) 1 LLN 487 (Mad) (DB). But see A.P. Dairy Development Corpn. *v.* Shivadas Pillay, (1992) 1 LLN 423: (1992) 1 LLN 423⊗(1992) 1 Cur LR 302: (1992) 1 LLJ 153 (AP) (DB).

26. Workmen *v.* Ashok Leyland Ltd., (1986) 2 LLN 1035 (Mad).

(b) requiring the provision in factories to which this section applies of additional facilities for the care of children belonging to women workers, including suitable provision of facilities for washing and changing their clothing;

(c) requiring the provision in any factory of free milk or refreshment or both for such children; and

(d) requiring that facilities shall be given in any factory for the mothers of such children to feed them at the necessary intervals.

Welfare Officers (S. 49)

(1) In every factory wherein five hundred or more workers are ordinarily employed the occupier shall employ in the factory such number of welfare officers as may be prescribed.

(2) The State Government may prescribe the duties, qualifications and conditions of service of officers employed under sub-section (1).

It cannot be said that this section cannot be applied to sugar factories or to other factories which employ over 500 employees only for a few months in the year and not continuously.[27]

Power to Make Rules to Supplement this Chapter (S. 50)

(1) The State Government may make rules—

(a) exempting, subject to compliance with such alternative arrangements for the welfare of workers as may be prescribed, any factory or class or description of factories for compliance with any of the provisions of this Chapter; and

(b) requiring in any factory or class or description of factories that representatives of the workers employed in the factory shall be associated with the management of the welfare arrangements of the workers.

(E) WORKING HOURS OF ADULTS

Weekly Hours (S. 51)

No adult worker shall be require or allowed to work in a factory for more than forty-eight hours in any week. If this provision is contravened the occupier of the manager is answerable.

Shall be required or allowed to work—The maximum number of hours of work that an 'occupier' or 'manager' can squeez out of a 'worker' is 48 hours in any week. If this provision is contravened the occupier or the manager is answerable.

27. Employer's Association of Northern India *v.* Secretary of Labour, AIR 1952 All 109: 6 DLR All 297.

It was held in *Superintendent and Remembrance of Legal Affairs, Bengal* v. *J.J. Andrews,*[28] decided under Act XII of 1911, that work done not in or about the factory, was not within the Act. "Where persons are found doing within a factory, work of a kind included in the definition given in Section 2(2) of the Factories Act, 1911 (repealed) they must be presumed to be employed in factory."[29]

Weekly Holidays (S. 52)

(1) No adult worker shall be required or allowed to work in a factory on the first day of the week hereinafter referred to as the said day unless—
  (a) he had or will have a holiday for a whole day on one of the three days immediately before or after the said day, and
  (b) the manager of the factory has, before the said day or the substituted day under clause (a), whichever is earlier,—
    (i) delivered a notice at the office of the Inspector of his intention to require the worker to work on the said day and of the day which is to be substituted, and
    (ii) displayed a notice to that effect in the factory:

  Provided that no substitution shall be made which will result in any worker working for more than ten days consecutively without a holiday for a whole day.

(2) Notices given under sub-section (1) may be cancelled by a notice delivered at the office of the Inspector and a notice displayed in the factory not later than the day before the said day or the holiday to be cancelled, whichever is earlier.

(3) Where, in accordance with the provisions of sub-section (1), any worker works on the said day and has had a holiday on one of the three days immediately before it, that said day shall, for the purpose of calculating his weekly hours of work, be included in the preceding week.

This section contemplates cases of only such workers over whom employer has control in the matter of taking work from them and also in the matter of their employment, leave, holidays, etc. A person cannot be held responsible for something over which he has no control.

"The Factories Act provides for weekly rest day. This ordinarily falls on Sunday but employers can substitute for Sunday any of the three days preceding or following it, subject to the condition that there must not be more than 10 days' continuous work. This proviso, which is designed to enable the more important religious festivals to be substituted for Sunday appears to give general satisfaction; and in a few centers there are more holidays or substituted days than on Sundays." (Report of the Royal Commission on Labour).

Sub-section (1) enjoins on a notice being delivered by the employer at the office of the Inspector of his intention to require the worker to work on the

28. (1931) ILR 50 Cal 519.
29. Ram Dett Mail *v.* Emperor, (1933) ILR 61 Cal. 322. Also see section 64.

said day, i.e. Sunday and of the day which is to be substituted. *Held*, that there was only one offence and not four offences where on a Sunday four offences four persons were employed in the same part of a factory without giving notice to the Inspector and without fixing notice in the manner prescribed by the Act.[30]

COMPENSATORY HOLIDAYS (S. 53)

(1) Where, as a result of the passing of an order or the making of a rule under the provisions of this Act exempting a factory or the workers therein from the provisions of Section 52, a worker is deprived of any of the weekly holidays for which provision is made in sub-section (1) of that section, he shall be allowed, within the month in which the holidays were due to him or within the two months immediately following that month, compensatory holidays of equal number to the holidays so lost.

(2) The State Government may prescribe the manner in which the holidays for which provision is made in sub-section (1) shall be allowed.

Daily Hours (S. 54)

Subject to the provisions of Section 51, no adult worker shall be required or allowed to work in a factory for more than nine hours in any day:

Provided that, subject to the previous approval of the Chief Inspector, the daily maximum hours specified in this section may be exceeded in order to facilitate the change of shifts.

Intervals for Rest (S. 55)

(1) The periods of work of adult workers in factory each day shall be so fixed that no period shall exceed five hours and that no workers shall work for more than five hours before he has had an interval for rest of at least half an hour.

The State Government or, subject to the control of the State Government, the Chief Inspector, may, by written order and for the reasons specified therein, exempt any factory from the provisions of sub-section (1) so however that the total number of hours worked by a worker without an interval does not exceed six.

There is no longer any distinction between seasonal and non-seasonal factories. "As the hours of daily work have been reduced to nine, the period of work before rest has been reduced to five and the Provincial Governments have been empowered to prescribe a higher limit of rest up to one hour in cases where they consider a longer rest interval is necessary."[31]

30. Chitness *v.* State, AIR 1953 MB 230.

31. *Id.* at 338.

"Merely because a factory enjoined an exception as regards this section, it cannot be presumed that it was not required to observe the provisions of Section 61."

The Factories Act has nowhere expressly or by necessary implication ruled out *mens rea* as an essential element of any offence in contravention of Section 55 thereof. Thus, the absence of *mens rea* is a good defense for the accused.[32]

Spread Over (S. 56)

The periods of work of an adult worker in a factory shall be so arranged that inclusive of his intervals for rest under Section 55, they shall not spreadover more than ten and a half hours in any day:

Provided that the Chief Inspector may, for reasons to be specified in writing, increase the [spreadover up to twelve hours].

Night Shifts (S. 57)

Where a worker in a factory works on a shift which extends beyond midnights,—

(a) for the purposes of Sections 52 and 53, a holiday for a whole day shall mean in his case a period of twenty-four consecutive hours beginning when has shift ends; and

(b) the following day for him shall be deemed to be the period of twenty-four hours beginning when such shift ends, and the hours he has worked after midnight shall be counted in the previous day.

Prohibition of Overlapping Shifts (S. 58)

(1) Work shall not be carried on in any factory by means of a system of shifts so arranged that more than one relay of workers engaged in work of the same kind at the same time.

The State Government or subject to the control of the State Government, the Chief Inspector, may, by written order and for the reasons specified therein, exempt on such conditions as may deemed expedient, any factory or class or description of factories or any department or section of a factory or any category or description of workers therein from the provisions of sub-section (1).

Where work of the same kind is carried out by two or more set of workers working during different periods of the day each of such sets is called a "relay" and each of such periods is called a "shift" [Section 2(r)].

This section prohibited multiple shifts except to the extent to which the State Government or subject to the control of State Government, the Chief Inspector may be deemed expedient.

32. State of Orissa *v.* Buhinipati, 1965 (1) LLJ 193.

The Royal Commission on Labour observes: "There are several objections to a system of multiple shifts from the point of view of labour. In the first place, the intervals bear no necessary relation to meal times and where different members of a family are working in different departments of mills, as is frequently the case, it is most unlikely that they will be able to have their meals together. In the second place, supervision becomes extremely difficult and the Chief Inspector, Factories, gave evidence of long services of infringements in these mills. It is stated that an appreciable number of the workers shown in the registers have no existence in fact. Not-existent workers are credited with pay, which is divided between the clerks, the jobbers and men who do the extra work. The proportion of such 'dummies' was estimated by competent witnesses at $7\frac{1}{2}$% or 10% of the total. The system increases the power and the illicit profits of the jobbers and it diminishes correspondingly the control over labour which the management can exercise."

Extra Wages for Over Time (S. 59)

(1) Where a worker works in a factory for more than nine hours in any day or for more than forty-eight hours in any week, he shall, in respect of overtime work, be entitled to wages at the rate of twice his ordinary rate of wages.

(2) For the purposes of sub-section (1), 'Ordinary rate of wages' means the basic wages plus such allowances, including the cash equivalent of the advantage accruing through the concessional sale to workers of foodgrains and other articles, as the worker is for the time being entitled to, but does not include a bonus and wages for overtime work.

(3) Where any workers in a factory are paid on a piece rate basis, the time rate shall be deemed to be equivalent to the daily average of their full time earnings for the days on which they actually worked on the same or identical job during the month immediately preceding the calendar month during which the overtime work was done, and such time rates shall be deemed to be the ordinary rates of wages of those workers:

Provided that in the case of a worker who has not worked in the immediately preceding calendar month on the same or identical job, the time rate shall be deemed to be equivalent to the daily average of the earnings of the worker for the days on which he actually worked in the week in which the overtime work was done.

Explanation: For the purposes of this sub-section, in computing the earnings for the days on which the worker actually worked such allowances, including the cash equivalent of the advantage accruing through the concesional sale to workers of foodgrains and other articles, as the worker is for the time being entitled to, shall be included but any bonus or wages for overtime work payable in relation to the period with reference to which the earnings and being computed shall be excluded.

(4) The cash equivalent of the advantage accruing through the concessional sale to a worker of foodgrains and other articles shall be computed as often as may be prescribed on the basis of the maximum quantity of foodgrains and other articles admissible to a standard family.

Explanation 1: "Standard family" means a family consisting of the worker, his or her spouse and two children below the age of fourteen years requiring in all three adult consumption units.

Explanation 2: "Adult consumption unit" means the consumption unit of a male above the age of fourteen years; and the consumption unit of a female above the age of fourteen years and that of a child below the age of fourteen years shall be calculated at the rates of 0.8 and 0.6 respectively of one adult consumption unit.

(5) The State Government may make rules prescribing—

(a) the manner in which the cash equivalent of the advantage accruing through the concessional sale to worker of foodgrains and to the articles shall be computed; and

(b) the registers that shall be maintained in a factory for the purpose of securing compliance with the provisions of this section.

House rent allowance, although payable to employees who were not provided with accommodation, cannot be taken into account to calculate overtime wages of the employees provided with such accommodation.

Section 59 does not postulate payment of extra wages of overtime when a worker does not work in the factory beyond the prescribed hours and is absent on tour on duty.

An employer requiring the workmen to work for more than the maximum number of hours or overtime work postulated by Section 64(4)(iv) cannot merely on that ground deny him overtime wages for the excess hours.[33]

A settlement denying the benefits of overtime wages contemplated by Section 59 cannot be treated as binding on the workmen in the garb of Section 19 of the I.D. Act, 1947.

The Chief Inspector of factories is not competent to order the employer to make a payment under Section 59 to the workers.

All persons, whether employed as 'worker' within the meaning of Section 2(1) or not, who are employed in or in connection with a factory, would be entitled to the benefits of the Act including Section 59 thereof.

Computation of cash equivalent—The basis for such computation is the maximum quantity of foodgrains and other articles admissible to a standards family.

Standard family—The expression means a family consisting of the worker, his or his spouse and two children below the age of fourteen years requiring in all three adult consumption units.

33. Hindustan Machine Tools Ltd. *v.* Labour Court, (1994) I Cur LR 137: (1994) 1 LLNB 256: (1993) 2 LLJ 1219 (Raj).

Adult Consumption Unit—Means the consumption unit of a male above the age of fourteen years, and the consumption unit of a female above the age of fourteen years and that of a child below the age of fourteen years to be calculated at the rate of .8 and .6 respectively of one adult consumption unit.

Accrual of advantage in cash equivalent as contemplated in this section arises through the concessional sale to a worker of foodgrain and other articles.

The State Government is empowered to prescribe rules governing the computation of such cash equivalent and the maintenance in a factory of the necessary registers for purpose of securing compliance with a provisions of this section.

Restriction on Double Employment (S. 60)

No adult worker shall be required or allowed to work in any factory on any day on which he has already been working in any other factory, save in such circumstances as may be prescribed.

Notice of Periods of Work for Adults (S. 61)

(1) There shall be displayed and correctly maintained in every factory in accordance with the provisions of sub-section (2) of Section 108, a notice of periods of work for adults, showing clearly for every day the periods during which adult workers may be required to work.

(2) The period shown in the notice required by sub-section (1) shall be fixed beforehand, in accordance with the following provisions of this section, and shall be such that workers working for those periods would not be working in contravention of any of the provisions of Sections 51, 52, 53, 54, [55, 56 and 58].

(3) Where all the adult workers in a factory are required to work during the same periods, the manager of the factory shall fix those periods for such workers generally.

(4) Where all the adult workers in a factory are not required to work during the same periods, the manager of the factory shall classify them into groups according to the nature of their work indicating the number of workers in each group.

(5) For each group, which is not required to work on a system of shifts, the manager of the factory shall fix the periods during which the group may be required to work.

(6) Where any group is required to work on a system of shifts and the relays are not to be subject to pre-determined periodical changes of shifts, the manager of the factory shall fix the period during which each relay of the group may be require to work.

(7) Where any group is to work on a system of shifts and the relays are to be subject to pre-determined periodical changes of shifts, the manager of the factor shall draw up a scheme of shifts where under the periods during which any relay of the group may be required to work and the relay which will be working at any time of the day shall be known for any day.

(8) The State Government may prescribe forms of the notice required to sub-section (1) and the manner in which it shall be maintained.

(9) In the case of a factory beginning work after the commencement of this Act, a copy of the notice referred to in sub-section (1) shall be sent in duplicate to the Inspector before the day on which work is begun in the factory.

(10) Any proposed change in the system of work in any factory which will necessitate a change in the notice referred to in sub-section (1) shall be notified to the Inspector in duplicate before the change is made, and except with the previous section of the Inspector, no such change shall be made until one week has elapsed since the last change.

Display and correct maintenance in every factory of a notice of periods of work for adults—This section insists on a correct notice to be displayed and correctly maintained. An incorrect notice, though complied with the requirements of this section, amounts to a failure to display as enjoined by this section.

Extension of time: It is entirely at the discretion of the manager to change the working hours, but that change cannot be exercised by the manager after the mill begins working for the period scheduled in advance, since hours of employment are to be fixed and should not be an object of sudden variation of casual alteration.

The extra time taken for the work involved in carrying ice to ships in the docks when required was held to be not worked done in or about the factory and that it did not fall within the prohibitory provisions of the Act.

Penalty—Where the manager of a factory employed eighteen workers beyond permitted hours, it was held that in 18 prosecutions brought against him, he could properly be convicted and sentenced on each.

Change in the hours of work—Where an intimation was sent to the Inspector of Factories about the change in the hours of work on the day of which the change was made and the letter did not reach the Inspector till two days later and where the notice under section 61(1) of the Act did not show the change in hours of work, held, that an offence has been committed under section 63. It is not protected by section 117.

System of work—If on a particular single day, there is departure from the system of work already notified under sub-section (1) then that cannot be said to be change in the system of work in the factory because a change in the system of work would mean either a permanent change or a change of a change for a fairly long time, duration of time in the hours of work or any other condition.

Register of Adult Workers (S. 62)

(1) The manager of every factory shall maintain a register of adult workers, to be available to the inspector at all times during working hours, or when any work is being carried on in the factory showing—
  (a) the name of each adult worker in the factory;
  (b) the nature of his work;
  (c) the group, if any, in which he is included;
  (d) where his group works on shifts, the relay to which he is allotted; and
  (e) such other particulars as may be prescribed:

Provided that, if the Inspector is of opinion that any muster-roll or register maintained as a part of the routine of a factory gives in respect of any or all the workers in the factory the particulars required under this section, he may, by order in writing, direct that such muster-roll or register shall to the corresponding extent be maintained in place of, and be treated as, the register of adult workers in that factory.

[(1-A) No adult worker shall be required or allowed to work in any factory unless his name and other particulars have been entered in the register of adult workers.]

The State Government may prescribe the form of the register of adult workers, the manner in which it shall be maintained and the period for which it shall be preserve.

Hours of Work to Correspond with Notice Under Section 61 and Register Under Section 62 (S. 63)

No adult worker shall be required or allowed to work in any factory otherwise than in accordance with the notice of periods of work for adults displayed in the factory and the entries made beforehand against his name in the register of adult workers of the factory.

This section prohibits employment of any worker on any work in the factory premises except in accordance with notice displayed and the contention that the work was not a part of manufacturing process or incidental to it is immaterial.

Power to Make Exempting Rules (S. 64)

(1) The State Government may make rules defining the persons who hold positions of supervision or management or are employed in a confidential position in a factory [or empowering the Chief Inspector to declare any person, other than a person defined by such rules, as a person holding position of supervision or management or employed in a confidential position in a factory if, in the opinion of the Chief Inspector, such person holds such position or is so employed] and the provisions of this Chapter, other than the provisions of clause (b) of

sub-section (10 of Section 66 and of the proviso to that sub-section, shall not apply to any person so defined [or declared]:

Provided that any person so defined or declared shall, where the ordinary rate of wages of such person does not exceed the wage limit specified in sub-section (6) of Section 1 of the Payment of Wages Act, 1936 (4 of 1936), as amended from time to time, [be entitled to extra wages in respect of overtime work under Section 59.]

The State Government may make rules in respect of adult workers in factories providing for the exemption, to such extent and subject to such conditions as may be prescribed—

(a) of workers engaged on urgent repairs, from the provisions of Sections 51, 52, 54, 55 and 56;

(b) of workers engaged in work in the nature of preparatory or complementary work which must necessarily be carried on outside the limits laid down for the general working of the factory, from the provisions of Sections 51, 54, 55 and 56;

(c) of workers engaged in work which is necessarily so intermittent that the intervals during which they do not work while on duty ordinarily amount to more than the intervals for rest required by or under Section 55, from the provisions of Sections 51, 54, 55 and 56;

(d) of workers engaged in any work which for technical reasons must be carried on continuously from the provisions of Sections 51, 52, 54, 55 and 56;

(e) of workers engaged in making or supplying articles of prime necessity which must be make or supplied every day, from the provisions of [Sections 51 and 52];

(f) of workers engaged in a manufacturing process which cannot be carried on except during fixed seasons, from the provisions of [Sections 51, 52 and 54];

(g) of workers engaged in a manufacturing process which cannot be carried on except at times dependent on the irregular action of natural forces, from the provisions of Sections 52 and 55;

(h) of workers engaged in engine-rooms or boiler-houses or in attending to power-plant or transmission machinery, from the provisions of [Sections 51 and 52];

(i) of workers engaged in the printing of newspapers, who are held up on account of the breakdown of machinery, from the provisions of Sections 51, 54 and 56.

Explanation: In this clause the expression "newspapers" has the meaning assigned to it in the Press and Registration of Books Act, 1867 (XXV of 1867);

(j) of workers engaged in the loading or unloading of railway wagons [or lorries or trucks], from the provisions of [Sections 51, 52, 54, 55 and 56]; and

(k) of workers engaged in any work, which is notified by the State Government in the Official Gazette, as a work of national importance, from the provisions of [Sections 51, 52, 54, 55 and 56.]

Rules made under sub-section (2) providing for any exemption may also provide for any consequential exemption from the provisions of Section 61 which the (State) Government may deem to be expedient, subject to such conditions as it may prescribe.

In making rules under this section, the State Government shall not exceed, except in respect of exemption under clause (a) of sub-section (2), the following limits of work inclusive of overtime—

(i) the total number of hours of work in any day shall not exceed ten;

(ii) the spread over, inclusive of intervals for rest, shall not exceed twelve hours in any one day:
Provided that the State Government may, in respect of any or all of the categories of workers referred to in clause (d) of sub-section (2), make rules prescribing the circumstances in which, and the conditions subject to which, the restrictions imposed by clause (i) and clause (ii) shall not apply in order to enable a shift worker to work the whole or part of a subsequent shift in the absence of a worker who has failed to report for duty;

(iii) the total number of hours of work in a week, including overtime, shall not exceed sixty; and

(iv) the total number of hours of overtime shall not exceed fifty for any one quarter.

Explanation: "Quarter" means a period of three consecutive months beginning on the 1st January, the 1st of April, the 1st of July or the 1st of October.

(5) Rules made under this section shall remain in force for not more than [five years.]

Power to Make Exempting Orders (S. 65)

(1) Where the State Government is satisfied that, owing to the nature of the work carried on or to other circumstances, it is unreasonable to require that the periods of work of any adult workers in any factory or class or description of factories should be fixed beforehand, it may, by written order, relax or modify the provisions of Section 61 in respect of such workers therein, to such extent and in such manner as it may think fit, and subject to such conditions as it may deem expedient to ensure control over periods of work.

(2) The State Government or, subject to the control of the State Government, the Chief Inspector, may be written order exempt, on such conditions as it or he may deem expedient, any or all of the adult workers in any factory or group or class description of factories from any or all of the

provisions of Section 51, factories to deal with an exceptional press of work.

(3) Any exemption granted under sub-section (2) shall be subject to the following conditions, namely—
   (i) the total number of hours of work in any day shall not exceed twelve;
   (ii) the spreadover, inclusive of intervals for rest, shall not exceed thirteen hours in any one day;
   (iii) the total number of hours of work in any week, including overtime, shall not exceed sixty; and
   (iv) no worker shall be allowed to work overtime, for more than seven days at a stretch and the total number of hours of overtime work in any quarter shall not exceed seventy-five.

Explanation: In this sub-section "quarter" has the same meaning as in sub-section (4) of Section 64.

The State Government is empowered to make exempting orders in cases where it is expedient. Such power is to be exercised to ensure control over periods of work, i.e. working hours. The exemption contemplated by sub-section (4), is subject to the maximum limits prescribed under sub-section (4) of Section 65. The exemption is to last in any year for a period or periods in all not exceeding in the aggregate three months.

Further Restriction on Employment of Women (S. 66)

(1) The provisions of this Chapter shall, in their application to women in factories, be supplemented by the following further restrictions, namely—
   (a) no exemption from the provisions of Section 54 may be granted in except of any woman;
   (b) no woman shall be [required or allowed to work in any factory] except between the hours of 6 a.m. and 7 p.m.:
   Provided that the State Government may, by notification in the Official Gazette, in respect of [any factory or group or class or description of factories], vary the limits down in clause (b), but so that no such variation shall authorize the employment of any woman between the hours of 10 p.m. and 5 a.m.;
   [(c) there shall be no change of shifts except after a weekly holiday or any other holiday.]

(2) The State Government may make rules providing for the exemption from the restrictions set out in sub-section (1), to such extent and subject to such conditions as it may prescribe, of women working in fish-curing or fish-canning factories, where the employment of women beyond the hours specified in the said restrictions is necessary to prevent damage to, or deterioration in, any raw material.

(3) The rules made under sub-section (2) shall remain in force for not more than three years at a time.

The Report of Royal Commission on Labour may be referred to the relevant observations.

"For every country the regulation of the hours of works for women follows suit to the regulation of the hours of work for children. The main arguments in favour of fixing the maximum hours for women at lower levels than those prescribed for men are that women have domestic duties to perform and that they find long hours a greater strain. For practice, too, their hours are shorter in a number of factories."

General Prohibition—The Inspector has to right to issue a general prohibition against he employment of women at night without going in the question whether the staff is sufficient. Here it may be noted that an owner of a factory can employ women for night work only if the inspector deems it fit.

In some women workers in a textile factory choose to dust of their own accord and regulate the spinning wheels for their own satisfaction and comfort some time before the starting of the work hour, although arrangement for such had been made by the occupier of the factory, it cannot be said that the women had been employed before the statutory hour.

(F) Employment of Young Persons

Prohibition of Employment of Young Children (S. 67)

No child who has not completed his fourteenth year shall be required or allowed to work in any factory.

Non-adult Workers to Carry Tokens (S. 68)

A child who has completed his fourteenth year or an adolescent shall not be required or allowed to work in any factory unless—

(a) a certificate of fitness granted with reference to him under section 69 is in the custody of the manager of the factory, and

(b) such child or adolescent carries while he is at work a token giving a reference to such certificate.

A child who has completed his 14th year or an adolescent can be required or allowed to work in any factory if a certificate of fitness granted with reference to him under section 49 is in custody of the manager of the factory, and such child or adolescent carries while he is at work a token giving a reference to such certificate. The obligation rests on the occupier as well.

Certificate of Fitness (S. 69)

(1) A certifying surgeon shall, on the application of any young person or his parent or guardian accompanied by a document signed by the manager of a factory that such person will be employed therein if certified to be fit for work in factory, or on the application of the

manager of the factory in which any young person wishes to work, examine such person and ascertain his fitness for work in a factory.

(2) The certifying surgeon, after examination, may grant to such young person, in the prescribed form, or may renew—

(a) a certificate of fitness to work in a factory as a child, if he is satisfied that the young person has completed his fourteenth year, that he has attained the prescribed physical standards and that he is fit for such work; and

(b) a certificate of fitness to work in a factory as an adult, if he is satisfied that the young person has completed his fifteenth year, and is fit for a full day's work in a factory:

Provided that unless the certifying surgeon has personal knowledge of the place where the young person proposes to work and of the manufacturing process in which he will be employed, he shall not grant or renew a certificate under this sub-section until he has examined such place.

(3) A certificate of fitness granted or renewed under sub-section (2)—

(a) shall be valid only for a period of twelve months from the date thereof; and

(b) may be made subject to conditions in regard to the nature of the work in which the young person may be employed, or requiring re-examination of the young person before the expiry of the period of twelve months.

(4) A certifying surgeon shall revoke any certificate granted or renewed under sub-section (2) if in his opinion the holder of it is no longer fit to work in the capacity stated therein in a factory.

(5) Where a certifying surgeon refuses to grant or renew a certificate or a certificate of the kind requested or revokes a certificate, he shall, if so requested by any person who could have applied for the certificate or the renewal thereof, state his reasons in writing for so doing.

(6) Where a certificate under this section with reference to any young person is granted or renewed subject to such conditions as are referred to in clause (b) of sub-section (3), the young person shall not be required or allowed to work in a factory except in accordance with those conditions.

(7) Any fee payable for a certificate under this section shall be paid by the occupier and shall not be recoverable from the young person, his parents or guardian.

Effect of Certificate of Fitness Granted to Adolescent (S. 70)

(1) An adolescent who has been granted a certificate of fitness to work in a factory as an adult under clause (b) of sub-section (2) of Section 69, and who while at work in a factory carries a token giving reference to the certificate, shall be deemed to be an adult for all the purposes of Chapters VI and VIII.

[1-A) No female adolescent or male adolescent who has not attained the age of seventeen year but who has been granted a certificate of fitness to work in a factory as an adult, shall be required or allowed to work in any factory except between 6 a.m. and 7 p.m.:

Provided that the State Government may, by notification in the Official Gazette, in respect of any factory or group or class or description of factories,—

(i) vary the limits laid down in this sub-section so, however, that no such section shall authorise the employment of any female adolescent between 10 p.m. and 5 a.m.; and

(ii) grant exemption from the provisions of this sub-section in case of serious emergency where national interest is involved.

(2) An adolescent who has not been granted a certificate of fitness to work in a factory as an adult under the aforesaid clause (b) shall, notwithstanding his age, be deemed to be a child for all the purposes of this Act.

Working Hours for Children (S. 71)

(1) No child shall be employed or permitted to work, in any factory—
 (a) for more than four and a half hours in any day; and
 (b) during the night.

Explanation: For the purpose of this sub-section "night" shall mean a period of at least twelve consecutive hours, which shall included the interval between 10 p.m. and 6 a.m.

(2) The period of work of all children employed in a factory shall be limited to two shifts which shall not overlap or spread over more than five hours each; and each child shall be employed in only one of the relays which shall not, except with the previous permission in writing of the Chief Insecptor, be changed more frequently than once in period of thirty days.

(3) The provisions of Section 52 shall apply also to child workers and no exemption from the provisions of that section may be granted in respect of any child.

(4) No child shall be required or allowed to work in any factory on any day on which he has already been working in another factory.

(5) No female child shall be required or allowed to work in any factory except between 8 a.m. and 7 p.m.

Notice of Periods of Work for Children (S. 72)

(1) There shall be displayed and correctly maintained in every factory in which children are employed, in accordance with the provisions of sub-section (2) of Section 108 a notice of periods may be required or allowed to work.

(2) The periods shown in the notice required by sub-section (1) shall be fixed beforehand in accordance with the method laid down for adult workers in Section 61, and shall be such that children working for this period would not be working in contravention of any of the provisions of Section 71.

(3) The provisions of sub-sections (8), (9) and (10) of section 61 shall apply also to the notice required by sub-section (1) of this section.

Register of Child Workers (S. 73)

(1) The manager of every factory in which children are employed shall maintain a register of child workers, to be available to the Inspector at all times during working hours or when any work is being carried on in a factory, showing—

(a) the name of each child worker in the factory,

(b) the nature of his work,

(c) the group, if any, in which he is included,

(d) where his group works on shifts, the relay to which he is allotted, and

(e) the number of his certificate of fitness granted under Section 69.

(1-A) No child worker shall be required or allowed to work in any factory unless his name and other particulars have been entered in the register of child workers.

(2) State Government may prescribe the form of the register of child workers, the manner in which it shall be maintained and the period for which it shall be preserved.

Hours of Work to Correspond with Notice under Section 72 and Register Under Section 73 (S. 74)

No child shall be employed in any factory otherwise than in accordance with the notice of periods of work for children displayed in the factory and the entries made before hand against his name in the register of child workers of the factory.

Power to Require Medical Examination (S. 75)

Where an Inspector is of opinion:

(a) that any person working in factory without a certificate of fitness is a young person, or

(b) that a young person working in factory with a certificate of fitness is no longer fit to work in the capacity stated therein, he may serve on the manager of the factory a notice requiring that such person or young person, as the case may be, shall be examined by a certifying surgeon, and such person or young person shall not, if the Inspector so directs, be employed, or permitted to work, in any factory until he has been so examined and has been granted a certificate of fitness or a fresh certificate of fitness, as the case may be, under Section 69, or has been certificate of fitness, as the case may be, under Section 69 by the certifying surgeon examining him not be a young person.

Power to Make Rules (S. 76)

The State Government may make rules—

(a) prescribing the forms of certificates of fitness to be granted under Section 69, providing for the grant of duplicates in the event of loss of the original certificates, and fixing the fees which may be charged for such certificates and renewals thereof and such duplicates;

(b) prescribing the physical standards to be attained by children and adolescents working in factories;

(c) regulating the procedure of certifying surgeons under this Chapter; and

(d) specifying other duties which certifying surgeons may be required to perform in connection with the employment of young person in factories, and fixing the fees which may be charged for such duties and the persons by whom they shall be payable.

(G) ANNUAL LEAVE WITH WAGES

Application of Chapter (S. 78)

(1) The provisions of this Chapter shall not operate to the prejudice of any right to which a worker may be entitled under any other law or under the terms of any award, agreement (including settlement) or contract of service:

Provided that if such award, agreement including settlement or contract of service provides for a longer annual leave with wages than provided in this Chapter, the quantum of leave, which the worker shall be entitled to, shall be in accordance with such award, agreement or contract or service or matters which are provided for in such award, agreement or contract of service or matter which are provided for less favourable therein, the provisions of Sections 79 to 82, so far as may be, shall apply.

(2) The provisions of this Chapter shall not apply to workers in any factory of any railway administered by the Government, who are governed any leave rules approved by the Central Government.

Annual Leave with Wages (S. 79)

(1) Every worker who have worked for a period of 240 days or more in a factory during a calendar year shall be allowed during the subsequent calendar year, leave with wages for a number of days calculated at the rate—

(i) if an adult, one day for every twently days of work performed by him during the previous calendar year; and

(ii) if a child, one day for every fifteen days of work performed by him during the previous calendar year.

Explanation 1: For the purpose of this sub-section—

(a) any days of lay-off, by agreement or contract or as permissible under the standing order;

(b) in the case of a female worker, maternity leave for any number of days not exceeding twelve weeks; and

(c) the leave earned in the year prior to that in which the leave is enjoyed; shall be deemed to be days on which the worker has worked in a factory for the purpose of computation of the period of 240 days or more, but he shall earn leave for these days.

Explanation 2: The leave admissible under sub-section shall be exclusive of all holidays whether occurring during or at either end of the period of leave.

(2) A worker whose service commences otherwise than on the first day of January shall be entitled to leave with wages at the rate laid down in clause (i) or, as the case may be, clause (ii) of sub-section (1) if he has worked for two-thirds of the total number of days in the remainder of the calendar year.

(3) If a worker is discharged or dismissed from service or quits his employment or is superannuated or dies while in service, during the course of the calendar year, he or his heir or nominee, as the case may be, shall be entitled to wages in lieu of the quantum of leave to which he was entitled immediately before his discharge, dismissal, quitting of employment, superannuating or death calculated at the rates specified in sub-section (1), even if he had not worked for the entire period specified in sub-section (1) or sub-section (2) making him eligible to avail of such leave, and such payment shall be made—

(i) where the worker is discharged or dismissed or quits employment, before the expiry of the second working day from the date of such discharge, dismissal or quitting; and

(ii) where the worker is superannuated or dies while in service, before the expiry of two months from the date of such superannuation or death.

(4) In calculating leave under this section, fraction of leave of half a day or more shall be treated as one full day's leave, and fraction of less than half a day shall be omitted.

(5) If a worker does not in any one calendar year take the whole of the leave allowed to him under sub-section (1) or sub-section (2), as the case may be, any leave not taken by him shall be added to the leave to be allowed to him in the succeeding calendar year:

Provided that the total number of days of leave that may be carried forward to a succeeding year shall not exceed thirty in the case of an adult or forty in the case of a child:

Provided further that a worker, who has applied for leave with wages but has not been given such leave in accordance with any scheme laid down in sub-sections (8) and (9) or in contravention of sub-section (10) shall be entitled to carry forward the leave refused without any limit.

(6) A worker may at any time apply in writing to the manager of a factory not less than fifteen days before the date on which he wishes his leave to begin, to take all the leave or any portion thereof allowable to him during the calendar year:

Provided that the application shall be made not less than thirty days before the date on which the worker wishes his leave to begin, if he is employed in public utility service as defined in clause (n) of Section 2 of the Industrial Disputes Act, 1947 (XIV of 1947):

Provided further that the number of times in which leave may be taken during any year shall not exceed three.

(7) if a worker wants to avail himself of the leave with wages due to him to cover a period of illness, he shall be granted such leave even if the application for leave is not made within the time specified in sub-section (6); and in such a case wages as admissible under Section 81 shall be paid not later than fifteen days, or in the case of a public utility service not later than thirty days from the date of the application for leave.

(8) For the purpose of ensuring the continuity of work, the occupier or manager of the factory, in agreement with the Work Committee of the factory constituted under Section 3 of the Industrial Dispute Act, 1947 (XIV), or a similar committee constituted under any other Act or if there is no such Work Committee or a similar committee in the factory, in agreement with the representatives of the workers therein chosen in the prescibred manner, may lodge with the Chief Inspector a scheme in writing whereby the grant of leave allowable under this section may be regulated.

(9) A scheme lodged under sub-section (8) shall be displayed at some conspicuous and convenient places in the factory and shall be in force for a period of twelve months from the date on which it comes into force, and may thereafter be renewed with or without modification for a further period of twelve months at a time, by manager in agreement with the Works Committee or a similar committee, or as the case may be, in agreement with the representatives of the workers as specified in sub-section (8), and a notice of renewal shall be sent to the Chief Inspector before it is renewed.

(10) An application for leave which does not contravene the provisions of sub-section (6) shall not be refused, unless refusal is in accordance with the scheme for the time being in operation under sub-sections (8) and (9).

(11) If the employment of a worker who is entitled to leave under sub-section (1) or sub-section (2), as the case may be, is terminated by the occupier before he has taken the entire leave to which he is entitled, or

if having applied for and having not been granted such leave, the worker quite his employment before he has taken the leave, the leave, the occupier of the factory shall pay him the amount payable under Section 80 in respect of the leave not taken, and such payment shall be not, where the employment of the worker is terminated by the occupier, before the expiry of the second working day after such termination, and where a worker who quits his employment, on or before the next pay day.

(12) The unavailed leave of a worker shall not taken into considera.ion in computing the period of any notice required to be given before discharge or dismissal.

Wages During Leave Period (S. 80)

(1) For the leave allowed to him under (Section 78 or Section 79, as the case may be), a worker shall be entitled to wages at a rate equal to the daily average of his total full time earnings for the days on which he actually worked during the month immediately preceding his leave, exclusive of any overtime and bonus but inclusive of dearness allowance and the cash equivalent of the advantage accruing through the confessional sale to the worker of food grains and other articles:
Provided that in the case of a worker who has not worked on any day during the calendar month immediately preceding his leave, he shall be paid at a rate equal to the daily average of his total full time earnings for the days on which he actually worked during the last calendar month preceding his leave, in which he actually worked, exclusive of any overtime and bonus but inclusive of dearness allowance and the cash equivalent of the advantage accruing through the concessional sale to the workers of foodgrains and other articles.

(2) The cash equivalent of the advantage accruing through the concessional sale to the worker of foodgrains and other articles shall be computed as often as may be prescribed on the basis of the maximum quantity of foodgrains and other articles admissible to a standard family.

Explanation: "Standard family" means a family consisting of a worker, his or her spouse and two children below the age of fourteen years; and the consumption unit of a female above the age of fourteen years and that of a child below the age of fourteen years shall be calculated at the rate of 0.8 and 0.6 respectively of one adult consumption unit.

(3) The State Government may make rules prescribing—
   (a) the manner in which the cash equivalent of the advantage accruing through the concessional sale to a worker of food grains and other articles shall be computed; and
   (b) the registers that shall be maintained in a factory for the purpose of securing compliance with the provisions of this section.

Payment in Advance in Certain Cases (S. 81)

A worker who has been allowed leave for not less than four days, in the case of an adult, and five days, in the case of a child, shall, before his leave begins, be paid the wages due for the period of the leave allowed.

Mode of Recovery of Unpaid Wages (S. 820)

Any sum required to be paid by an employer, under this Chapter but not paid by him shall be recoverable as delayed wages under the provisions of the Payment of Wages Act, 1936 (IV of 1936).

Power to Make Rules (S. 83)

The State Government may make rules directing managers of factories to keep registers containing such particulars as may be prescribed and requiring the registers to be made available for examination by Inspector.

Power to Exempt Factories (S. 84)

Where the State Government is satisfied that the leave rules applicable to workers in a factory provide benefits which in its opinion are not less favourable than those for which this Chapter makes provision of this Chapter subject to such conditions as may be specified in order.

Explanation: For the purposes of this section in deciding whether the benefits which are provided for by any leave rules are less favourable than those for which this Chapter makes provision, or not, the totality of the benefits shall be taken into account.

16

Sale of Goods Act, 1930

A. INTRODUCTION

The present act came into force on Ist July, 1930. Until that date the law relating to sale of goods was contained in Chapter VII (Sections 76 to 123) of the Indian Contract Act, 1872. The Sale of Goods Act is applicable throughout India.

B. DEFINITION OF CONTRACT OF SALE

Section 4(1) defines a contract of sale as under—

A contract of sale of goods is a contract whereby the seller transfers or agrees to transfer the property in the goods to the buyer for a price. The essentials to constitute such a contract are:

1. It is a contract between two parties, one known as the seller and the other the buyer.
2. The subject matter of a contract is "goods."
3. The seller should transfer or agree to transfer the property (ownership) in the goods to the buyer.
4. The transfer of property (ownership) in the goods from the seller to the buyer is for consideration known as "price."

To provide valid sale under the sale of Goods Act, there must be cogent and convincing evidence of:

(i) agreement between the competent parties,
(ii) the price of goods, and
(iii) passing of property in the goods.

Unless all these ingredients of sale are duly proved, mere entry or endorsement made by the registering authority under section 31 of the Motor Vehicles Act showing transfer of ownership of the vehicle does not amount to sufficient proof of sale of that vehicle.[1]

1. See R.K. Bangia, *'Sale of Goods Act'* (1999) at 2. Also See New India Ass. Co. Ltd. *v.* T.H. Deva Kumar, AIR 1996 Kant. 345, at 349.

A. GOODS

The subject matter of a contract of sale of goods Sec. 2(7) of the Act defines the same as under:

Goods means every kind of movable property other than actionable claims and money; and includes stock and share, growing crops, grass, and things attached to or forming part of the land which are agreed to be severed before sale or under the contract of sale.

The sale of goods act deals with the sale of goods, i.e., movable property. The sale of immovable property is dealt with in the transfer of Property Act, 1882. Although the term "goods" means every kind of movable property but certain things have been specifically excluded and certain other things specifically included in the term, by the definition.[2]

D. CONDITIONS AND WARRANTIES

In a contract of sale of goods there may be various terms or stipulations. Such stipulations may be either conditions or warranties. If a stipulation forms the very basis of the contract, or, as stated in Sec. 12(2), is essential to the main purpose of the contract, it is called a condition. On the other hand, if the stipulation is not essential to the main purpose of the contract but is only of secondary importance, or as Sec. 12(3) put it, is collateral to the main purpose of the contract, it is called a warranty.

ILLUSTRATION

(i) A lady orders for a red saree, it being agreed between her and the seller. That it will be sent by a registered parcel, and that she will pay the price by 15th January, the day of her marriage. In this illustration the stipulations regarding the colour of the saree as well as the date of supply are essential to the main purpose of the contract and are conditions where as stipulations regarding the time of payment of the price and the mode of despatch of the goods are not essential to the main purpose of the contract but are only collateral, they are warranties.

There is no hard and fast rule as to which stipulation is a condition and which one is a warranty. Whether a stipulation in a contract of sale is a condition or a warranty depends in each case on the construction of the contract.[3]

(ii) A agrees to supply a suit to B by 15th November, which the latter wants to bear on the day of his marriage to be held on 16th November, the time of the delivery of the suit is a condition. On the other hand, if the suit which A agrees to deliver to B by 15th November, is required by the buyer to be used in the following winter season the time of delivery is a warranty.

2. *Id.* at 4.
3. *Id.* at 27.

(a) Stipulations as to time

According to section 55 of the Indian Contract Act, if the time of the performance of the contract is of the essence of the contract and the promisor makes a delay in the performance of the contract, the contract is voidable at the option of the promisor. On the other hand, if the time of performance is not of the essence of the contract the delayed performance by the promisor entitles the promisee to claim damages only for the loss occasioned to him.[4]

(b) Consequences of the Breach of a Condition or a Warranty

Since a condition is a stipulation essential to the main purpose of the contract its breach by one party entitle the other to treat contract as repudiated.[5]

ILLUSTRATION

If the seller makes a breach of condition, the buyer may reject the goods. Similarly, if the breach is made by the buyer, seller, the seller may treat it as a breach of contract and not perform his own part of the obligation.

A agrees to supply B 1000 bags of first quality wheat at the rate of Rs. 100 per bag but supplies only second quality wheat, the price of which is Rs. 90 per bag. There is breach of condition by the seller and the buyer can reject the goods, but if the buyer so likes he may treat it as a breach of warranty, accept the second quality wheat and claim compensation at the rate of Rs 10. per bag.

(c) Difference between Condition and Warranty

S.N.	*Condition*	*Warranty*
1.	It is a stipulation, which is essential to the main purpose of contract.	It is stipulation, which is not essential to the main purpose of contract.
2.	It goes direct to the root or substance of the contract.	It does not direct to the root of the contract.
3.	Its breach gives the buyer right to repudiate the contract.	Its breach does give right to buyer to repudiate the contract.
4.	The buyer has an option to claim damages, instead of repudiating the contract.	The buyer can in no case repudiate the contract, if there is a breach of warranty. He can only claim damages.

(d) Express and Implied Conditions

Parties may expressly provide any conditions or warranties in their contract. A part from what may be provided by the parties in the contract,

4. *Ibid.*
5. Sec. 12(2).

certain conditions and warranties, as provided in sections 14 to 17, are impliedly therein every contract of sale of goods. The implied conditions and warranties provided in the act are binding in every contract of sale unless they are inconsistent with any express conditions and warranties agreed to by the parties.[6]

(e) Implied Conditions as to Title (S. 14(9))

In every contract of sale, unless the circumstances are such as to show a different intention, there is an implied condition on the part of the seller that in the case of sale he has a right to sell the goods and in the case of an agreement to sell he will have a right to sell the goods at the time when the property in them is to pass.

Generally a person who is the owner of the goods or who is owner's agent may sell the goods. If a person has no title to the goods or otherwise does not have a right to dispose-off certain goods, the buyer of such goods has a right to reject them and to claim back the price. If the same has already been paid and refuses to pay. If the price has not been paid till then.

In *Rowland* v. *Divall*,[7] the plaintiff purchased a motorcar from the defendants and used the same for several months. The defendant had no title to the car and, therefore, the plaintiff was compelled to give it up to the true owner. The plaintiff used the defendant to recover back the price, which he had already paid. It was held that even though the buyer had used the car for some months he was entitled to recover back the whole of the price paid by him as consideration had totally failed.

(f) Implied Condition in Sale by Description (S. 15)

When the goods are sold by description there is an implied condition that the goods supplied shall correspond what the description. In case the goods are not in accordance with the description there is a breach of implied condition and the buyer has right to reject them. He has, however, an option under section 13, to accept the goods by treating the breach of condition as a breach of warranty and claim damages.

In *Antory Thomas* v. *Ayuppunni Mani*,[8] there was a contract for the supply of cashew nuts, one of the terms of the contract being that bad nuts shall not exceed twenty per cent of the total, when the goods were supplied the bad nuts exceeded the stipulated percentage. It was held that the stipulation regarding the proportion of the bad nuts made a basic element of the description of goods, the seller had made a breach of the implied condition contained in Sec. 15 and the buyer was, therefore, entitled to reject the goods and claim back the part of the price already paid by him.

6. Sec. 16(4).
7. (1923) 2 K.B. 500.
8. AIR 1960, Kerala, 176.

(g) Implied Condition in Sale by Samples as well as Description (S. 15)

When the goods are sold by sample as well as description it is not sufficient that the bulk of the goods corresponds with the sample if the goods do not also correspond with the description. In the contract of sale by sample, the following conditions must be satisfied:

(i) The bulk quantity must correspond with the sample.
(ii) The buyer must be given opportunity to compare the bulk with the sample.
(iii) Goods shall be free from any defect and not apparent on examination.

In *Nichol* v. *Godts*[9], there was sale of "foreign refined rape oil, warranted only equal to the samples." The oil supplied though corresponded with the sample, was adulterated with hemp oil. The Jury found that the admixture was not commercially known as "foreign refined rape oil" and therefore, it was held that since the oil supplied was not in accordance with the description the buyer was entitled to reject the same.

E. THE RULE OF CAVEAT EMPTOR (S. 16)

Sometimes the goods purchased by the buyer may not suit the particular purpose for which the buyer wants them. The question which in such a case arises is, whether the buyer can reject the goods or he is supposed to take the risk of the goods turning out not suitable for the required purpose. The section provides that as a general rule there is no implied warranty or condition as to the quality or fitness for any particular purpose of goods supplied under a contract of sale. It is incorporation of the rule contained in the maxim caveat emptor, which means buyers beware. According to this rule the buyer himself should be careful while purchasing the goods and he should himself ascertain that the goods suit his purpose. If the goods are subsequently found to be unsuitable for his purpose he cannot blame the seller for the same, as there is no implied undertaking by the seller that he shall supply such goods as to suit the buyer's purpose. For example, A purchases a horse from B. The horse is not suitable for riding but is suitable only for being driven in a carriage. A can neither reject the horse nor can he claim any compensation from B.

In *re Andrew Yule & Co.,*[10] the buyer ordered for Hessian cloth without specifying the purpose for which he wanted the same. It was in fact needed for packing. Because of unusual smell it was unsuitable for the purpose. It was held that the buyer had no right to reject the same, even if it did not suit his purpose.

Section 16 also incorporates the following two exceptions to the rule of caveat emptor, which are two further implied conditions.

9. (1854), DEX. 191: R.R 523.
10. AIR 1932, Cal. 879: 140 I.C. 877.

(a) Implied Conditions as to Quality or Fitness (Being First Exception to the Rule of Caveat Emptor—S. 16(1))

There is no implied condition or warranty as regards the quality or fitness of the goods for any particular purpose. To this rule there is an exception. If the following requirements as mentioned in S. 16(1) are satisfied, there is considered to be an implied condition from the side of the seller that the goods supplied shall be reasonably fit for the purpose for which the buyer wants them;

(i) The buyer, while purchasing the goods, expressly or impliedly makes known to the seller the particular purpose for which the goods are required by him, so as to show that the buyer relies on the seller's skill or Judgement; and
(ii) The goods supplied are of such a description which it is in the course of the seller's business to supply.[11]

(b) Implied Condition of Merchantable Quality (Being Second Exception to the Rule of Caveat Emptor—S. 16(2))

Section 16(2) contains another implied condition which is by way of exception to the rule of caveat emptor. It has been noted above in Sec. 15 that when the goods are bought by description there is an implied condition that the goods supplied shall answer that description. According to this sub-section there is a further implied condition in such a case and that is that the goods supplied shall be of merchantable quality. Where—

(1) The goods are bought by description.[12]
(2) From a seller who deals in the goods of that description (whether he is the manufacturer or producer or not.)

There is an implied condition that the goods shall be of merchantable quality. The terms 'merchantable quality' has not been defined in the Act. It means that the article is of such quality and in such condition that a reasonable man acting reasonably would after a full examination accept it under the circumstances of the case in performance of his offer to buy that article, whether he buys for his own use or to sell again. It is not sufficient that the goods are marketable or saleable (that is no doubt the dictionary meaning or the word) for, in the statutory sense the significance of the word 'merchantable' is relative, the test being, are the goods merchantable or not under the particular description in the contract. If the goods are not saleable in the market as the goods of a certain description, they are not of merchantable quality.

11. Raghava Menon *v.* Kuttappan Nair, AIR 1962, Kerla, 318.
12. See *Supra* Note 39.

In *Grant* v. *Australian Knitting Mills. Ltd.*,[13] the underwears contained certain chemicals, which could cause skin disease to a person wearing them next to skin, it was held that because of such a defect the underwears were not of merchantable quality. Even when the goods are purchased by their trade name and the implied condition as to their quality or fitness is not there, another implied condition as to merchantable quality could still be invoked.

F. EFFECTS OF THE CONTRACT

(i) When there is a contract for sale of unascertained goods, no property in the goods is transferred to the buyer unless and until goods are ascertained.
(ii) If the intention of the parties as to the time when the property in the goods has to pass, is not clear from the contract the following are the rules.

G. SPECIFIC OR UNASCERTAINED GOODS

Existing goods may be further classified into specific goods and unascertained goods:

> "Specific Goods" means those goods which have been identified and agreed upon at the time of contract of sale. If the exact thing which is the subject matter of the contract is known to the parties it is known as specific goods. For example, A has a number of horses and out of them he sells his white horse to B, the particular horse being identified and agreed upon at the time of the contract, the same is considered to be specific goods. Similarly, if A agrees to sell 100 bags of wheat to B and for the purpose of that contract out of 1,000 bags, which he has in his godown, he earmarks 100 bags at the time of making his contract with B, the goods sold are specific. For specific goods it is necessary that such goods must be identified and agreed upon at the time of making of the contract and not subsequently.

If the goods are not identified and agreed upon at the time of making of the contract they are known as unascertained goods. For example, A having 1,000 bags of wheat in his godown sells only 100 bags to B without specifying those which he wants to deliver to B, it is a sale of unascertained goods. It becomes relevant to see whether the goods are specific or unascertained when we want to know as to when does the property in the goods pass from the seller to the buyer. In case of specific goods there is a possibility of the property in the goods passing to the buyer at the time of making of the

13. (1936) A.C. 85.

contract, whereas in the case of unascertained goods the property in the goods does not pass to the buyer unless and until the goods are ascertained.

In *Vinay Minerals Pvt. Ltd.* v. *Bakash Chandra Deb,*[14] there was a contract for the sale of Manganese and Iron Ores which were excavated and raised for delivery from mines *ex pit* mouth. In other words, only such ores were sold and to be delivered as had been excavated and raised. It was held to be sale of specific goods. In this case the sale was of specific goods specific performance of the contact could be granted.

H. TRANSFER OF PROPERTY (OWNERSHIP) IN THE GOODS

In every contract of sale there is to be transfer of property in the goods from the seller to the buyer. According to the Sale of Goods Act, "property" means 'general property' in the goods rather that mere 'special property'. The term general property means ownership and special property means only some of the rights, e.g., the right of possession and use. If under a contract the ownership in the goods is transferred from one person to another, it may be a contract of sale, but when mere right of possession is transferred the transaction may be by way of hire or pledge.

(i) A contract of sale of goods is a contract whereby the seller either transfers the property (ownership) or agrees to transfer the property in the goods to the buyer. Transfer of property, i.e., the ownership in the goods from the seller to the buyer, is the essence of the contract. A contract under which there is neither a transfer of property in the goods nor there is an agreement to transfer the same cannot be considered to be a contract of sale. The transfer of property in the goods may be there either at the time of making of the contract or at a later time. According to Sec. 4, sub-sec. (3), if the property is transferred at the time of the making of the contract the contract is known as a sale. But if, on the other hand, the transfer of property in the goods is to take place at a future time or subject to some conditions thereafter to be fulfilled, the contract is called an agreement to sell. In an agreement to sell it may be provided that the ownership will pass either on the lapse of a certain time or on the fulfilment of specified conditions. For example, the agreement entered into on first January may say that the ownership will pass after two months, or on the payment of the price, or when the goods are delivered. According to Sec. 4, sub-sec. (4), an agreement to sell becomes a sale when the time elapses or the conditions are fulfilled subject to which the property in the goods is to be transferred.

(a) Delivery of Goods in Wrong Quantity

Seller's duty is to deliver the goods in accordance with the terms of the contract. That includes a duty to deliver goods of the same quality, in the

14. AIR 1996, Cal. 67.

required quantity and in accordance with their description given in the contract. Section 37 covers the following cases of delivery of goods, where the performance is not in accordance with contract, i.e. where he—

(i) delivers a quantity less than he contracted to sell;
(ii) delivers a quantity large than he contracted to sell; and
(iii) delivers the goods he contracted to sell mixed with goods of a different description not included in the contract.

(b) Delivery of Less Quantity

If the seller supplies less quantity than he contracted to sell the buyer has a right to reject the goods. The buyer is, however, free to waive his right of rejecting the goods. In case the buyer waives his right of rejection and accepts the goods he has to pay at the contract rate. For example, if there is a contract to supply 100 bags of wheat and 80 bags are supplied the buyer may reject those 80 bags, but if he accepts them he should pay for them, at the contract rate. The buyer's right of rejection is subject to the *rule de minimis non curat lex* (the law does not take trival deviation into account) and therefore, it is slight deficiency in the goods supplied that must be overlooked. Thus, if in a contract to supply 16,000 kgs. of rice there was shortage of only 522 kgs. The *"de minimis"* rule was applicable, and the buyer could not refuse to take delivery of the goods.

In case the supply of certain specified quantity is the essence of the contract, then any short supply is the breach of a condition, for which the buyer may reject the goods.

If there is a contract for delivery of a specified quantity by instalments, the buyer may return the deliveries first made if the seller fails to deliver the subsequent instalments, but if the buyer keeps the goods delivered in the first instalment after the expiration of the time fixed for the delivery of the remainder, the seller can recover for the same. He could not bring such an action before the expiry of the time of the delivery of the remaining goods.

(c) Delivery of Larger Quantity

Where the quantity of the goods supplied is larger than that was contracted for the buyer may accept the goods included in the contract and reject the rest, or may reject the whole of the goods, or may accept the whole of the goods. If the goods are more than that were contracted for are accepted, the buyer has to pay for them at the contract rate. If against an order for two dozen bottles of wine four dozen are sent by the seller, the buyer has a right to reject the whole.

In *Vilas Udyog Ltd.* v. *Prag Vanaspati Product*[15], the paintiff Company of Ahmedabad agreed to supply 120 barrels of groundnut oil to the defendant

15. AIR 1975, Guj. 112.

firm of Aligarh. The plaintiff dispatched 140 barrels, i.e., 20 barrels in excess. The defendant refused to take delivery and pay for the goods, one of the contentions being that the goods dispatched were in access of the contract quantity. The court agreed with the right of the buyer. The seller in such a case can again supply the contract quantity.

In this case the buyer not only refused to take delivery but also even before the goods reached the destination unilaterally and unjustifiably cancelled and repudiated the contract, whereby the seller was prevented from tendering again the contract quantity. It was held that the buyer has only a right to reject the goods but not to cancel the contract and since in this case the buyer had cancelled the contract, he was liable for damages for breach of contract. The principle is subject to the rule *de minimis non curat lex,* i.e., the law does not take trivial deviations into account.

(d) Mixed Delivery

It has already been observed under Sec. 15 that in a contract of sale by description there is an implied condition that the goods supplied by the seller shall correspond to the description the buyer has a right to reject the goods. The question may sometimes arise about the buyer's remedy, when the seller delivers to the buyer the goods he contracted to sell mixed with the goods of a different description not included in the contract. In such a case the buyer may accept the goods which are in accordance with the description and reject the rest, or may reject the whole.

In *Moti Lal* v. *The Netha Cooperative Spinning Mills Ltd.*[16], there was a contract for the supply of 500 bales of cotton of a certain variety. The first instalment of 50 bales was supplied and accepted but the buyers rejected the second instalment of 50 bales as they were adulterated with waste cotton mix and the cotton was of inferior quality, and asked the sellers not to supply further goods. It was held that the buyer was justified in repudiating the whole contract. Moreover, the sellers were not entitled to claim any damages, as they did not tender any further instalments within the contract period but agreed to the repudiation of the contract made by the buyer.

16. AIR 1975, A.P 169.

Index